STUDIES IN THE ECONOMICS
OF TRANSPORTATION

Prepared by the Cowles Commission for Research in Economics, at the University of Chicago, under a contract with the RAND Corporation.

The Bensenville Yard, Chicago.

Courtesy of the Chicago, Milwaukee, St. Paul, and Pacific Railroad

STUDIES IN THE

ECONOMICS
OF
TRANSPORTATION

by

MARTIN BECKMANN

C. B. McGUIRE

CHRISTOPHER B. WINSTEN

With an Introduction by

TJALLING C. KOOPMANS

Published for the COWLES COMMISSION

for RESEARCH in ECONOMICS by

YALE UNIVERSITY PRESS: NEW HAVEN, 1956

LONDON: GEOFFREY CUMBERLEGE: OXFORD UNIVERSITY PRESS

CONTENTS

INTRODUCTION

The exploratory studies presented in this report are addressed to analysts in various professions, including economists, traffic and railroad engineers, management scientists, operations researchers, and mathematicians who are interested in assessing the capabilities and studying the efficient operation of transportation systems. Studies relating to two systems, highway traffic and railroad transportation, are offered.

The tasks indicated — assessing capabilities and appraising efficiency of operation — are as vast and complicated as the transportation systems themselves. The purpose of the present studies is to develop and illustrate certain concepts, methods, and models that may have usefulness as points of departure for the execution of these tasks. While the aim of these studies is thus both modest and provisional, they are offered in the hope of stimulating further factual, conceptual, mathematical, and computational research into the efficient utilization of transportation systems.

The method employed is to construct and study simple models. The word "model," frequently used in engineering studies to mean a physical model — that is, an accurate copy of the system studied (often with the scale altered) — is here used in the more general meaning attached to it by physicists as well as social scientists: a simplified conceptual counterpart of the system studied. In such a model the most important variables of the system studied are enumerated and defined and the relevant relationships between them specified. Variables and relationships thus express the most essential aspects of the system in question but leave out many other aspects, so that an opening wedge for analysis may be provided.

This analysis is often mathematical. However, the mathematical underpinning of the studies here presented has been set off in separate sections, marked by an asterisk. These sections can be passed over by the reader interested mainly in results, which are fully described in sections without that symbol.

The application of the method of model construction to operating or business problems has increased substantially in recent years. To name first a few examples unrelated to transportation, we refer to two studies on inventory policy by Arrow, Harris, and Marschak (1951) and Dvoretzky, Kiefer, and Wolfowitz (1952), in which models are designed to help balance inventory costs against losses from stock depletion. Another family of models constitute the general field of "linear programming," a technique to compute programs for the interdependent activities of a large organization. Besides the original presentations by Wood and Dantzig (1951a) and by Dantzig (1951b, c, d) we mention an expository discussion by Dorfman (1953) in terms of a problem of automobile production and an application to gasoline blending by Charnes, Cooper, and Mellon (1952).

Similar studies in terms of a very simple linear model of transportation have also been made. Two mathematicians, F. L. Hitchcock (1941) in the United States and L. Kantorovitch (1942)[1] in Russia, and one economist (the author of this introduction) independently of one another formulated the problem of the most economical execution of a given transportation program between a number of locations if the per unit cost of transportation between each pair of locations is independent of the amount transported. This model belongs to the class of "linear programming" models and has served as one of the stock examples of this class. Dantzig (1951d) explored the computational aspects of the above (linear) transportation problem, which were carried further and applied to a military tanker fleet problem by Flood (1953, 1954). Economists studied various implications of this model, such as the relative costs of alternative possible changes in the transportation program and the relationship of these cost ratios to freight rates formed in competitive markets (Koopmans, 1947; Koopmans and Reiter, 1951) as well as the relation of freight rates to interregional price differences and movements of goods (Enke, 1951; Samuelson, 1952; Fox, 1953). An extension of the model to a situation where places of origin and destination are continuously distributed in a plane was given by Beckmann (1952). An important general result of the studies mentioned is that under the circumstances of the simple model described, a competitive market solves the most economical routing problem as efficiently as a centrally directed transportation organization could.

From the point of view of the efficient utilization of the transport systems of road and rail, the applicability of the simple linear ("constant cost") model is rather limited. It ignores all phenomena of congestion, either at terminals, or en route. Perhaps the most important case where this assumption is approximately satisfied is that of ocean or lake shipping between uncongested ports. The linear model further ignores indivisibilities, such as those which arise from the bunching of a number of railroad cars into a train for which one indivisible engine provides traction. To extend the analysis of transportation systems by model construction, it will therefore be desirable to set aside the linear model, and take a fresh look at the technological and organizational circumstances of various transportation systems. Before leaving the linear model, however, let us point out one practical application of importance for the individual business firm that has plants in several locations. This application arises irrespective of whether unit cost of transportation on each route actually depends on the amount transported, whenever a public carrier makes the service in question available at a constant freight rate. The linear model then suffices to show this firm how to minimize its bill for transportation from plants to

---

1. This reference was brought to our notice by M. M. Flood (1954).

customers, even though the minimum-billed-cost flows of goods so computed have no necessary relation to the best utilization of the transportation system.

In our study of highway traffic the main emphasis is on the effects of traffic congestion. Congestion phenomena have been subjected to mathematical analysis in the theory of telephone systems by Erlang (in Brockmeyer, et al., 1948) and Palm (1943) and more recently in a more general analysis by Kendall (1951) of queues that arise in many situations: people waiting for service in a bank, ships waiting for access to port or repair facilities, airplanes circling to land, pedestrians waiting for an opportunity to cross a street, etc.

The main purpose of these studies has been to determine, by means of the calculus of probability, how the average waiting time and the extent of fluctuation in individual waiting times depend on the opportunities for servicing (number of servers, average of and fluctuations in service time) and on the amount and irregularity of the inflow of claimants for service. In Chapter 1 of this report queue theory is applied to such traffic situations as the flow of cars through an intersection and the passing of slower cars by faster cars by using gaps which occur in the opposing traffic stream. In addition, in Chapters 3 and 4 the main results of such studies are incorporated into the assumptions of a (nonlinear) model of highway traffic on a road network.

It was said at the beginning of this introduction that one important objective to which our studies are ultimately directed is the determination of the capabilities of transportation systems — in the present case, of a road network. It will now be clear that this cannot be expressed in a single number, such as so many vehicle-miles per day. It is an essential aspect of congestion phenomena that — up to a limit beyond which overloading starts — more "service" can always be obtained at higher unit cost. Hence, the capability concept to be analyzed has more dimensions than a single number. Even for one individual one-way road, it is represented by a curve, which gives the relationship between the flow of traffic through the road and the cost encountered on it, and possibly risk or other sacrifices measurable in money equivalents. The higher the flow, the greater the cost encountered. The time element alone, probably the most important cost factor, is represented in the "capacity curve" of the traffic engineer. In this curve, flow is set off against average speed, the reciprocal of travel time. This curve and the concepts associated with it are presented and discussed in Chapter 1, which is based on study of the relevant traffic engineering literature. For a road network, the capabilities are expressed by the relationship between traffic flows on all routes and the costs encountered on each as a result of these flows.

A theory of highway traffic should of course go beyond a description of the capabilities of a network to a study of how these capabilities are utilized. This introduces the concept of demand for transportation. The flows of highway traffic are the result of a great many individual decisions about destinations, routes, and preferred speeds. There is a certain degree of analogy between highway traffic equilibrium and the models used by the economist to explain quantity sold in a market by the interaction of demanders and suppliers. The behavior of demanders is summed up in a "demand curve," which states the amounts taken off the market at various alternative prices. Similarly, the supply curve states amounts offered for the various possible prices. The point of intersection of the curves then indicates the price at which demand equals supply.

On the supply side the analogy is not a close one. Except for toll roads, there is no party in the market selling access to roads for a price. Each piece of road not occupied or endangered by another vehicle is free for use by whoever is near. However, there is a cost of transportation, incurred individually in terms already discussed. If we regard this cost as the "price" in the transportation "market," the economist's notion of a demand curve does become applicable. For a single one-way road it would state what flow of traffic is demanded at any given cost encountered on that road. The higher the cost, the smaller the flow demanded, other things being equal. For a road network the demand function would state what flows are forthcoming on each route in response to given transportation costs along these routes. Equilibrium is established if the flows on all roads arising in response to given costs have precisely the magnitudes that produce these same costs.

The demand concept is developed in Chapter 2. It is applied in Chapter 3 to a study of traffic equilibrium on a highway network. The stability of this equilibrium is also discussed, and some observations are made about the use of the analysis in the prediction of traffic flows.

Mathematical tools used in this analysis (in particular Sections 3.1.2, 3.1.3, and 3.2.1) may also have an interest to the mathematical economist apart from their present application to highway traffic.

The analysis of demand and of equilibrium recognizes that freedom of choice of destination, time of departure, route, and speed, within the traffic laws and general safety considerations, are part of the services rendered by the road network. Completely regulated traffic, such as in the truck convoys of an advancing army, can wrench higher rates of flow out of a given network than can a traffic system that secures these choices to the individual because they have value to him. There is, however, one particular aspect of this freedom of choice which does the totality of road users more harm than good: the choice of route — once a trip is decided on — is quite naturally made so as to minimize cost (in terms of delay, risk, nuisance of congestion, etc.) to the individual driver who makes the choice, without reference to delays caused to other users of the roads in question as a result of his choice. We can illustrate the effect of this circumstance by imagining a completely selfless driver, who (a) is fully aware of all delays and other costs he causes others and (b) gives the same weight to everyone else's cost of transportation that he gives to his own. Let such an ideal driver be

faced with a choice between two routes, one congested, the other uncongested but with somewhat higher travel time. Then our Mr. Milque-
toast will choose the more time-consuming route if the extra time and
other cost of that choice to him amounts to less than the extra delays
and other costs he would cause to others by choosing the congested
route.

It is argued in Chapter 4 that if all drivers were of this highly in-
formed and selfless type, more valuable service could be obtained in the
aggregate from the road network. Perhaps not much can be done about
this particular inefficiency of the traffic system. However, it should be
emphasized that the difficulty arises not from free choice as such but
from the fact that the chooser does not bear the full cost (to others as
well as to himself) of his choice. If there were a way to collect tolls
from the users of congested roads at rates that would measure the cost
to others caused by the average road user, a better use of the highway
system would be obtained (the collected revenue could be used to lower
gasoline taxes or in some other way benefit all road users). Chapter 4
analyzes as a theoretical proposition how the amounts of such "efficiency toll rates" could be determined. It also contains some observations on how closely maximum efficiency can be approached by proper
choice of the toll rates on roads that are at present toll roads, and by
other ways of penalizing additions to traffic congestion.

In this discussion tolls are looked upon as a means not of financing
road construction but of bringing about the best utilization of the highway network. This is in keeping with the growing acceptance among
modern economists of the proposition that best use of facilities requires
methods of pricing the services of these facilities that reflect the incremental cost attributable to each service demanded by an individual user.
Because of the nonlinearity in the relation between amount of use and
cost, such pricing does not necessarily produce revenues equal to the
total cost of operating and financing the facility. This same principle
has been applied by William S. Vickrey (1952) in formulating proposals
for fares in the New York subway which would diminish congestion by
providing incentives for traffic to shift from peak to off-peak hours and
to encourage fuller use of off-peak service by lower fares at these
times when incremental costs are low. It is also basic to contemporary
theory of electricity rates; see, e.g., H. S. Houthakker (1951).

It will be clear that these considerations leave unanswered the
question of criteria for extensions or improvements of the network to
relieve congestion. Some observations on the latter question that flow
from the present analysis are given in Chapter 4, Section 4.4.6, and
also in Chapter 5, which makes brief mention of many unsolved problems of traffic theory and analysis. The main part of the present study,
however, concentrates on what the economist calls "short run" problems. The road network, represented by a configuration of roads and a
capacity curve for each road, is taken as given. Demand for traffic on
each route is represented by a fixed function of current cost — that is,
if after considerable fluctuation, cost were to return to its former level

on each road, demand would also return to its former level on each route. Thus the more gradual responses of demand to changes in cost that arise from relocation of residences, stores, or plants are not taken into account. It is believed, however, that the present analysis can be useful as a starting point in developing a theory of balanced extension of the highway network, concurrently with industrial expansion or relocation. The increased vulnerability of metropolitan areas under modern warfare adds a note of urgency to the development of such a theory, already highly desirable before this complication arose.

Differences between our studies of railroad transportation and those of highway traffic reflect the different characteristics of the two transportation systems. The fact that highway traffic results from the interdependent choices of many decision makers, each with an objective of his own, gives to traffic theory a strong social science flavor. In a railroad system, operations are at least in principle centrally directed. On the other hand, the technical aspects of railroad operation are a great deal more complicated than those of highway use. Hence, our exploratory study of models of certain railroad operations is somewhat closer to physics or engineering. In order to assess and describe the capabilities of a railroad network, it is again necessary to construct simple conceptual models of various parts of railroad operation. Our study, which makes a start with this task, confines itself almost entirely to the supply side of railroad services. One exception to this is the discussion in Chapter 6, Section 6.1 of the value to the shipper of speedy transportation. Another exception is the discussion in Chapter 12 of best routing patterns for empty cars, to which we return below.

It is probable that congestion phenomena, which hold the center of attention in our analysis of highway traffic, are important also in railroad operations. However, it has appeared to the authors that other aspects of railroad operation require prior attention. One of these arises from the fact that in most circumstances it is economical to haul cars in trains rather than individually. This introduces the problem of "accumulation delay," the car time spent waiting for enough traffic to accumulate so that a train can economically be formed. Another is the problem of classification — that is, the problem of sorting cars that arrive in incoming trains or are delivered from loading tracks, so as to make up new trains that will take these cars to the next sorting point, closer to or at their destination. The problem is how to distribute this sorting work over classification yards in a way that minimizes cost of classification plus the money equivalent of accumulation delay.

Basic concepts to make possible an accurate formulation and treatment of problems of this kind are introduced in Chapter 7. In Chapter 8 the operations of classification yards are described, and simple approximative formulae are proposed for the dependence of classification cost on the classification task performed. These formulae are used in Chapter 9 in a general discussion of the distribution of classification work over yards.

An earlier version of the material in this chapter and the one preceding it was presented to a meeting of the Railway Systems and Procedures Association, held in Chicago on November 5, 1953, and published as an appendix to the proceedings of that organization (Beckmann, et al., 1953). The material is here reused and extended with the permission of the R.S.P.A. Chapters 10 and 11 are more detailed studies of specific problems. Each of these chapters ignores what the other concentrates on. Chapter 10 is devoted to the problem of distributing classification work between a hump yard and a flat yard located down the line from the hump yard, when problems of scheduling are ignored. In Chapter 11 classification cost is ignored, and instead the problem of scheduling trains between yards to minimize accumulation delay is discussed in detail for a single-line railroad, and in more general terms for more complicated railroad networks.

From this summary the reader will see that time and resources available for the study did not permit us to construct a model that simultaneously incorporates all the main aspects of railroad operations, on the basis of which one could, for instance, discuss the best dovetailing of classification, scheduling, and line-hauling operations. For that purpose further "partial" models would be needed first, such as a model for the study of track capacity. In addition, mathematical problems belonging to underdeveloped areas of mathematics would arise in the attempt to put the partial models together into one model that would fully express the interdependence of the main elements of railroad operation. It is felt, however, that the first steps on the road to a more integrated model have been made, and that this in itself justifies the publication of these studies.

A more integrated model would have several uses. It would help in computing the capabilities of a given railroad network, and the rolling stock requirements of any transportation program that is within the capabilities of the network. It would also facilitate estimating the "incremental" or "marginal" cost (i.e. the cost increase) occasioned by the rendering of an extra unit of service.

The importance of the latter consideration lies in the fact that freight rates are an important element in business decisions about industrial locations and about modes of transportation used. Only if the rate on each unit of service reflects its incremental cost can we expect that such decisions, taken by profit-seeking entrepreneurs in response to freight rates and geographical price differences, will lead to the most efficient utilization of the nation's resources. It is true that this view, held by most economists (e.g. Dupuit, 1844; Hotelling, 1938), has not been accepted by regulatory bodies as relevant to rate making. However, the economist's case is likely to remain just a nice point of theory unless the operations of railroads are analyzed to the extent necessary to provide a method of estimating the incremental costs of transportation services rendered.

It may be useful here to recall the main properties of incremental cost in the very simplest linear model of transportation mentioned at the beginning of this introduction, where both congestion and the fact that cars are lumped into trains are ignored. In this model "efficiency freight rates" — that is, rates reflecting incremental cost — are relatively low per mile in directions in which empty cars proceed regularly, and relatively high in opposite directions. On routes not traveled by empty cars the efficiency freight rates have intermediate values, which can be determined in the same calculation by which the best routing plan for empty cars is determined (see Koopmans and Reiter, 1951; Dantzig, 1951e). In any more refined model incremental cost freight rates are likely to exhibit these main features, with the effects of congestion and lumpiness superimposed as modifications. It is therefore worth while to examine the pattern of empty car originations and terminations associated with the movement of goods on U.S. railroads, the pattern of best routing of empty cars between origination and destination points, and the stability or variability of this pattern between years. The examination of this question in Chapter 12 reveals a substantial stability of best routing patterns of empty boxcars — and hence of incremental costs of transportation of goods shipped in these cars — during peacetime years in contrast to remarkable changes connected with war-time movements of supplies to Pacific coast ports.

This report has resulted from a research project carried out by the Cowles Commission for Research in Economics under contract with the RAND Corporation. Tjalling C. Koopmans was the research leader of the project. The several authors came to this study with different skills and backgrounds, and accordingly contributed in different and complementary ways to their common task. Martin Beckmann, a mathematical economist especially interested in linear programming and economic activity analysis, contributed most of the chapters of the highway traffic analysis, with the exception of Chapter 1 on capacity. Christopher Winsten, mathematician and economist with a special interest in applications of probability calculus to industrial phenomena, contributed the analysis of queues reported in Chapter 1 and the analysis of the division of sorting work between yards given in Chapter 10. C. B. McGuire, economist, was assigned primary responsibility for the degree of "realism" of the models developed by the group. For this purpose he gave most of his time in earlier phases of the project to study of the literature on traffic analysis and railroad operation, to interviews with traffic specialists and railroad officials, to visits to classification yards, and, assisted first by Marc Nerlove and later by Thomas Goldman, to the analysis of operating records. Most of the chapters on railroad problems are the result of joint work by McGuire and Winsten. Chapter 11 was contributed by Koopmans. Chapter 12 was prepared by McGuire on the basis of earlier work by Kirk Fox, Marc Nerlove, Harlan Suits, and Thomas A. Healy. The computations for a simple example of a highway network were prepared, and the report thereon in Section 3.3.2 written, by Goldman.

This dry enumeration of contributions does not indicate the extent to which practically every chapter has been affected by the thinking of all members of the group. A good deal of group discussion has been devoted in particular to choice of concepts and models of railroad operations. During the later stage of preparation of manuscript the group met in weekly sessions for criticism and evaluation of successive drafts. Final editing of the manuscript was done by McGuire with the assistance of James M. Terrell.

Proper acknowledgment cannot be given in this space to all those who helped the authors in their project. Especially deserving of mention for the patient way they dealt with the authors' questions are the following men in the railroad industry: C. H. Bremhorst, L. H. Dyer, and E. P. Stine of the Chicago, Burlington, and Quincy; Arthur H. Gass of the Car Service Division, Association of American Railroads; C. E. McCarty and R. M. Zimmermann of Potomac Yard; T. J. O'Connell and C. E. Bertrand of the Baltimore and Ohio; W. A. McClintic of the Pere Marquette Division of the Chesapeake and Ohio; E. E. Foulkes of the Rock Island; and Val Rice of *Modern Railroads*. For the frontispiece, an aerial photograph of Bensenville Yard on the outskirts of Chicago, we are indebted to the Milwaukee Road.

Discussions with other member of the Cowles Commission research staff and with visiting scholars have also been stimulating and helpful. Among these we wish to mention in particular W. Feller of Princeton University; H. S. Houthakker, formerly of the Commission and now of Stanford University; D. G. Kendall of Oxford University; Harry Markowitz, George Dantzig, and T. E. Harris of the RAND Corporation; and William S. Vickrey of Columbia University. Professor Vickrey has read the entire manuscript and given the authors the benefit of many detailed comments. Of course, responsibility for what is offered rests with the respective authors alone who will feel their endeavor has been fully rewarded if these studies stimulate others to improve on them.

PART I

A STUDY OF
HIGHWAY TRANSPORTATION

Chapter 1

ROAD AND INTERSECTION CAPACITY

1.1. Introduction

In most cases where an attempt has been made to measure the capacity of a road or intersection this capacity has been taken to be a number representing the highest possible flow of traffic through the facility being studied. Accepting this view for a moment, let us examine a particular case in some detail and see into what complications we are led. Suppose a certain unsignaled intersection is used by eastbound and northbound traffic only. What is its capacity? Obviously no one number will suffice to describe the capacity of the intersection for northbound flows alone, for it is quite clear that the more eastbound traffic there is, the less will be the amount of northbound traffic that can get through

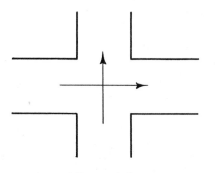

Figure 1.1

unless this latter flow in some way dominates the intersection, and we rule this out for the present. Perhaps, however, it is possible to express the capacity in terms of a number, say 1600 vehicles per hour, which is not to be exceeded by the sum of the two flows. If this is so, then this capacity can be expressed in the following lengthier but more instructive way. The capacity is

       0 vehicles per hour northbound and 1600 vehicles per hour eastbound
or 100 vehicles per hour northbound and 1500 vehicles per hour eastbound
or 200 vehicles per hour northbound and 1400 vehicles per hour eastbound

     .
     .
     .
     .
     .

or 1600 vehicles per hour northbound and   0 vehicles per hour eastbound.

This set of combinations written out in full says precisely the same thing as the shorter defining sentence preceding it; we can if we wish therefore always describe such capacities in terms of the various highest possible combinations of flows. Since the set of such combinations is rather tedious to write down, it is convenient to describe it graphically in the following way:

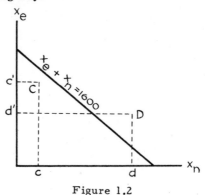

Figure 1.2

The set of capacity flow combinations can be represented graphically in Figure 1.2 as all those points with non-negative coordinates x_e, x_n which lie on the downward sloping line whose equation is $x_e + x_n = 1600$. The whole set of combinations is therefore completely described by that line. The capacity expression has thus changed from a simple number to a set — the set of points on the 45^0 line.

At this point there arises the very natural question of whether the line must always have a 45^0 slope, or whether in fact it need always be a straight line. Without further information there are no reasons to reject the possibility of capacity curves like those in Figures 1.3 and 1.4. Where the capacity curves are of this nature we begin to see some of the advantages of capacity formulations in terms of sets of alternatives rather than single numbers. The capacities described in the last two curves can be represented by sets of combinations just as before, but they cannot readily be represented in a straightforward way by a single number. If we look at the points A and B in Figure 1.3, we notice that while both represent capacity flow combinations, the total flow represented by A is less than the total flow represented by B. Total flow in these examples is no longer an important element in capacity considerations.

Before leaving this simple intersection example it is worth pointing out that the curve, or set, we have been talking about represents capacity in the sense that it forms a part of the boundary of all those points representing possible flow combinations. Thus in Figure 1.2, the point C with coordinates c and c' is a possible flow combination, since the sum of c and c' is less than 1600, while the point D with coordinates d and d' is an impossible flow combination, since the sum of d and d' is greater than 1600. The possible combinations are those represented by

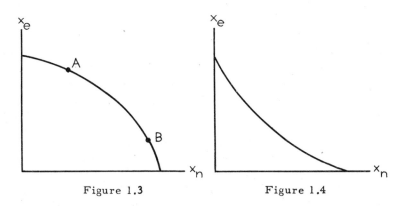

Figure 1.3　　　　　　　　　Figure 1.4

points on or below the capacity curve; the impossible ones by points above the curve.

The reader may object at this point that all of this elaboration has been unnecessary, because for most of the important cases the capacity curve does in fact just happen to be a straight line sloped at 45°, so that capacity expressed as a limitation on total flow is really all that is needed. If every interesting case were like the ones in Figure 1.2, the objection would indeed be well taken. We intend to show, however, that as soon as the capacity notion is complicated in order to make it more useful from an economic point of view, the interpretation as a set of possibilities becomes imperative. To make this clear another simple and rather artificial example will be described. So far we have not considered the driving conditions which the traffic will meet, even when the flows are possible ones. One way of introducing these conditions into a definition of capacity is given in the *Highway Capacity Manual* (Normann and Walker, 1949; pp. 6-7), where, very briefly:

basic capacity is the maximum flow under "most nearly ideal roadway and traffic conditions";

possible capacity is the maximum flow under "prevailing roadway and traffic conditions";

practical capacity is the maximum flow short of causing "unreasonable delay, hazard, or restriction to the drivers' freedom to maneuver."

Thus for each traffic condition specified there is a corresponding maximum flow.

Alternatively, capacity may be defined as a relation showing how traffic conditions depend on flow, a definition that is to be preferred if the ambiguity of terms like "unreasonable" is to be avoided. This procedure means that no two or three arbitrarily selected traffic conditions are concentrated on, but rather the whole range of traffic conditions is examined, just as the whole range of flows is.

The word "delay" in the description of the traffic conditions that define practical capacity covers what is probably the most important element in traffic conditions. Conditions are good if delay is small; they are bad if delay is large. In the following example, in fact in nearly all of the subsequent discussion in this chapter, we shall suppose that "traffic conditions" are fully described by an assessment of the delays that occur.

Let us imagine a certain vehicle inspection station at which all vehicles traveling a particular road must stop. Suppose that the inspection takes exactly two minutes for each vehicle, that only one vehicle can be inspected at a time, and that the arrival of vehicles at the station is known to be random. What is the capacity of the station?

The example would be completely uninteresting were it not for the fact that as flows become larger, "traffic conditions" — that is, delays — get progressively worse. Any particular car has to wait not only the two minutes until its own inspection is completed, but until the inspections of all cars waiting when it arrived are finished as well. The heavier the traffic, the more cars it is likely to find waiting ahead of it. If the average delay that cars suffer is plotted as a function of flow, a curve like ABCD in Figure 1.5 results. For very small flows the station will seldom be occupied, and the average delay will be close to two minutes. As flow approaches 30 vehicles per hour, the station will usually have several vehicles waiting in line and the average delay is likely to be large.

Proceeding just as in the intersection example we can express the capacity as the set of combinations

> 0 vehicles per hour and 2 minutes average delay
> or b′ vehicles per hour and b minutes average delay
> or c′ vehicles per hour and c minutes average delay
> or d′ vehicles per hour and d minutes average delay
>   etc.

Now imagine another station at which two vehicles can be inspected simultaneously, but where such inspection takes exactly three minutes. The capacity curve for this station is EF in Figure 1.5. With flows close to zero the average delay is three minutes, a little greater than for the other station. At C, where the two curves cross, the advantage of the first station in terms of a shorter service time is exactly compensated for by the second station's ability to deal with congestion. Thus, in a sense, for small flows the first station has the greater capacity; for high flows the second station has the greater capacity. Such a capacity comparison would be arbitrary indeed if it were made on the basis of knowledge of delays at the two stations corresponding to one particular flow, or on the basis of knowledge of the flows at the two stations corresponding to one particular value of average delay.

Note that if we were to plot a similar function for the intersection example given above, then for each combination of flows which the intersection could handle, we would have an average delay. The capacity curve shown in the figure might now be supposed to separate the

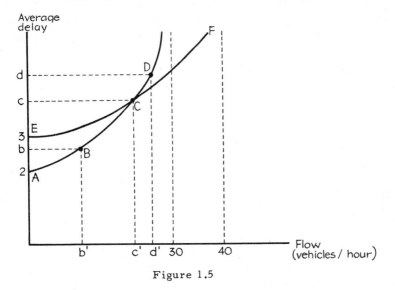

Figure 1.5

combinations of flows which had acceptable delays from those where the average delays were too large to be acceptable. When we are considering two flows in this way, we could break this average delay down into two parts, those experienced by each of the two streams. What kind of functions of the traffic densities these delays are depends especially on the traffic rules governing the intersection. This question will be discussed in Section 1.2 below.

With this introduction it is time to enter into a more detailed discussion of the capacities of various types of intersections and roads.

1.2. *The Capacity of Intersections*

We have sketched above the notion of capacity we intend to use. Before we can develop quantitative expressions for this capacity notion, we must consider in more detail the rules governing traffic at intersections, and we must specify the simplifications inevitably involved in constructing a model of traffic behavior. Some of the previous work on intersection capacity will be discussed, and a new model will be given which, it is hoped, will be useful for quantitative prediction in some situations.

1.2.1. *The Stop-Sign Intersection*

In a simple type of such an intersection a minor road crosses a major road. It is assumed that traffic in the minor road must not interfere with major-road traffic. Hence a car ready to cross the major road must wait until there is a sufficient gap in the major-road traffic. The burden of judging when a gap is sufficient lies on the minor-road driver. It is possible for these judgments to vary considerably, both between one driver and the next, and between different intersections. Drivers may vary because of different degrees of cautiousness, ability to pick up speed, and so on. Intersections vary in visibility, width, and many other factors. It is necessary to consider which of these factors to bring into a quantitative model, and just how they should be brought in.

1.2.2. Intersections Controlled by Traffic Lights

Traffic lights may have various rules of operation, and the delay will depend on which of these is being used. The most common is the fixed repeated cycle. With this rule a green interval of fixed length is followed by a red interval of fixed length (though the length of the red interval may differ from the length of the green one). The whole cycle is repeated indefinitely. There may be additional warning intervals between the green and the red intervals or between the red and the green. There are some possible variations — for example, lights can be made to change their cycle according to the densities of the traffic in the two roads, and some types of lights give priority to one of the roads — but we do not discuss them here.

In both the stop-sign case and the traffic-light case, cars turning left or right are an additional cause of variation. Suppose, for example, that at a stop sign the driver of a car in the minor road wishes to make a left turn into the major road. He will have to wait for a gap in the major-road traffic, and also for a gap in the minor-road traffic in the opposing stream. Thus on the average he will have to wait longer than a car going straight ahead and is likely to delay traffic behind him longer. Hence the delay at the intersection may well depend on the number of cars making left turns and on the density of traffic in the opposing stream in this situation. Similar considerations apply to the traffic-light case. These complications are mentioned to show that quantitative statements about delays at intersections and their relations to traffic flows will not be of completely general application, whether they are derived from theory or from experimental observation of actual road conditions. Many intersections may present special features which call for modification of the results.

1.2.3. Related Work in the Literature

Before we present our contribution to the theory of intersection capacity, we will give some very brief references to related work described in the literature. The discussion has no intention of being exhaustive; it is meant only to call attention to some attempts to develop a quantitative theory of congestion at intersections.

In order to develop a theory of delay we have to have some way of describing traffic flow. Because of the various unrelated factors which determine whether there will be a car at a particular point at a particular time, it was suggested by Adams (1936) that a special type of probability model called the Poisson process might yield a description of the times at which cars pass a particular point. His experimental work confirms that this process gives an adequate description for some roads, and for some purposes. It has since been used in work on traffic congestion by other writers, for example Garwood, Greenshields, Raff, and Tanner.

A theoretical treatment of stop-sign intersection delays is given in papers by Raff (1951) and Tanner (1951). Both use the same assumptions and simplifications. It is supposed that cars in the minor road do not interfere with each other, for instance. This assumption will be a valid one if traffic in the minor road is sparse. Tanner frames his discussion in terms of pedestrians crossing a road; since pedestrians can usually cross in groups if necessary, all those waiting can cross almost as soon as there is a sufficient gap in the traffic. Thus it seems a good approximation to suppose that the length of time a pedestrian will have to wait to cross does not depend materially on how many other pedestrians are using the crossing. In other words, the assumption of noninterference seems a valid one in this case too.

It is also necessary to have some more precise definition of "sufficient gap." In the theories developed so far the notion of a fixed critical time gap is used. It is supposed that the driver in the minor road will cross only if there is no car in the major road due at the intersection in the next w seconds, say. Under these circumstances w is called the critical gap.

We can represent the arrivals at the intersection of cars in the major road as points of a time axis, as in Figure 1.6.

Figure 1.6

By using the notion of a fixed critical gap we can, if we are given a plot of the traffic of this sort, say whether a car in the minor road can or cannot cross at any given time. It is natural to call the time interval during which a car in the minor road is not able to cross a *red interval* and the time interval in which it can cross a *green interval*. Thus if we have a plot of arrivals in the major road, with our assumption of a fixed critical gap we can divide the time into a sequence of intervals, alternating red and green. This procedure is illustrated in Figure 1.7, where the cars on the left end of the time axis are later arrivals than those on the right. A car arriving in the green interval will not have to wait, but a car arriving in the red interval will have to wait just until the end of that interval. As we are supposing there is no other car in the minor road in front of it to delay it, it will be able to leave at the start of the green interval.

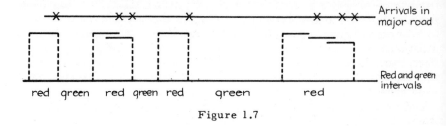

Figure 1.7

To find the average wait in the minor road, we have to study the distribution of the lengths of red and green intervals. The papers by Raff and Tanner do this for the case in which the arrivals in the major road can be described as a sequence formed by a Poisson process. The assumption that sufficiently large spaces occur between vehicles is the only one necessary for the minor road.

Notice that the reasoning in this case can easily be extended to the case where the critical gap accepted varies from car to car. If we know the relative frequencies of the different critical gaps, we can find the mean delay for each one and then average the results, using these relative frequencies as weights. In fact, Raff presents empirical evidence which shows very clearly that there is considerable variation in the gaps drivers consider long enough to allow them to cross, so that a refinement of this sort may be useful. In the case of dense traffic in the minor road, which we treat later, there is no such easy generalization to the case of a variable critical gap, and we must for the time being be content with the approximation that supposes it to be constant.

Some methods of calculation for the repeated-cycle traffic-light case are presented by Garwood (1940-41) and Raff (1950). In these papers an attempt is made to deal with the phenomenon of "sluggishness." If a line of cars is waiting when the light turns green, it will take some time to clear. Below we suggest a new method of dealing with this case, which gives us a useful approximate formula when traffic is sparse, and can be used to give results when traffic is heavy.

1.2.4. A Model of Intersection Delays

The results we have mentioned above for the stop-sign intersection were restricted to the case for which traffic in the minor road was sparse. In this section we give a method of extending this type of model to the case where the traffic in the minor road is dense, and cars are delayed not only by the traffic in the major road, but by cars in front of them in the minor road too. The type of model we develop turns out to be useful for the repeated cycle traffic light case also.

The basic fact we have tried to express in the model is that a queue of cars waiting to cross a road cannot clear all at once, and the longer the queue the longer it will take to clear (the phenomenon already described as sluggishness). The reason for this effect is that the cars as they leave maintain a certain spacing between each other. In our model we also take account of the fact that cars arrive spaced out too.

In constructing the model, a device has been used which may at first sight seem to have a slightly artificial look about it but which, in fact, expresses the spacing between traffic in a very convenient way. We suppose that events such as the arrival or departure of a car can only happen at discrete points in time, rather as if they were being shown by a motion picture film which moved in jerks. Each of the discrete time-points can be considered a frame of the film. At each time-point, at most one car can arrive, and at most one car can cross the road. These conditions make sure that traffic is spaced out as it should be. They also imply the restriction that the minimum time spacing between cars arriving at the intersection and cars leaving it is the same.

In addition we suppose that each time-point is either a red time-point or a green time-point. A red time-point is a point at which a car cannot cross the stop sign or traffic light. At a green time-point a car will cross, provided that a car has just arrived or that one or more cars have been held over from the last time-point.

With these conditions we can represent a sequence of events at the intersection in a very simple way symbolically. Suppose we represent the arrival of a car at the intersection by the symbol 1, and that the symbol 0 means that no car arrives. Then, for example, a sequence of the type

$$1 \quad 1 \quad 0 \quad 0 \quad 1 \quad 0 \quad 0 \quad 0 \quad 1 \quad 0$$

shows that cars arrived at the first two time-points but not at the next two, a car arrived at the fifth time-point but not at the next three, and so on.

If we represent red time-points by the symbol r, and green time-points by the symbol g, then a sequence of the form

$$r \quad r \quad r \quad g \quad g \quad g \quad g \quad r \quad r \quad g$$

shows the first three time-points were red and were followed by four green ones, and so on.

We are primarily interested in the delay which cars suffer. To find this delay we must calculate another sequence: the *queue* sequence. For our purposes the queue at any particular time-point is defined as the number of cars held over from that time-point to the next. With the simple rules of traffic behavior given above, once we know the arrival sequence, the red/green sequence, and the number of cars waiting at the intersection at some initial time-point, we can calculate the queues for all later time-points successively. We illustrate such a calculation below.

There is one more sequence of interest: that of departures. How does the process of crossing the intersection alter the spacing of cars? The departure sequence too can be calculated from the others.

We can now illustrate these sequences. The time-points are numbered t = 1, 2, 3 . . . . . and we will suppose that at the beginning of the period no cars were waiting to cross.

Time	1	2	3	4	5	6	7	8	9	10	11	12	13	14	15	16	17	18
Arrivals	0	1	1	0	0	1	0	0	0	1	1	1	0	1	0	0	0	1
Red/green sequence	g	g	r	r	r	r	g	g	g	r	r	r	g	g	r	r	r	g
Queue held over to next period	0	0	1	1	1	2	1	0	0	1	2	3	2	2	2	2	2	2
Cars waiting to cross	0	1	1	1	1	2	2	1	0	1	2	3	3	3	2	2	2	3
Departures	0	1	0	0	0	0	1	1	0	0	0	0	1	1	0	0	0	1

The cars waiting to cross at any time-point are those held over from the previous time-point, together with any car that arrives at the time-point considered.

In previous analysis of traffic delays the assumption was made that the arrivals of cars could be considered as generated by a Poisson process. This assumption, when it was checked against observation, was found quite adequate in many circumstances. Now that, for our present model, we have distorted nature slightly by making time move in jumps, we have to find an appropriate modification of this way of describing the structure of traffic. The modification we use, a very close analogue of the Poisson process for discrete time measurement, can be called the *binomial process*. The nature of the process can perhaps be seen most easily by the following way of deriving a sequence from it. Suppose that the flow of traffic is such that on the average 37 cars arrive per 100 time-points. Suppose we draw numbers at random from the set of numbers 1 to 100, replacing each one before drawing the next. When a number from 1 to 37 is drawn we write down 1; when a number greater than 37 is drawn we write down 0. If, as above, we consider 1 to represent the arrival of a car and 0 the nonarrival, then the sequence of 0's and 1's we obtain in this way can be taken to represent a possible flow of traffic having the specified average density. To obtain a different average density of traffic, a correspondingly different classification of the numbers 1 to 100 would be used. This average density in the minor road we have represented by α. It is defined as the ratio of the number of cars which arrive in a long period of time to the maximum number which could arrive provided the proper time spacing between cars is maintained. The corresponding quantity for the major road we have called ρ.

We have calculated the average delay for the case when "statistical stability" has been reached. This average is the same as the average over a period of time sufficiently long for the particular state of the intersection at the beginning of our observation to become unimportant. However, the calculations involve the assumption that congestion will not tend to increase indefinitely. The probability model we have used has the property that this event will in fact almost certainly not happen provided the average number of green points exceeds the average number of cars arriving at the intersection in the minor road. If this condition is satisfied, the queue of cars will certainly vanish again and again, even though at times it may build up to a considerable length.

The critical gap also needs redefining for the purposes of our discrete model. We have called it w and defined it as the number of time-points before the arrival of a car in the major road which are blocked by the closeness of that car. For example, if w = 2, the two time points before the arrival of the car in the major road will be blocked, and also the time-point at which it actually arrives.

The curves in Figures 1.8, 1.9, and 1.10 present the results of the calculations for this model. Based on the mathematical analysis given in Section 1.5, they show the mean delay in the minor road as a function of the traffic densities α and ρ in the minor road and major road, and the critical gap w. For a given value of ρ and w, as α increases, the mean delay increases, until at a certain value of α the congestion increases indefinitely. The intersection is not able to accommodate a density of traffic corresponding to that value of α or greater for an indefinite length of time.

It is important to note for purposes of analysis in other chapters that these average delay functions possess a curvature property called convexity (see Section 3.1.3).

The same type of analysis has been made in Section 1.5 for the repeated-cycle traffic-light case. The traffic lights are supposed to be red for r time-points and green for g time-points. The density of arrivals is represented by α as in the stop-sign case. As in that case the average wait over a long time period is calculated. Again congestion will certainly build up indefinitely unless the number of green points exceeds the number of arrivals over a long period. Thus the average delay is calculated on the supposition that this condition is satisfied.

A most striking by-product of our calculations is the adequacy of an approximation which has been used in the past for sparse traffic. The approximation is based on the supposition that the queue of cars has vanished at the beginning of each red period. Though this would seem a drastic assumption, the results calculated by using it turn out to be valid for nearly all the values of α, r and g for which we have carried through the calculations. The stability condition for queues not to grow indefinitely is $\alpha < \dfrac{g}{r+g}$, and the approximation is valid even when α is quite close to this limiting value.

1.3. The Uniform-Speed Capacity of a Road

In discussing road capacity we shall first examine a particular type of capacity curve which will be called the uniform-speed capacity curve. Among our reasons for giving some attention to this curve are

1) Its possible usefulness in the planning of large *directed* traffic movements such as army convoys, urban evacuations, etc.
2) Its very distinct difference from, and relation to, the more complicated notion of a capacity curve which is to follow. This

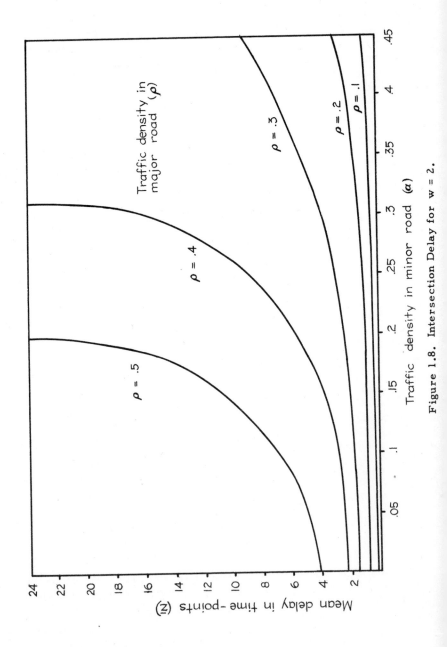

Figure 1.8. Intersection Delay for w = 2.

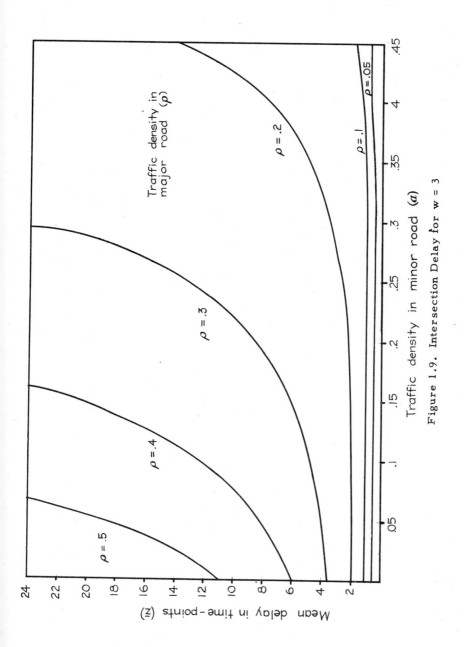

Figure 1.9. Intersection Delay for w = 3

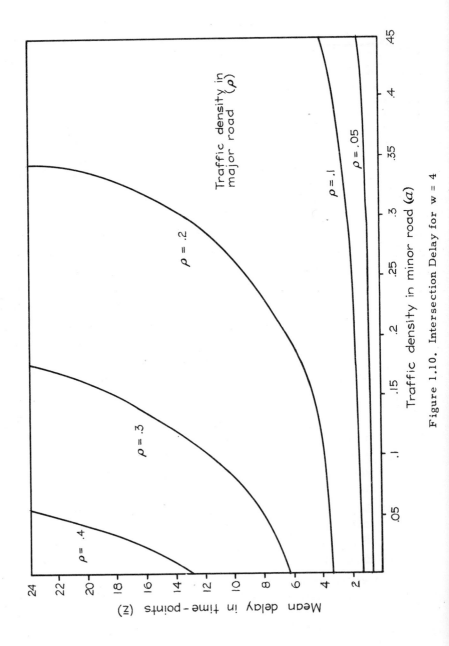

Figure 1.10. Intersection Delay for w = 4

difference is of some interest in itself, for it demonstrates the fact that the "capacity" of a facility must be defined with an eye toward the use to which the facility is put.

Consider a single-lane road over which traffic moves in one direction. A *uniform speed* will be said to exist when every vehicle moves at the same speed. At a given point on the road, the *uniform-speed capacity* at a given uniform speed is defined as the maximum traffic flow (measured in vehicles per hour) which can pass that point at that speed under certain assumed conditions. Obviously flow will depend on the distance-spacing between vehicles and will be at a maximum for any given speed when spacing is at a minimum, since flow equals speed divided by spacing.

The assumed conditions are those that affect the minimum spacing between vehicles at each uniform speed. These include not only such things as the physical characteristics of the road being examined but also some characteristics of the vehicle population being studied, and in addition a statement of whether the spaces between vehicles shall be determined by reference to some standard of safety or by observing the spacing actually maintained by drivers or perhaps in some other manner. The main problem involved in determining these capacities comes from the fact that by any realistic criterion the spacing between vehicles must increase with speed. The form this spacing function takes will seriously affect the shape of the curve relating uniform-speed capacity and uniform speed.

Four ways of determining these capacities suggest themselves:

1) Hypothetical spacing functions can be constructed and substituted in the relation

$$\text{flow} = \frac{\text{speed}}{\text{spacing}}$$

to give the maximum flow at each uniform speed.

2) Empirical spacing functions can be determined by observation of existing traffic flows, and they can be substituted in the relation of method (1).

3) Empirical estimates of uniform-speed capacities can be attempted by direct observation of flows, bypassing a determination of spacing.

4) Experiments can be performed.

To our knowledge the experimental method, interesting as it is, has never been carried out. Each of the others will be described below.

1.3.1. Hypothetical Spacing Functions

A minimum "safe" spacing function may be postulated on the basis of information about the distances required to decelerate vehicles from various speeds, and also on the basis of one's beliefs as to what constitutes safety. This has been the most common approach (Herrey and Herrey, 1945; Hess, 1950; extensive bibliography in Normann, February, 1942, p. 122). Without much justification it has usually been assumed that safety requires a distance between vehicles at least equal to that necessary to bring a vehicle to a full stop.[1] The mathematical form typically given this spacing function has been

$$(1.1) \qquad a + bu + cu^2$$

where

$$a = \text{average length of vehicle}$$

$$b = \text{perception plus reaction time}$$

$$(1.2) \qquad c = \frac{1}{2r}, \text{ where } r \text{ is the maximum rate of deceleration}$$

$$u = \text{speed}$$

All three values are affected by the composition of traffic (number of trucks, age of drivers, etc.). Time of day and location affect b; and road surface, weather, and grade and curvature of the road affect c. Some of the most careful studies of b have been made by De Sylva (1937), and of c by Moyer (1947). Various values used in constructing these spacing functions are interestingly compared by Normann and Walker (1949, p. 120). While much disagreement is evident, the values

$$(1.3) \qquad \begin{aligned} a &= 2.84 \times 10^{-3} \text{ miles} &&(15 \text{ feet}) \\ b &= 2.78 \times 10^{-4} \text{ hours} &&(1 \text{ second}) \\ c &= 9.47 \times 10^{-6} \text{ hours}^2/\text{mile} &&(\text{i.e. deceleration} \\ &&&= 21.6 \text{ ft./sec.}^2) \end{aligned}$$

are fairly typical and give an idea of the magnitudes involved. It will be seen that the "safe" trailing distance grows more and more rapidly as speed increases. The resulting uniform-speed capacity function which can be written

$$(1.4) \qquad \frac{u}{a + bu + cu^2}$$

reaches a maximum at some intermediate speed and declines thereafter. This means that at high levels of speed, the added spacing that is necessary for a further speed increase more than offsets the direct effects of speed itself in bringing about an increase in flow. The curve OA'A in Figure 1.11 is a uniform-speed capacity curve of this type.

---

1. The most notable exception to this statement is the work of Greenshields and Weida (1952), pp. 152-154, where it is argued that full-stop spacing is too conservative an interpretation of safety.

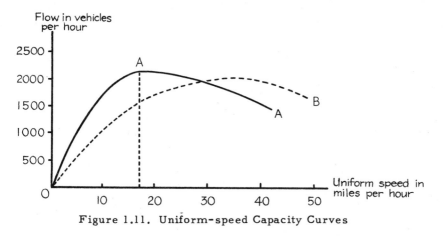

Figure 1.11. Uniform-speed Capacity Curves

In most of these studies the uniform speed corresponding to the point (.A' in Figure 1.11) of maximum flow has been found to be surprisingly low, in the 11-25 mph range;[2] the maximum flow itself is usually around 1800 vehicles per lane per hour   (Normann and Walker, p. 120).

A criticism which might be leveled against this kind of uniform-speed capacity curve concerns the concept of safety it uses. Minimum safe spacing is a difficult quantity to define to start with, and further-more, there is ample reason to believe that drivers do not space them-selves at distances which are perfectly safe anyway (Normann, 1939, pp. 226-227). While some attempts have been made to refine this concept of safety in order to secure a better correspondence between theory and observation, these attempts are more properly classified under the method to be described next.

1.3.2. Empirical Spacing Functions

An empirical spacing function can be found, and used in the same way as above to determine the uniform-speed capacity curve. One such procedure, reported by Normann (*ibid.*), was as follows. Of 8,500 vehi-cles recorded at one location, about 2,000 were traveling at the same speed as the vehicles just ahead of them. These were classified into speed groups. The next step was to find for each speed group the mean spacing between vehicles. To ensure, however, that the mean spacing thus derived was an accurate estimate of the mean *minimum* spacing for that speed group, it was necessary to exclude from the sample as many as possible of those vehicles which just happened to be moving at the same speed as preceding vehicles, without in any way being impeded by these preceding vehicles. In order to perform this elimination the

---

2. Perhaps the feeling that the speed at which flow is maximized must be greater than 11 or 12 mph accounts for the rather high value of deceleration cited as typical in formula 1.3 above.

time spacing, that is, the space in front of a vehicle divided by its speed, was calculated for all members of the sample.

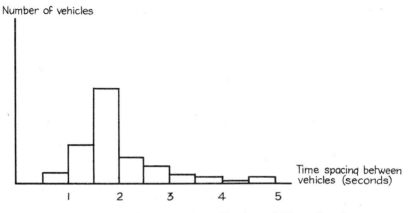

Figure 1.12.   A Frequency Distribution of Time Spacings
for a Single Speed Group

The histogram of Figure 1.12 gives a general indication of the relative frequencies of various time spacings in a single speed group. Since, in the case pictured, most of the time spacings are concentrated at the low values, and a very few are to be found at levels greater than four seconds, the investigators were probably justified in throwing out of the sample those vehicles with time spacings greater than four seconds. These, they assumed, were not traveling at minimum spacing. The same procedure was followed for all the speed groups, and the mean *distance* spacing of the reduced sample for each speed group was determined.

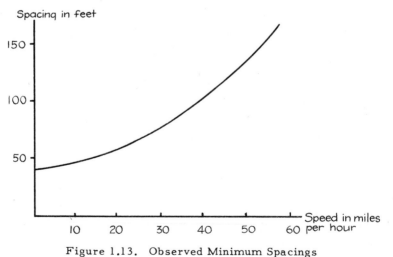

Figure 1.13.   Observed Minimum Spacings

Figure 1.13 shows, for each speed group, this mean minimum spacing in the feet of all vehicles spaced at less than four seconds. Using the data in Figure 1.13, a uniform-speed capacity curve was constructed which indicates for each speed the maximum flow possible if all traffic moved at just that speed. The resulting curve, OB in Figure 1.11, differs from a typical theoretical curve, OA'A in Figure 1.11, mainly in indicating greater flows at the higher speeds. Notice also that the uniform speed at which this curve attains its maximum flow is higher than before.

1.3.3. Direct Observations of Flows

The uniform-speed capacity curve might be estimated directly by fitting a curve to a set of maximums of observed flows for several different uniform speeds. The main difficulty encountered here is that very seldom are the higher *uniform* speeds observed. When speeds are high, some passing nearly always takes place. This difficulty points up one of the rather artificial features of a uniform-speed capacity function. No roads of importance are one-lane roads, yet the function is defined with the latter as a basis. A multiple-lane road is quite a different thing from a sum of single lanes. The complications introduced by passing will be dealt with in Section 1.4.

One of the reasons for the variety of methods used to determine uniform-speed capacity functions is that congestion often appeared to be present when flows were far short of the maximal levels indicated by the particular curve being used. It was then thought that a more careful procedure would lead to a function without this defect. But the trouble in many cases probably was that an average rather than a uniform speed was being used as the independent variable in the capacity function. The difference between the two cannot be neglected, as we shall see.

Difficulties such as these make it impossible to use a uniform-speed capacity curve alone to explain speed and flow limitations. There are, however, some reasons for finding realistic uniform-speed capacity curves for typical roads or points. Such information would be useful to an authority (such as the army) which had complete control of a traffic movement, so that all speeds could be specified. These functions also represent useful points of reference in the sense that they show the loss in terms of flow when drivers select a variety of speeds. In addition, they will be found useful below in the discussion of capacity concepts which take into account the fact that uniform speeds are not ordinarily found in practice.

1.4. The Free-Speed Capacity of a Road

For the reasons indicated the uniform-speed capacity curve was never found to be very useful. People do not all drive at the same speed ordinarily, and in those cases where they do some of them at least wish to go faster and will pass the cars ahead of them as soon as the opportunity arises. This leads to a bunching of traffic which the uniform-speed capacity curve does not take into account.

The capacity notion to be described here is the very different one developed by O. K. Normann and his associates in the Bureau of Public Roads and described in the *Highway Capacity Manual* (Normann and Walker, 1949). For a particular road a capacity curve is derived empirically which relates *average* speed and flow. The curves which have been published show that flow increases only at the expense of a marked reduction of average speed. Further work is necessary before this mechanism can be fully understood, but it seems plausible that at higher flows more passing per car is required to maintain a given distribution of speeds, that limited opportunities for passing prevent the maintenance of the higher speeds, and that flow reaches a maximum when all cars are traveling at very close to the same speed, which then is necessarily a relatively slow one.

1.4.1. Free-Speed Distribution

Before discussing this matter further, a word should be said about the way drivers' preferences affect the capacity relations we are about to discuss. Nearly every kind of capacity curve imaginable depends in some way on the characteristics of the vehicle and driver population it pretends to describe.

When this population changes, the capacity curve also changes and the problem is to relate the capacity curve to the underlying vehicle population in some simple way. The uniform-speed capacity curve depended on the minimum between-vehicle spacing required at different speeds by drivers, and it probably sufficed in this case to define "different vehicle populations" to mean "different spacing functions." While the populations may have differed in other respects as well, these were not important so far as uniform-speed capacity curves were concerned.

For the free-speed capacity curve the characteristic we have chosen to describe the vehicle population is (as the name of the curve indicates) its free-speed distribution. A driver's *desired* or *free* speed on a given road is that speed at which he chooses to travel when "alone" on the road, that is, when the preceding car is so far ahead as to have no influence whatsoever on the speed of the car in question. Since the matter is discussed again in Section 2.2.2 we shall only say here that the free speeds drivers select probably depend on the physical characteristics of the road and on their estimates of the risks and costs involved and the value they place on time. The "distribution" of free speeds over a given road for a specified group of drivers is simply a summary description of the free speeds of the group; it tells us what fraction of the drivers have free speeds between any two given limits. A graphic representation of a free-speed distribution is given in Figure 1.14 where the total area under the curve is equal to one and the fraction of drivers with free speeds between 30 mph and 40 mph is represented by the area ABDC, the fraction with free speeds between

40 mph and 50 mph by the area CDFE, etc. The reader who is interested in the actual free-speed distributions found to prevail in certain
instances is referred to the *Highway Capacity Manual* (Normann and
Walker, p. 32, Fig. 6).

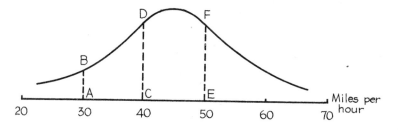

Figure 1.14. Graphic Representation of a Speed Distribution

To describe, as we are doing, a vehicle population by its free-speed
distribution is very obviously an oversimplification; for certainly there
are many other real differences which may be quite important, such as
the proportion of trucks in the population being considered, or the
lengths of opposing-lane gaps demanded for passing by the drivers.
However, the simple description will probably do for our purposes.
Whether or not more of the characteristics that distinguish different
groups of drivers should be used is a question that can only be decided
in practice. Once the reader is convinced of the usefulness of description by means of free-speed distributions, it should not be difficult for
him to imagine how other more complicated descriptions might be
handled.

1.4.2. Realized Speed Distribution

We shall now attempt both to summarize and to enlarge somewhat
upon the work of Normann and Walker in examining highway capacity in
terms of speed reductions. It should be made clear that while much of
what follows is based directly on material in the *Highway Capacity
Manual* and related publications (Normann, 1939, 1941; June, 1942), the
authors of that report are not to be held responsible for possible mis-
interpretations on our part, nor for additions we have made with which
they may not agree. The description will refer to a two-lane road which
carries traffic in both directions. The free-speed distributions of the
two streams of traffic will be assumed known, and we shall suppose that
a vehicle will move at its free speed whenever traffic conditions permit.
The distribution of desired speeds will ordinarily not be the same
as the distribution of actual speeds. For a fast car to pass a slow car
some empty space in the opposing lane is necessary. If the density of
vehicles (i.e. the number of vehicles per mile of road at any instant) in
this opposing lane is high, such spaces will seldom be available and the

passing maneuver will be delayed or prevented. As a result, the actual speed distribution will differ from the free-speed distribution, the lower speeds being relatively more frequent in the former.

Another way of looking at this effect that heavy traffic has on actual speeds is to concentrate our attention for a moment on a one-mile stretch of road with unrestricted visibility. Suppose that the southbound traffic flow is very low, so low in fact that for northbound traffic the free-speed distribution is the same as the actual speed distribution. Now let us ask ourselves how the total number of passing maneuvers per hour carried out by northbound vehicles on this one-mile stretch varies with the level of northbound flow. Suppose northbound flow doubles. A 50 mph driver will now find it necessary to complete twice as many passing maneuvers over the one-mile stretch as before, due to the doubling of the flow of vehicles moving at less than 50 mph. But since the flow of 50 mph vehicles has also doubled, this means the hourly number of passing maneuvers by 50 mph vehicles has increased by a factor of four. The same holds for all speeds, and it is only a step further to the conclusion that the total number of passers per mile of road per hour increases with the square of flow if the free-speed distribution remains unchanged.

If now the assumption of negligible southbound flow is dropped, it becomes clear that at some level of northbound flow, the number of northbound passing maneuvers required to maintain the free-speed distribution will be more than the gaps in the opposing traffic stream permit. As a result, some vehicles will be impeded and the realized speed distribution will no longer be the same as the free-speed distribution. Investigations have revealed roughly the way speed distributions change with increases in flow for some cases and have shown that the actual total number of passings per mile of road per hour increases with flow up to a certain point and then decreases gradually down to zero as flow becomes so great that all vehicles are forced to move at the same speed (Normann, June, 1942, p. 70).

The realized speed distribution for northbound traffic is clearly influenced by the flows of traffic in *both* directions on the road. If northbound flow increases, maintaining the same speed distribution requires more passing opportunities than before; if southbound flow increases, fewer passing opportunities present themselves than before. Both phenomena cause a change in the realized speed distribution. An elegant theory of road capacity would be one which described just this relationship. Given the two flows and the two free-speed distributions we could determine the two corresponding realized speed distributions. With this information we would be able to assess the effect of congestion on vehicles of each speed-class in the two traffic streams. However, this is obviously asking too much, at least in our present stage of developing a body of information on the behavior of traffic. A speed distribution is a rather large assembly of information. We shall settle for a simpler, substitute measure of the degree to which speeds have been affected by flows. The measure we use is the mean realized speed. Normann's group has in fact attempted more than this by making use to some extent of the standard deviation of realized speed, in addition to mean speed (Normann, 1939, p. 228). In subsequent discussion we shall for the most part ignore these more sophisticated descriptions of the speed-flow mechanism. It should of course be borne in mind that here is a possible weakness in our theory. Practical work may well indicate that mean speed is too gross a measure of the consequences of increased flow, in which case it will be necessary to incorporate additional measures such as standard deviation of mean speed, or one of the others suggested by Normann.

1.4.3. *Mean Speeds and the Free-Speed Capacity Function*

The question now becomes, how do northbound and southbound mean speeds depend on the two flows? When we move in the direction of further simplification we are faced with a situation much like adding together the two intersection flows in the example in Section 1.1. Northbound mean speed depends on southbound as well as northbound flow; is it going too far to suppose that northbound mean speed depends only on the sum of the two flows? Or, indeed, can we drop the final complication and say that speed averaged over both northbound and southbound traffic depends only on the sum of the two flows?

Of course these progressively simpler representations are at most approximations, and a final answer as to which of them is best for the purpose cannot be given here. In practice the choice will be dictated by the cost of obtaining data, the reliability of the resulting flow-speed relationships in making predictions, and the consequences of errors when the estimated relationships are applied to specific problems.

In any case, such questions as these, important as they are, need not be decided here. The analysis that follows may be applied to any of the various representations of the flow-speed relation. It is to make this last point clear that we emphasize these differences.

In one of the earliest articles (Normann, 1939, p. 229, Fig. 11) on the subject Normann chose one of the more complicated relationships for one particular road and by the method of least squares he fitted a plane to a set of observations on northbound mean speed, northbound flow, and southbound flow. Since the coefficients he estimated are of interest, we reproduce his result:

$$(1.5) \qquad \bar{u}_n = 44.92 - .01044x_n - .00719x_s$$

where $\bar{u}_n$ is in miles per hour and x_n and x_s in vehicles per hour. This plane, shown graphically in Figure 1.15, is an example of what we shall call a *free-speed capacity function* or where no confusion is likely to result simply a *capacity function* (or plane or curve, depending on the number of dimensions involved). The term *free speed* in this use does not mean (as in the case of the uniform-speed capacity function) that the function applies only to vehicles traveling at free speeds; we retain the

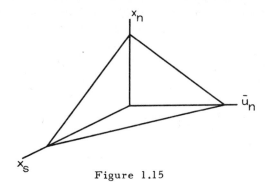

Figure 1.15

term here only to emphasize the fact that the function is based on a free-speed distribution.

More generally, a free-speed capacity function is the function relating flows and mean realized speeds on a particular road for a particular population of vehicles. Other and simpler examples are presented in the *Highway Capacity Manual*[3] where mean speed of all traffic on the road is made to depend on the *total* flow on the road. Graphs of these curves (which in fact have usually been assumed to be straight lines) are quite a bit easier to draw and to visualize, the number of dimensions being less. Figure 1.16 is one example. For reasons to be discussed below, the curve has not been extended all the way to the flow axis. Notice also

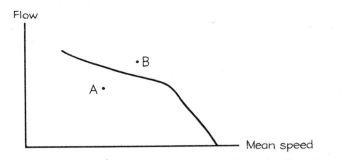

Figure 1.16. An Example of a Free-Speed Capacity Function

that in this example the curve is not a straight line; we have drawn it the way it is merely to emphasize the fact that from a theoretical point of view there is no reason to believe it to be so. We shall, nevertheless, often draw it as though it were, if only for convenience. Most investigators have found that a straight line provides a fairly good fit to observations.

---

3. *Op. cit.*, p. 31 Fig. 5, Curve 2 on p. 33 Fig. 7. Other similar examples are to be found in: Normann, June, 1942, p. 61 Fig. 6, p. 63 Fig. 8; Normann, 1939, p. 229 Fig. 12; Wardrop, Feb. and Mar., 1952, p. 2 Fig. 1; Glanville, 1949, p. 41 Fig. 9; Forbes, 1952, pp. 6, 7 Figs. 5, 6, respectively.

The important characteristic of all these curves, no matter what their degree of complication, is that they are negatively sloped — that is, mean speed decreases as flow increases. It should be emphasized that apart from sampling errors and errors of observation, only points *on* the curve are possible flow-speed combinations for the vehicle population with the assumed free-speed distribution. Points below the curve, such as A in Figure 1.16, would imply that some drivers are not going as fast as they both can and wish to, and the width and condition of the road and the presence of traffic prevent points such as B from occurring.

1.4.4. Relation Between the Free-Speed Capacity Curve and the Free-Speed Distribution

The position of a capacity curve at levels of flow approaching zero will vary with the vehicle population that the curve describes. When very little congestion is present nearly every vehicle will be able to travel at its free speed. At zero flow, therefore, mean realized speed is equal to mean free speed. If for a certain road it is known that Sunday drivers have a lower mean free speed than weekday drivers, we should expect the capacity curves for the two days to differ in a fashion like that indicated in Figure 1.17 (assuming the curves to be of the same simple functional form as the one in Figure 1.16). Here the points A and B, the mean speeds corresponding to zero flows for the Sunday and weekday traffic respectively, are also equal to the respective mean free speeds of those two days. The capacity curves both slope upward and to the left from these points.

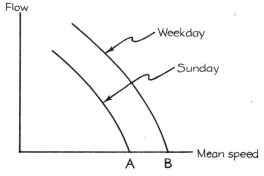

Figure 1.17. Capacity Curves Corresponding to Different Free-Speed Distributions

The difference in capacities between wide roads and narrow roads should show up in these curves more as a difference in slope than intercept. Suppose an improvement program is contemplated for a certain road whose capacity is represented by the curve AB in Figure 1.18. If the proposed improvements are effective in reducing congestion, a new capacity curve CB will result which will indicate for each level of flow a

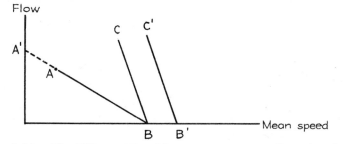

Figure 1.18.   The Effect of Road Improvement on a Capacity Curve

higher mean speed than before. As we should expect, the difference is greatest where congestion is high — that is, at high levels of flow. When flows approach zero, mean free speed prevails for both curves by the preceding arguments, and if we have reason to believe that people's free speeds will not be altered by the road improvement, these two points will be the same. The type of shift described seems to agree very well with some of the results of highway studies carried out by England's Road Research Laboratory (Wardrop, February and March, 1952, p. 2, Fig. 1).

It is quite conceivable of course that free speeds will change with the improvement. Wider roads are very likely to cause an upward shift in the whole free-speed distribution, with a consequent shift in the mean free speed from B to B' in Figure 1.18. The capacity curve in this case might look something like C'B', where the road improvement has changed (1) the slope of the curve through its direct effect on, say, passing opportunities; and (2) the speed intercept of the curve through its indirect effect on drivers' choices as to speeds.

Before further discussion of the influence of free speeds on the slope of capacity curves, we must cover a point we have so far glossed over. In Figures 1.16, 1.17, and 1.18 the curves have not been extended all the way to the flow axis. If in Figure 1.18 the dotted section AA' were added to the capacity curve AB, the whole curve would seem to tell us that for the appropriate road and vehicle population mean speed will be zero if flow rises to the level A'. But if mean speed is zero, all speeds are zero and flow cannot be positive. Clearly, the upward extension of the curve must end at some point such as A.

Generally speaking, as flow increases from very low levels, mean speed declines and the spread of the realized speed distribution grows smaller and smaller. Figure 1.19 portrays, in a very rough way, this change in the realized speed distribution. If flow continues to increase until the point is just reached where every vehicle is traveling at the same speed, the end point, referred to above, of the free-speed capacity curve will have been attained. The mean speed at this point will, under

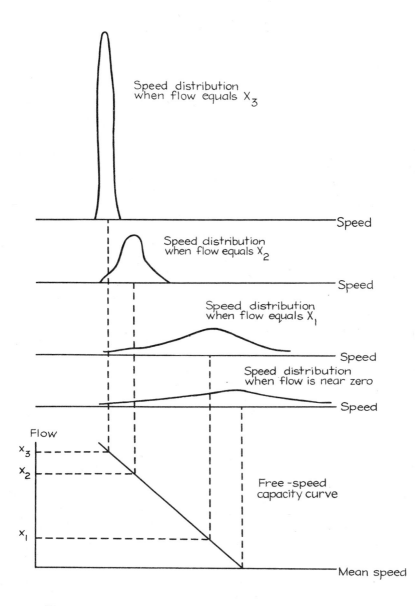

Figure 1.19. Effect of Changes in Flow on the Realized
            Speed Distribution

our assumptions, be the free speed of the slowest vehicle present.[4] It will not be less, for the free-speed capacity curve as we have defined it only describes speed reductions brought about by the absence of passing opportunities. Any reduction in the speed of this slowest vehicle, which has no need to pass, cannot therefore be explained by the capacity curve we have been discussing. It is true that flow-speed combinations above and to the left of the free-speed capacity curve's end point are possible, but a mechanism other than that of free speed and passing opportunity must be called upon to account for them. About this matter we shall have a word to say in a moment when we come to examine the relation between the free-speed and the uniform-speed capacity curves.

In Figure 1.19 the flow which corresponds to the end point of the curve drawn there is attained just above x_3. The mean speed at this point is meant to be equal to the lowest speed in each of the speed distributions pictured. The speed distribution at the end point cannot be drawn in the picture; the whole distribution would be lumped at one point.

It is clear that the complete specification of a particular free-speed capacity curve must include the location of this end point representing the flow and mean speed at which passing becomes impossible.[5] With Figure 1.19 before us it becomes a little easier to get a rough idea of how the shape of a capacity curve depends on the free-speed distribution behind it. A free-speed distribution with the same mean but less spread will be indicated by a more sharply rising capacity curve. Figure 1.20 gives such a comparison. A distribution with a higher mean but with the same spread will shift the capacity curve to the right. This effect is portrayed in Figure 1.21.

1.4.5. Some Shortcomings of the Free-Speed Capacity Concept

The importance of the effects described above comes from the fact that changes in flow may give rise to changes in the vehicle population and the underlying free-speed distribution. The reasons for such changes and the difficulties they occasion will become clearer in later chapters, but one rather extreme example here may serve to illustrate the point. Suppose on a certain road the usual traffic consists of passenger automobiles with fairly high free speeds. The capacity curve for this vehicle population on this road we shall suppose is well enough known to enable accurate predictions of the consequences of increases in

---

4. If we remember that the capacity curve of Fig. 1.19 is the simplified type which relates the average of the speeds of both north and southbound traffic to the sum of the two flows, the statement above is not strictly correct. Speeds will be reduced in both lanes by the increase of flow, but not necessarily to the same lower limits. In Fig. 1.19 the mean speed at the end point of the curve should really be regarded as the average (weighted by the flows) of these two lower limits, which in turn are the speeds at the low ends of the two free-speed distributions.

5. Normann and Walker (1949, pp. 31-33) indicate how these points may be located in practice by considering mean differences of speeds of successive vehicles.

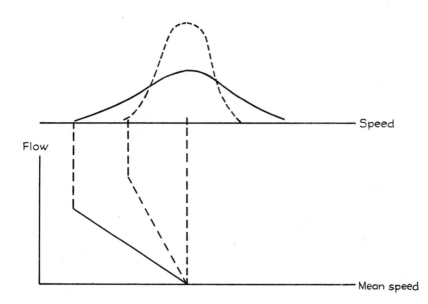

Figure 1.20. The Slope of the Capacity Curve is Greater When the Free-Speed Distribution Is More Concentrated

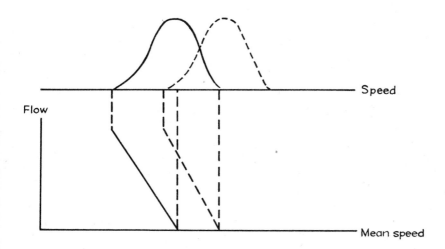

Figure 1.21. The Location of the Free-Speed Distribution Affects the Location of the Capacity Curve

flow *from this population*. But if the increment of flow is from another population, one, say, of trucks with low free speeds, then the capacity curve we started with is no longer the relevant one. A new capacity curve must be determined on the basis of the new free-speed distribution, which now describes the free speeds of the mixed population of passenger automobiles and trucks. In principle this procedure could be followed with each new increment of flow, but it is clear that much of the simplicity and convenience of the notion of a free-speed capacity curve is gone. In addition, the procedure introduces the practical difficulties of determining just how the free-speed distribution changes at each point. The analogue of this problem in economic theory is the simultaneous shifting of demand and supply curves.

A quite similar sort of difficulty comes about if the speeds at which drivers choose to travel when not immediately behind other vehicles depend on the level of traffic flow. The way we have made use of the free-speed distribution in defining capacity curves rules this type of phenomenon out of our theory, but it may well be too important to ignore. If increases in flow tend to slow down unimpeded drivers, the effect is the same as in the preceding example; it is just as though an influx of vehicles from a "slower" population had been let into the road.

The difference between these two sources of shifts in the capacity curve with changes in flow is that the second refers to a single population and the first to a change in the population itself. The second difficulty could be eliminated by a more or less complicated redefinition of the capacity curve. We have not attempted to resolve this second difficulty and unless a statement to the contrary is made it will be assumed throughout the rest of this study that changes of this kind in the free-speed distribution are negligible. While for many cases this assumption is quite realistic, enough exceptions exist for it to merit serious consideration.[6]

1.4.6. Relation between a Uniform-Speed Capacity Curve and a Free-Speed Capacity Curve

A moment ago we stated that speed-flow combinations above and to the left of the end point of the free-speed capacity curve are sometimes possible. For this to be the case the end point must fall below rather than on the corresponding uniform-speed capacity curve; it cannot be above the curve of course, for the spacing of cars prohibits such speed-flow combinations. At the rather extreme state of congestion represented by this end point all cars on the road are moving at very nearly the same speed. However, while a uniform speed can therefore be said to prevail, the flow corresponding to this speed need not be the (uniform-speed) capacity flow indicated by the uniform-speed capacity curve. This can be seen most easily if this congested situation is pictured as a series of queues of cars moving along in both directions. At

---

6. Cf. Section 2.1, where the concept of the *average road user* is introduced.

the head of each queue is a car with a relatively low free speed; the cars in each queue wish to pass this slow one but passing opportunities occur only rarely. Thus even though the gaps in the opposing traffic are so few as to cut down passing nearly to zero, they can still be sufficient for the flow to be below the level of the uniform-speed capacity curve.

Traffic from side roads could of course enter these gaps, thus raising flow above that level given by the end point of the free-speed capacity curve. In addition, as flows approached uniform-speed capacity, further reductions in mean speed might occur through more complicated mechanisms than the one we have described.[7]

1.5. Delay at an Intersection

In this section we find an analytic expression for the delay at a stop-sign intersection and also at a repeated fixed-cycle traffic light. In both cases the model is formulated in terms of discrete time points, as explained in Section 1.2.

1.5.1*. The Stop-Sign Case

1.5.1.1. With a General Major-Road Arrival Distribution.* For the arrival distribution in the minor road the assumptions are as follows. At most one car can arrive at any time-point. The arrivals at successive time-points form a binomial sequence with parameter α. By this statement we mean than the chance of a car arriving at any particular time-point is α, and is independent of what has happened at any previous time-point. The discrete formulation ensures that cars are spaced out. This probability model is very close to one that has been found to give a quite adequate description of traffic.

We suppose at first that the green intervals and red intervals generated by the traffic in the major road are formed as follows:

(i) The distribution of the lengths of green intervals is geometric — that is, the relative frequency of an interval of length x is $\pi^{x-1}(1-\pi)$, (x = 1, 2, . . .), where π is the parameter of the geometric distribution.

(ii) The relative frequency of red intervals of length b is f(b), (b = 1, 2, ...). This distribution is completely unrestricted for the present (except that it will be supposed to have both first and second moments).

(iii) The sequence of red and green intervals is such as would be obtained from a probability model in which red and green intervals were drawn alternately from their respective distributions, each drawing being quite independent of other drawings.

The red/green interval sequence generated by a binomial sequence of traffic in the major road, when there is a constant minimum safe interval in front of each car, is a special case of such a sequence. After finding the mean waiting time for cars in the minor road for the general sequence specified above, we will give the results for that case.

---

7. The work of Reuschel (1951) and Pipes (1950) appears to have some relevance to these states of severe congestion.

As was shown above, to find the mean wait per car in the minor road it is necessary to find the mean queue length $E(q_x)$. We will find this for the case for which the probability mechanism which is supposed to be generating the queue has settled down to equilibrium. Either the system will do this after a sufficient time or else the queues will tend to build up indefinitely, so that the mean waiting time will become longer and longer, the later a car arrives. The theory below shows that a necessary and sufficient condition for the attainment of equilibrium is that the average number of green time-points exceeds the average number of cars arriving. By q_x we will denote the queue which has to wait from time x to time x + 1.

We will find $E(q_x)$ in two stages, first taking averages over green points, and then over red points.

Let the green time-points be numbered consecutively, t_1, t_2, ..., t_g, ..., regardless of whether there is a red interval between them or not. Because green intervals have a geometric distribution with parameter π, the probability of a red interval occurring between any two consecutive time-points t_g and t_{g+1} in the green sequence is $(1 - \pi)$ and is independent of where other red intervals are interspersed in the sequence. This is the same as saying that the probability of one green point being followed by another is π.

Define the variables

$b_g \equiv$ the number of consecutive red points immediately following t_g, that is, the number of red points between t_g and t_{g+1}

$\beta_g \equiv$ the number of arrivals at red points between t_g and t_{g+1} ($\beta_g \leq b_g$);

$\alpha_g \equiv$ number of arrivals at t_g (so α_g is either 0 or 1).

If $b_g = 0$, then necessarily $\beta_g = 0$. Generally, $q_{g+1} = \max [(q_g + \alpha_{g+1} + \beta_g - 1), 0]$, which we may also write

(1.6) $$q_{g+1} = q_g + \alpha_{g+1} + \beta_g - 1 + \delta_g$$

where

(1.7)
$$\delta_g = 0 \text{ if } q_g + \alpha_{g+1} + \beta_g > 0$$

$$\delta_g = 1 \text{ if } q_g + \alpha_{g+1} + \beta_g = 0 .$$

Thus q_g is generated by a Markoff process of a type discussed in the literature. The necessary and sufficient condition for such a process to settle down to statistical equilibrium is that

$$E(\alpha_{g+1} + \beta_g) < 1 .$$

That is, on the average, less than one car arrives per green point. The necessity is obvious; the sufficiency was shown in Kendall's paper (1951).

The mean queue at green points, $E(q_g)$, can now be found by a device used for a similar problem by Kendall.

When the process has settled down to statistical equilibrium $E(q_{g+1}) = E(q_g)$. Therefore, taking expectations in (1.6),

(1.8) $\qquad E(\delta_g) = 1 - E(\alpha_{g+1}) - E(\beta_g)$

and also

(1.9) $\qquad E(\delta_g^2) = E(\delta_g)$ since $\delta_g = 0$ or 1 .

By (1.7)

(1.10) $\qquad E\,\delta_g\,(q_g + \alpha_g + \beta_g) = 0$.

Squaring (1.6) we have

(1.11) $\qquad q_{g+1}^2 = q_g^2 + (\alpha_{g+1} + \beta_g - 1)^2 + \delta_g^2 + 2\delta_g\,(q_g + \alpha_{g+1}$
$\qquad\qquad + \beta_g) - 2\delta_g + 2q_g\,(\alpha_{g+1} + \beta_g - 1)$.

Taking expectations in (1.11) and using (1.8), (1.9), (1.10), and the further equilibrium condition $E(q_{g+1}^2) = E(q_g^2)$ we obtain:

(1.12) $\qquad E\,[(2q_g + 1)(1 - \alpha_{g+1} - \beta_g)] = E\,[(\alpha_{g+1} + \beta_g - 1)^2]$.

To find $E(\beta_g)$ notice that the probability that there is a red interval between t_g and t_{g+1} (i.e. that the point $t_g + 1$ is red) is $(1 - \pi)$, and the mean number of arrivals, if there is a red interval, is $\alpha E(b_g)$, $E(b_g)$ being the mean of the distribution $f(b_g)$ from which the red intervals are considered to be drawn. Accordingly,

(1.13) $\qquad E(\beta_g) = (1 - \pi)\,\alpha\,E(b_g)$.

Similarly, by just taking expectations over red intervals of length b, and then over red intervals of all lengths, we get

(1.14) $\qquad E(\beta_g^2) = (1 - \pi)\,\alpha^2\,E(b_g^2) + \alpha\,(1 - \alpha)\,E(b_g)$.

Also

(1.15) $\qquad E(\alpha_g) = E(\alpha_g^2) = \alpha$.

Using the independence of α_{g+1}, β_g, and q_g, (1.12) can be written

(1.16) $\qquad [2\,E(q_g) + 1]\,[1 - E(\alpha_{g+1}) - E(\beta_g)]$
$\qquad\qquad = E(\alpha_{g+1}^2) + E(\beta_g^2) + 1 - 2E(\alpha_{g+1}) - 2E(\beta_g)$
$\qquad\qquad\qquad + 2E(\alpha_{g+1})\,E(\beta_g)$.

Substituting the values given in (1.13), (1.14), and (1.15) and solving for $E(q_g)$ we get

$$(1.17) \qquad E(q_g) = \frac{\alpha^2(1 - \pi) \left[E(b_g^2) + E(b_g)\right]}{2[1 - \alpha - \alpha(1-\pi) \ E(b_g)]} \quad .$$

Now we must consider the queue length at red points. Suppose[8] a red interval of length b comes between t_g and t_{g+1}. We can number the points of the interval $t_{g_1}, t_{g_2}, \ldots, t_{g_b}$. The queue length just before the start of the interval will be q_g, and these cars will remain throughout the interval. Since b_g and q_g are independent, (1.17) gives the expected size of this "initial queue" over red as well as over green time-points. We require therefore only the expected length of that part of the queue made up of cars that arrive during red intervals.

If there is an arrival at t_{g_1}, it will be in the queue at $t_{g_1}, t_{g_2}, \ldots,$ t_{g_b}. It will thus add b to the sum of the queues over the red interval. Similarly, an arrival at t_{g_2} adds b-1 to the sum. Thus the mean addition to queues per red interval of length b caused by arrivals during such intervals is $\frac{b(b+1)}{2} \alpha$, and the mean addition per point in red intervals of length b caused by arrivals in those intervals is $\frac{b+1}{2} \alpha$.

A proportion $\frac{b \ f(b)}{E(b)}$ of red points lies in red intervals of length b. Therefore the mean addition per red point caused by arrivals during red intervals is

$$(1.18) \qquad \underset{b}{\Sigma} \ \frac{b(b+1)}{2} \ \frac{f(b)}{E(b)} \ \alpha = \frac{\alpha}{2E(b)} \ [E(b^2) + E(b)] \ .$$

Thus the proportion of red points in the total is

$$(1.20) \qquad \frac{(1-\pi) \ E(b)}{1 + (1-\pi) \ E(b)}$$

and the mean addition to the queue per time-point is

$$\frac{(1-\pi)\alpha}{2} \cdot \frac{E(b^2) + E(b)}{1 + (1-\pi) \ E(b)} \quad .$$

Adding this to (1.17) we get

$$(1.21) \qquad \frac{\alpha(1-\pi) \ [E(b^2) + E(b)]}{2[1 + (1-\pi) \ E(b)] \ [1 - \alpha - \alpha(1-\pi) \ E(b)]}$$

as the mean queue size over all time-points.

---

8. For simplicity, we shall drop the subscript g in the rest of this section.

1.5.1.2*. *Binomial Arrivals on the Major Road.* In this section we consider the case for which the traffic in the major road is also described by a binomial sequence, of parameter ρ. In front of each car in the major road there is a minimum safe interval of time-points. By this statement we mean that if a car arrives in the major road at time t, then no car in the minor road can cross at time t - w + 1, t - w + 2, ..., t, that is, an interval of w points up to and including t red points.

Under these conditions we can examine the structure of the sequence of red and green intervals generated by the traffic in the major road. The length of the green intervals has a geometric distribution, with parameter $1 - \rho$. If we put $1 - \rho \equiv \pi$ in the preceding analysis, this case turns out to be a special case of the more general one treated above. The result for the mean waiting time given by (1.21) shows that for our present purposes we only require the first two moments of the distribution of the lengths of red intervals. We find these below and are thus enabled to exhibit the mean waiting time per car as a function of the densities in the minor and major roads respectively, and of w, the minimum safe interval. This function is shown in Figures 1.8, 1.9, and 1.10.

1.5.1.3*. *Distribution of the Lengths of Green Intervals.* We will suppose from now on that the time-points are numbered in sequence t = ..., -1, 0, 1, ... For the sake of brevity, if a car in the major road arrives at the intersection at the time-point t = t', we will say that there is a car at t = t'. The safe interval w is supposed an integer and is defined as follows. Suppose the point t = 1 is the first point of a green interval; then there must be a car at t = 0, and no cars at t = 1, 2, ..., w. The point t = 2 is also a green point if and only if there is no car at t = (w + 1). Thus, given that t = 1 is a green point, the probability that t = 2 is a green point is $\pi = (1 - \rho)$. Similarly, the probability that the green interval will continue from t = 2 to t = 3 is π. By induction, the probabilities of green interval lengths of 1, 2, 3, ... are proportional to 1, π, π^2, ... and so must be

(1.22) $(1 - \pi), \pi(1 - \pi), \pi^2(1 - \pi), \ldots$

and these probabilities define a geometric distribution.

Now to derive E(b) and E(b^2), suppose t = 1 is the first point of a red interval. This means that there is a car at t = w, but none at t = 0, 1, 2, ..., w - 1. The red interval will end at t = w if there is no car at t = w + 1, w + 2, ..., 2w. However, if the red interval does go on, suppose the next car after the one at t = w is at t = w + x_2, where $1 \leq x_2 \leq$ w. We can say that the second car contributes a length x_2 to the length of the interval. We can also say that the first car always contributes a length x_1 = w to the interval. If the red interval continues to a third car, we can consider the contribution, x_3, of the third car to the length of the red interval, and so on.

We will now find the probability that the red interval is formed by just r cars. If there are already r - 1 cars in the interval, the probability that there will be no more is $\pi^w \equiv P$, say. Thus the probability that the interval will continue is 1 - P. Hence the probability that the interval will contain just r cars is $(1 - P)^{r-1} P$.

If the red interval is formed by just r cars, the number of points it covers is $x_1 + \ldots + x_r$, where $x_1 = w$ and $1 \leq x_i \leq w$, $i = 2, \ldots, r-1$.

The distribution function of each x_i is the same for $i > 1$. Therefore if the moment generating function (m.g.f.) of x_i is $\phi(u)$, say, ($i = 2, 3, \ldots$), then, since the m.g.f. of $x_1 = w$ is e^{wu}, the m.g.f. of $x_1 + x_2 + \ldots + x_r$ is

(1.23) $\phi^{r-1} e^{wu}$

and the m.g.f. of red-interval length if the red interval can contain any number of cars is

(1.24) $X(u) = \sum_{r=1}^{\infty} \phi^{r-1} e^{wu} P(1 - P)^{r-1} = \dfrac{e^{wu} P}{1 - (1-P) \phi}$.

It is also necessary to find $\phi(u)$. Since

(1.25) $\text{Prob } (x_i = x) = \dfrac{\pi^{x-1}}{\sum_{x=1}^{w} \pi^{x-1}} = \dfrac{1 - \pi}{1 - P} \pi^{x-1}$ $(i \geqq 2)$

we have

(1.26) $\phi(u) = \dfrac{\sum_{x=1}^{w} e^{ux} \pi^{x-1}}{\sum_{x=1}^{w} \pi^{x-1}} = \sum_{x=1}^{w} e^{ux} \left[\dfrac{1-\pi}{1-P} \cdot \pi^{x-1} \right]$

$= \dfrac{1 - Pe^{wu}}{1-P} \cdot \dfrac{1 - \pi}{1-\pi e^u} \cdot e^u$.

Hence

(1.27) $X(u) = \dfrac{e^{-u} - \pi}{P^{-1} [e^{-(w+1)u} - e^{-wu}] + 1 - \pi}$.

We have to find $E(b) = X'(0)$ and $E(b^2) = X''(0)$. By straightforward but somewhat tedious evaluation we obtain

(1.28) $E(b) = X'(0) = \dfrac{1-P}{(1-\pi) P}$

and

$$(1.29) \qquad E(b^2) = X''(0) = \frac{1}{1-\pi} - \left[\frac{3-\pi}{(1-\pi)^2} + \frac{2w}{(1-\pi)}\right]\frac{1}{P} + \frac{2}{(1-\pi)^2 P^2} \; .$$

Putting these values in (1.21), we find the mean queue size per time-point to be

$$(1.30) \qquad E(q) = \frac{\alpha\,[1-P(1 + w\rho)]}{\rho\,(P - \alpha)} \; .$$

Dividing this waiting time by the α cars per time-point we get

$$(1.31) \qquad \frac{1 - P\,(1 + w\rho)}{\rho\,(P-\alpha)}$$

as the mean waiting time per car, where $P = \pi^w = (1 - \rho)^w$. The necessary and sufficient condition for the system to settle down to statistical equilibrium is

$$(1.32) \qquad \alpha < (1 - \rho)^w \; .$$

The function (1.14) is the one plotted in Figures 1.8, 1.9, and 1.10 for various values of ρ, α and w.

1.5.1.4*. Two-Way Traffic in the Main Road. If there is a two-way stream in the main road, the results still apply with suitable reinterpretation of the parameters, provided both streams are binomial. We assume the safe distance for crossing, w, is the same for both streams. If ρ_1, ρ_2 are the densities in the two streams, the probability that a time-point will be occupied by a car in either of the streams is $\rho_1 + \rho_2 - \rho_1\,\rho_2$ and we can set ρ equal to this value in the formulae above.

We have not yet fitted these formulae to actual data, as we have not yet found any data in a suitable form. It is therefore difficult to tell just what the effects of the simplifications we have made will be. However, from the data in the papers by Raff and Greenshields it can be seen that w may not be constant but may sometimes vary fairly widely from car to car. The formula may still be fairly accurate if we use, in place of w, some parameter of the distribution of w. Previous suggestions as to what parameter to use include the mean of the w distribution (Greenshields) and the median (Raff), but neither of these need necessarily be the best, as the following argument will show.

Consider the mean waiting time when α is small. In this case

$$(1.33) \qquad \bar{z} = \frac{1}{\rho P}\,(1 - P - w\rho\,P)$$

approximately. Expressing P in terms of ρ we have

$$(1.34) \qquad \bar{z} = \frac{1}{\rho}\,(1-\rho)^{-w} = \frac{1}{\rho}\left[(1 + w\rho) + \frac{w(w+1)}{2}\,\rho^2 + \ldots\right] - \frac{1}{\rho} - w.$$

approximately. If ρ is also small then

$$(1.35) \qquad \bar{z} = \frac{\rho}{2} w (w + 1)$$

approximately. When α is small, there is a negligible chance that a queue will form. Thus if w has a distribution, the mean waiting time can be obtained by averaging (1.35) over the distribution of w. Then

$$(1.36) \qquad \bar{z} = \frac{\rho}{2} E \left[w (w + 1) \right] \quad ,$$

suggesting that the constant $\bar{w}$ which gives the best fit is the solution of the equation $\bar{w} (\bar{w} + 1) = E \left[w (w + 1) \right]$.

1.5.2*. Repeated-Cycle Traffic-Lights Case

In this case a red interval of length r is followed by a green interval of length g time-points, and then the whole cycle is repeated. To find the mean waiting time it is necessary to find the average queue length over all time-points. First we find the queue length at the start of the xth red interval, q_x say.

Let u_x be the number of cars arriving in the xth cycle consisting of a red interval and the succeeding green interval. If q_{x+1} is the queue at the start of the next red interval, then

$$(1.37) \qquad q_{x+1} = \max (q_x + u_x - g, 0) \quad ,$$

where u_x is distributed over $0, 1, 2, \ldots\ldots, r + g$ in a binomial distribution with parameter α, that is,

$$(1.38) \qquad \text{Prob} (u_x = n) = \binom{r + g}{n} \alpha^n (1 - \alpha)^{r + g - n} \quad .$$

Thus the q_x are generated by a Markoff chain. The condition that this process should settle down to statistical equilibrium is

$$(1.39) \qquad u_x < g.$$

It is simple to find a complete analytic solution for the distribution of q_x when the system has attained statistical equilibrium as the solution of a finite difference equation. However, we will confine this discussion to the calculation of mean queue length over all time-points. We will do this calculation in two parts, first considering the mean car-points of waiting during red intervals, and then during green intervals.

For the red interval the calculation is similar to that in (1.21) above. The queue which is waiting over until the first point of the interval stays throughout the interval, and thus contributes $r E(q_x)$ to the average car-points of waiting during each red interval. A car arriving at the first point of the interval contributes r, and as the probability of a car arriving at that point is α, the mean contribution to the wait is αr.

The mean contribution per interval from the second point is $\alpha(r-1)$, etc., the contribution from arrivals at the last red time-point being α. So the total red-interval waiting of cars arriving in the red interval averages $\dfrac{\alpha\ r(r+1)}{2}$ per red interval and the mean amount of waiting during each red interval by all cars is

(1.40) $$r\left[E\left(q_x\right) + \frac{\alpha}{2}\left(r + 1\right)\right] .$$

Now we must find the mean amount of waiting during green intervals. Suppose the queue at the beginning of the green interval is q_g. Consider the mean wait of cars in the queue if all subsequent time-points were green. The time taken for the queue to diminish by one (if it is not zero in the first place) is the number of green points to and including the first one in which a car does not arrive; this time is thus distributed geometrically, with parameter α and mean $\dfrac{1}{1-\alpha}$. The queue during all but the last of these time-points is q_g; during the last time-point it is $q_g - 1$. The mean car-points of waiting during this time is thus $\dfrac{1}{1-\alpha}\ q_g - 1$.

The time taken for the queue to diminish by one more is distributed in the same way, and the queue during all but the last of these time-points is $q_g - 1$. If all subsequent time-points were green, the process would continue until the queue had vanished altogether. The total wait for that time would have the mean

(1.41) $$\sum_{x=1}^{q_g}\left[\frac{1}{1-\alpha}\ x - 1\right] = \frac{1}{2(1-\alpha)}\left[q_g(q_g + 1)\right] - q_g ,$$

so that, averaging over the q_g distribution, the mean wait would be

(1.42) $$\frac{1}{2(1-\alpha)}\ E\left[q_g^2 + (2\alpha - 1)\ q_g\right] .$$

However, the green interval is not in fact infinite, and we must subtract the wait that would reach over into the next red interval. To do this we subtract the wait attributable to the queue at the beginning of the next red interval. This will average

(1.43) $$\frac{1}{2(1-\alpha)}\ E\left[q_x^2 + (2\alpha - 1)\ q_x\right] .$$

Thus the mean wait over the finite green interval is

(1.44) $$\frac{1}{2(1-\alpha)}\ E\left[q_g^2 - q_x^2 + (2\alpha - 1)\ (q_g - q_x)\right] .$$

Suppose v_x is the number of cars arriving in the xth red interval; v_x = 0, 1, 2, ..., r. Then $q_g = q_x + v_x$ and $E(q_g) = E(q_x) + E(v_x)$. Since v_x is independent of q_x it follows that

(1.45) $\qquad E(q_g^2) = E(q_x^2) + 2\,E(v_x)\,E(q_x) + E(v_x^2)$.

Cars arrive with frequency α in both red and green intervals, so $E(v_x)$ = r α. And since v_x is binomially distributed, we have

(1.46) $\qquad E(v_x^2) = r\,a(1 - a) + r^2\,\alpha^2$.

Thus the mean car-points of waiting during each green interval becomes, by substituting these values,

(1.47) $\qquad \dfrac{\alpha\,r}{1-\alpha}\left[\,E(q_x) + \dfrac{\alpha}{2}\,(r+1)\,\right]$.

Adding the amounts of waiting given by (1.40) and (1.47) for the red and green intervals, the mean amount of waiting per cycle is

(1.48) $\qquad \dfrac{r}{1-\alpha}\left[\,E(q_x) + \dfrac{\alpha}{2}\,(r+1)\,\right]$

and the mean wait per car will be

(1.49) $\qquad \dfrac{r}{(1-\alpha)(g+r)}\left[\,\dfrac{E(q_x)}{\alpha} + \dfrac{r+1}{2}\,\right]$.

Thus we only need to find $E(q_x)$. It seems, however, that the simplest way to find $E(q_x)$ is not from the analytic solution. The q_x distribution can be found numerically from the generating equation by a simple iteration. (The matrix is infinite, so it has to be truncated. It can be proved that this type of truncation can still give approximations to the ergodic probabilities of the infinite matrix however.) The mean wait can then be calculated by the formula given.

1.6. An Application of the Intersection Model to Road Capacity

When fast cars pass a slow car on a two-lane highway, the situation shows some rather close similarities to the case of a car in a minor road crossing a major road at a stop sign. A fast car coming up behind a slow car must wait until there is a sufficient gap in the opposing traffic. When such a gap appears it may be able to pull over into the other lane and pass. If, ahead of it, there are other cars also waiting for an opportunity to pass the slow car, then our car will usually be able to pass only after these other cars have done so. The relation with the wait at a stop sign is clear. Passing the slow car corresponds to crossing the intersection. The opposing traffic, which has the right of way in its own lane, corresponds to the major-road traffic. The fast cars coming up behind the slow car correspond to the minor-road traffic.

And we can suppose, as a simplified description of drivers' behavior, that fast cars will only pass when there is no car due to come in the opposing lane for at least some fixed time interval, which we can call the critical gap.

The analogy is close enough to give some hope that the quantitative theory developed for the stop-sign case may also be useful in giving a theoretical basis for the free-speed capacity curve on a two-lane highway. As a first and perhaps rather drastic simplification, we might suppose that in one of the lanes there are just two types of cars, slow and fast, and that the slow cars are distributed sparsely on the road. In the opposing stream the traffic all goes at roughly the same speed. If we could know the average delay to fast cars in passing each of the slow cars as a function of the densities of fast cars and the density of the opposing stream, we could then derive a free-speed capacity curve for this simple case. We show how this can be done in the next section.

1.6.1*. Free-Speed Capacity Derived from the Average Delay

Suppose that the speed of the slow cars is v_1, and that they are, on the average, a distance d apart. The speed of the fast cars is v_2.

We will for simplicity make an extra assumption, that the average delay of a fast car in passing a slow car is the same for each slow car, W say. Such an assumption is probably adequate if, for example, the fast traffic and slow traffic are both sparse, so that the fast cars do not interfere with each other in passing a slow car. We have tried to test the validity for denser fast traffic by means of "Monte Carlo" experiments (that is, numerical experiments designed to simulate traffic behavior). The results of these experiments are discussed later in this section. W is a function of the opposing traffic density and of the critical gap. However, we will not show this dependence in our notation.

We want to find the average speed of the fast cars, taking into account their delay. The speed of the other traffic is unchanged by the congestion on the road. To do this we will find the distance covered by a fast car in a period of time of length T. T can be divided into T_2, the time during which the car is going at its free speed, v_2 and T_1, the time during which it is delayed behind a slow car traveling at v_1. The average speed v of a fast car can then be written

$$(1.50) \qquad v = \frac{v_1 T_1 + v_2 T_2}{T_1 + T_2} \ .$$

If by N we denote the average number of slow cars overtaken by one fast car in time T, then we have

$$(1.51) \qquad N = \frac{T_2}{d/(v_2 - v_1)} \ ,$$

since on the average a fast car takes a time $d/(v_2 - v_1)$ to travel between one slow car and another at its free speed, and it spends a time T_2 traveling at its free speed. We can now write $T_1 = NW$ and

$T_2 = Nd/(v_2 - v_1)$. Substituting for T_1 and T_2 in the expression for v, canceling the N's, and multiplying numerator and denominator by $(v_2 - v_1$ we find

$$(1.52) \qquad v = \frac{Wv_1(v_2-v_1) + dv_2}{W(v_2 - v_1) + d} \ .$$

A similar formula can be derived if we suppose that there is sparse traffic traveling at more than two speeds on the road.

The average speed of both kinds of traffic, fast and slow, taken together, is given by

$$(1.53) \qquad M_1 \ v_1 + M_2 \ \frac{W(v_2 - v_1) \ v_1 + dv_2}{W(v_2 - v_1) + d} \ ,$$

where M_1 and M_2 are the relative numbers of the fast and slow cars. This formula gives a theoretical form to the free-speed capacity curve in the case which we consider.

1.6.2*. A Monte Carlo Experiment

We have assumed above that the mean delay of traffic in passing each slow car is the same. This assumption needs examination if the fast traffic is dense. Our theory of passing behavior leads us to question it for the following reason. The mean delay of cars crossing an intersection (or passing a slow car) depends on the distribution in time of the arrivals of such cars. In our derivation of a theoretical formula we have assumed a particular form for this distribution: that the arrivals form a binomial sequence. However, if cars arrive in a binomial sequence, they do not leave the cause of congestion (the intersection or slow car) in a binomial sequence. Thus their average wait behind this next slow car may be different from the previous one. In the same way the spacing distribution may change again in passing this obstacle; so the average wait behind the next slow car may be still different.

Thus far we are expressing theoretical possibilities. We have not yet succeeded in treating analytically this type of question about passing through successive queues. We therefore decided to resort to "Monte Carlo" experiments, that is, experiments with simulated traffic streams generated by random devices, to get a feel for the problem and to judge the importance of these effects. These experiments did not have very positive results. However, we will report them very briefly here, as they may give some useful information to others faced with the same sort of problems. When we started the experiments we had two alternative hypotheses, either of which would be useful in deriving a free-speed capacity curve.

The first was that despite the modification of the spacing sequence in passing through each queue, the formulae derived from the binomial assumption were satisfactory in any case.

The second was that, failing the first assumption, the mean delay changes for the first few queues through which the fast car passes, but

fairly quickly settles down to be more or less constant for later cars,
though this constant might be different from the result derived for the
binomial sequence.

To explore these possibilities the experiments we performed were
as follows. Initially, a sequence of minor-road (or "fast-car") arrivals
was generated over 500 time-points by drawings from a binomial distribution. The output from this distribution was passed through a
red/green sequence also derived from a binomial sequence, with the
assumption of a constant critical gap.

The departure sequence, derived by using the method described in
Section 1.2.4, was used as the arrival sequence of an exactly similar
type of queueing process. Since all the fast cars would take the same
time to cover the distance between slow cars, we could neglect this time
in our calculations. The whole process was repeated fifteen times,
representing the traffic successively passing fifteen slow cars on the
road.

In computing the average waiting time, that is, the average queue
length over the period, it was decided to neglect the first time-points,
while the process was starting up. An arbitrary rule was used that for
each process the waiting time would be computed from a time-point 40
time units after the queue first became non-zero. The mean waiting
time was calculated by taking the average queue length over time-points
from that point to the last (the 500th).

The sequences fluctuated rather heavily from one process to the
next. Part of these fluctuations may be due to the relative shortness of
the series. The queue series are necessarily highly autocorrelated and
this means that, as a statistical sample, the series are equivalent to a
much smaller number of "effective" or "independent" observations than
the original 500 time-points. In any case, the experiments we performed give no evidence of stability of mean waiting time.

The work was done on a punched-card machine. The results show
that if Monte Carlo methods are to be used in this type of work, the experiments would have to be on a still larger scale, so that an electronic
computer would probably be appropriate. But it does not seem that such
experiments will give very useful results without more theoretical
knowledge of repeated queue processes.

Chapter 2

DEMAND

One of the striking features of traffic is its resemblance to physical flows. The relations between speed and volume and such phenomena as the propagation of waves of stopping and acceleration are understandable in large part from the mechanics of motion (see, e.g., Herrey and Herrey, 1945; Pipes, 1952). However, appealing as this physical view of the matter is, it neglects the purposive aspect of traffic, which becomes particularly important when attention is shifted from the single road to an entire network, that is to say, when we are interested in understanding the generation and distribution of traffic within a system of interconnected roads.

The point of view to be adopted from here on is that vehicles are operated by people who (1) have a range of choices available to them and (2) are motivated by economic considerations in their decisions. This element of choice prevails even though, once committed to the road, the movement of vehicles is strongly circumscribed by the traffic conditions around them. For there is always the question why people, anticipating these constraints, and particularly the irritations of congestion, still choose to go when, where, and in the manner they go.

The study of rational behavior in the presence of choice leads into the domain of economics. In this and the following three chapters some applications of economic theory to highway transportation will be explored. The purpose is not to exhaust all economic aspects that seem relevant or important. Rather the argument is constructed with reference to two points which may be regarded as but two aspects of the same matter: that it is possible to give some economic explanation of the distribution of traffic in a network; and that this distribution, as it forms itself spontaneously, falls short of efficiently utilizing the available capacity. For a fairly systematic development of this topic, a number of concepts must be introduced and some principles postulated, which may seem rather trivial if looked at in isolation. But emphasis here is on the fitting together of all relevant concepts into a theory. The discussion of fundamental concepts falls for the most part into the present chapter. It has been labeled *Demand*, because this seems to be the most characteristic notion that an economic viewpoint can contribute.

The fundamental question in capacity theory, discussed in the preceding chapter, is how flow on a road determines the traffic conditions, mainly average speed. This puts flow into the role of a cause. We can, however, raise the reverse question: how do traffic conditions affect the public's decisions of which the flow is the actual result? This is the problem of the current chapter on demand. The actual determination of the flows through the interaction of demand for transportation and capacity for accommodating it is deferred to the following chapter on equilibrium. Unless otherwise noted we shall deal with the problem of passenger traffic only.

2.1. Decisions of Road Users

A first step toward economic analysis is to disaggregate flow and take notice of the various *road users*. These fall into classes that are distinguished by origin, by destination, and by behavior characteristics such as free speed. Whenever we speak of the demand for road transportation we mean the demand, on the part of road users (or sometimes only the road users in a particular free-speed class), for transportation from a particular origin to a particular destination. Whenever we disregard the different free speeds of road users we shall employ the convenient fiction of an *average road user*. It presumes that the composition of traffic by free speeds follows some constant pattern on each road.

With most other means of transportation, once a traveler has chosen his destination his remaining freedom of choice is usually limited to a relatively small number of routes and departure times. If he chooses to go by road, however, he faces decisions about his route, the speed under various roadway and traffic conditions, and more decisions each time he wants to pass a vehicle or an intersection or desires to weave into another lane. The temporal order of the actual decisions is that in which they were mentioned. But in exercising a rational choice, a road user normally anticipates his speed and passing behavior under various conditions when choosing a route, and he also has some notion about the route when deciding whether or not to travel by road. A situation where the logical order of decisions may run counter to their sequence in time is not unusual in economics. The location and size of a power dam, for instance, can be determined optimally only after the desirable policy of water storage for any given reservoir location has been specified, which in turn is influenced by the demand for power as affected by the chosen rate structure. Here again the "natural" sequence of events is the reverse of the logical dependence of decisions.

In this chapter we shall follow the logical order of decisions; that is, we shall discuss the choice of individual free speeds first, the selection of routes (the demand for the use of roads) next, and finally the demand for road transportation between locations. Before this, however, another concept which is central to economic thinking has yet to be introduced, namely the notion of cost. This will be done in the following section.

2.2. Costs

To state that economic considerations influence drivers' decisions is another way of saying that road users are conscious of costs. Cost must be understood here, in the wide sense of economics, to include everything of value that is foregone to attain a certain end.

In this study we are interested in the transportation cost to road users only; that is, we exclude from consideration all cost to public bodies incurred through the maintenance or construction of road capacities. For demand depends on cost to road users only. And we shall not go so far as to analyze the tax component in gasoline costs, say, which would reflect to some extent the cost of maintenance and expansion of the road system. For doing this means going into the "long run."

The term transportation cost needs to be delimited also in spatial respects. Thus a distinction will become necessary between cost of transportation on specific roads and trip cost. In this section we consider the first cost only.

2.2.1. Composition of Transportation Cost

For purposes of the analysis of demand, the cost of transportation on a road includes not only the operating cost of a vehicle over the length of the road, but also such things as the travel time and the risks incurred.

Operating cost consists of all outlays directly attributable to vehicle use on a mileage basis. This includes fuel, oil, tire wear, deterioration and maintenance as far as these are dependent on mileage; it excludes vehicle taxes and license fees, depreciation due to time, and obsolescence. Certain money costs will be considered separately from operating cost, namely as *risk cost*.

Time costs will include the times-in-transit of vehicle and driver, and perhaps of passengers and loads. The value of a vehicle-hour is determined by the alternative uses of the vehicle that are possible. In private use the availability of a vehicle at times other than those of its ordinary use may have some value, but typically a low one. In commercial transportation the value of driver time is set by the wage rate of the driver, and the value of vehicle time is the earning power, after all operating cost, of the vehicle per unit of time. But this earning power is not an independent variable. A brief excursion into the long run is necessary here. In the long run the value of the vehicle hour tends to be equal to depreciation plus interest on the investment in a vehicle. Except insofar as average speed affects the rate of depreciation — an effect which may well be disregarded here — the value of the vehicle hour is thus independent of the prevailing speed of traffic.

For commercial transportation it is obvious that there exist definite money equivalents of vehicle, driver, and cargo times. That drivers in private cars tend to mind their time also and at least implicitly assign some money value to it can be seen in their choice of a free speed. For an example, let us accept an estimate in *Toll Roads and Free Roads* (1939, p. 39), according to which "Tests on several makes of modern passenger cars show that with steady driving on concrete pavements at a speed of 40 miles per hour the consumption is

0.0575 gallon per mile. At 60 miles per hour the consumption becomes 0.082 gallon per mile." It follows that a driver preferring to go at 60 rather than at 40 miles per hour values a saving of one hour by at least the price of 2.9 gallons of gasoline, which is in the neighborhood of 85 cents. Unawareness on the driver's part may blur and possibly diminish this figure somewhat. On the other hand, the fact that we have interpolated linearly a curve which is bent upward, and that risk and other operating costs are increasing with speed also, is likely to raise the figure again. The estimate conveys, however, an idea of the order of magnitude of the value of time, as applied to driving.

Under *Risk Cost* we shall include the losses from accidents in terms of life, health, and property, as well as the irritation from the threat of such accidents, which is particularly manifest under conditions of road congestion.

2.2.2. *Transportation Cost as a Function of Flow*

It is for the elementary reason that the transportation cost on a road varies with the flow of traffic that economic considerations of a short-run character are relevant at all to transportation in highway networks. This dependence may be described very simply by saying that an individual road user is the worse off, the more traffic there is on the road he is traveling. This is so because the presence of other traffic causes delays, added risks, and extra operating cost as expended in passing maneuvers. The road user incurs a higher transportation cost the larger the flow, even though a lower average speed may actually reduce his operating cost and although risks, as measured in accidents per vehicle mile, may start falling off at a flow level where passing becomes increasingly rare.

The explanation is of course that these latter cost reductions, if any, from congestion are more than offset by the accompanying losses of time. By congestion we mean here traffic conditions which occur at flows that "substantially" reduce average speed on the road. If it is assumed, for instance, that below a certain flow level average speed is "practically" independent of flow, so that a vertical section of the capacity curve is appropriate, then congestion would begin at the flow level where the vertical section of the capacity curve terminates.

On this apparently obvious point that costs increase because delays do, a few remarks are in order. One might ask why road users do not seek compensation for congestion in higher free speeds. Although the uniform-speed capacity curve shows that this is physically possible only within certain narrow limits, economic considerations also suggest that it is not feasible for the individual road user to try to stretch his possibilities to this limit. An increase in the free speed is either out of the question because the road user recognizes an absolute speed limit imposed on him by risk considerations or by the law, or else an increase of speed is possible but increasingly costly in terms of both risk and operating cost (Beakey, 1937). The conclusion is that both travel time and transportation cost increase or at best remain constant for each road user with increasing flow.

That the average travel time should be increasing (or constant) with respect to flow is just a restatement of the facts described by the free-speed capacity curve. The other relationship, that average cost is also increasing or constant with flow, will prove important enough for our analysis to warrant the introduction here of a corresponding average-cost capacity function. By this we mean the average transportation cost on a road for all road users entering during a unit period of time regarded as a function of the traffic flow. It differs from the previously considered capacity functions only by the inclusion of operating and risk cost.

2.3. Demand for Road Use

2.3.1. Choice of Routes

So far we have been concerned with the behavior of road users on a single road. We did not have to consider in detail the economic motivations that underlie the main decision, that about free speed. Principles of choice must be considered, however, when it comes to the behavior of a road user in a network. The outstanding problem is the determination of choices of routes. Let us introduce some concepts pertaining to networks first.

We start with a set of locations which we shall call *points*. All origins and destinations will be at these points, and every *road* will be a direct link between a pair of points. In general of course not every pair of points will be connected by a road, and some points will neither originate nor terminate traffic. By including all intersections in the set of points, we ensure that each road is a distinct segment of our network.

The rate at which traffic originates at a location, i.e. the net outflow to all destinations per unit of time, will be referred to as (*net*) origination. Similarly (*net*) termination denotes the rate at which traffic terminates, or the net absorption of traffic at a location per unit of time.

A *trip* denotes the path of a vehicle starting at one point, the *origin*, and terminating at another one, the *destination*. The roads traversed in succession on a trip are said to constitute its *route*. The traffic flow in both directions on a road is the sum of all traffic flows to the various destinations which enter this road from either direction.

Vehicles are now distinguished not only with regard to their free speed, but more importantly with respect to their destination. Flow and transportation cost remain variables defined with reference to a road. The notion of the cost of a trip between locations is introduced later and set in relation to transportation cost on roads.

The simplest possible assumption about choices of route would be that drivers select the geographically shortest one. But this would disregard roadway and traffic conditions entirely. If traffic conditions are to bear at all on the choice, an obvious next assumption is that the route should be chosen so as to minimize total travel time.[1] A completely rational route in the economic sense would be one that minimizes cost to the road user (in the broad sense defined above). We shall assume that actual choices of route approach this ideal to the extent that routes chosen are those of smallest *average* cost of transportation (averaged over users of each road). This amounts to considering a fictitious *average road user,* who incurs on every road the transportation cost that is indicated by the capacity function at the prevailing flow. While the errors committed in this way do not exactly cancel out, it seems a plausible and simple approximation to the actual routing of traffic flow.

Henceforth, for brevity, we shall call a route that is optimal in terms of average cost a *shortest* route. It need not be unique, of course. A shortest route defined with reference to an origin and a destination contains within it the shortest route that leads from any intermediate point to the destination. The notion of a shortest route now permits us to define transportation cost from any origin to any destination, simply called the *trip cost,* as the average cost along a shortest route. Then, along a shortest route, this trip cost to a given destination decreases as the origin is moved from one road end point to the next by exactly the average transportation cost on the road cut out. Along roads not on a shortest route, trip cost to a given destination decreases by less or even increases. The converse is also true. If there exist numbers, associated with all conceivable trips, which decrease by the full amount of transportation cost along roads that belong to certain routes, and which decrease by no more along all other roads, then the routes so distinguished are shortest routes and the numbers are the trip costs, provided that they have value zero where origin and destination coincide.

This is best seen graphically. In Figure 2.1, let 1-2-3-4-5-6 denote the shortest route between 1 and 6. Now the fact that this route continues from 2 via 3 rather than via 7 means that the trip cost from 7 to 6 plus the transportation cost on road 2-7 is more than the trip cost

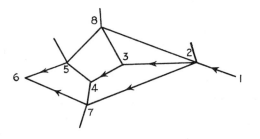

Figure 2.1

---

1. See Trueblood (1952), where this hypothesis is tested.

from 2 to 6. In other words the trip cost to 6 decreases along road 2-7 by less than the transportation cost on that road, whereas it decreases by exactly the transportation cost incurred on any road that is part of the shortest route 1-2-3-4-5-6.

Let us assume that the route 1-2-8-5-6 is a shortest route also. Then the cost from 2 to 5 is the same for both of the alternatives, 2-3-4-5 and 2-8-5. Counting transportation cost on roads positive in the direction toward the destination and negative in a direction away from the destination, the sum of costs on roads along the closed circuit 2-3-4-5-8-2 is zero. A closed cycle of this kind has been called a *neutral circuit* (Koopmans and Reiter, 1951, pp. 247-248). Neutral circuits indicate the existence of more than one shortest route.

In the following section we shall formulate mathematically the relationship between shortest routes and trip costs, and demonstrate our assertion that shortest routes are completely characterized by this relationship.

2.3.2*. Shortest Routes and Trip Costs

Let locations be indicated by single letters i, j, k, where i usually stands for an origin and k for a destination. Roads are designated by the pair of adjacent locations they connect, ij for instance (Figure 2.2).

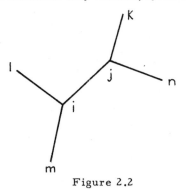

Figure 2.2

Transportation costs y on roads ij are written y_{ij}. Since we do not distinguish between costs in the two directions, $y_{ij} = y_{ji}$. For points i and j that are not contiguous, y_{ij} is left undefined. Trip costs from origin i to destination k are denoted by $y_{i,k}$. (Notice that the subscripts are separated by a comma.) Now

$$(2.1) \qquad y_{i,k} = Min \ (y_{ij} + y_{jl} + y_{lm} + \ldots + y_{nk})$$

that is, the minimum of all chain sums of y_{rs} starting at i and terminating at k in which consecutive elements have one subscript in common. In particular $y_{k,k} = 0$. (Since all $y_{rs} > 0$, it follows incidentally that these minimum chain sums do not contain any closed subchains.)

Consider $y_{m,k}$ for two locations $m = i$ and $m = j$ connected by a road ij. Extending the minimum chain that leads from j to k by adding y_{ij}, we have a chain from i to k, but not necessarily a minimum chain. Thus

$$(2.2) \qquad y_{i,k} \leqq y_{ij} + y_{j,k}.$$

To summarize: for every pair of points i,k there exists a uniquely determined number $y_{i,k}$ such that

$$(2.3) \qquad y_{i,k} - y_{j,k} \leqq y_{ij} \text{ and "=" for some } j; \quad y_{k,k} = 0 \quad .$$

We next show the converse. If for every pair of points i,k there is a unique number $y_{i,k}$ satisfying (2.3), then the $y_{i,k}$ represent shortest distances:

$$(2.4) \qquad y_{i,k} = \min (y_{ij} + y_{jl} + \ldots + y_{nk}) \quad .$$

Let i-j'-$1'$-....-n'-k denote a shortest route. Then

$$
\begin{aligned}
y_{i,k} - y_{j',k} &\leqq y_{ij'} \\
y_{j',k} - y_{1',k} &\leqq y_{j'k'} \\
&\vdots \\
y_{n',k} - y_{k,k} &\leqq y_{n'k} \quad .
\end{aligned}
$$

(2.5)

Since $y_{k,k} = 0$, one obtains by addition of these inequalities

$$(2.6) \qquad y_{i,k} \leqq y_{ij'} + y_{j'1'} + \ldots + y_{n'k} \quad .$$

On the other hand, since the $y_{i,k}$ satisfying (2.3) are assumed to be unique, there must, between every pair of points i and k, exist a sequence of pairs of points starting at i and ending at k for each of which the "=" sign holds in the inequalities (2.3). Let one such sequence be denoted $i - j'' - 1'' - .... - n'' - k$. Then

$$(2.7) \qquad y_{i,k} = y_{ij''} + y_{j''1''} + \ldots + y_{n''k} \quad .$$

By definition of a shortest route,

$$(2.8) \qquad y_{ij'} + y_{j'1'} + \ldots + y_{n'k} \leqq y_{ij''} + y_{j''1''} + \ldots + y_{n''k}.$$

Combining inequalities (2.6), (2.7), and (2.8) we obtain that

$$
\begin{aligned}
(2.9) \qquad y_{i,k} &= y_{ij'} + y_{j'1'} + \ldots + y_{n'k} \\
&= \text{Min} (y_{ij} + y_{jl} + \ldots + y_{nk})
\end{aligned}
$$

so that the numbers $y_{i,k}$ indeed denote the shortest distances (in terms of transportation costs).

In the economic theory of industrial location the points i of common $y_{i,k}$ for a given k are referred to as *isodistants* if cost is measured in terms of distance, *isochrones* if measured in terms of time, and *isovectures* if measured in terms of transportation cost (Palander, 1935, pp. 337-360).

2.3.3. Induced Demand for Use of a Road

Once the shortest routes for traffic between each pair of locations are found at prevailing traffic conditions, flow on each road can be determined. It is the sum of the numbers of trips per unit of time for all those origin-destination pairs whose shortest route goes through the road. As explained more fully in Section 2.4.1 below, we assume that the amount of flow demanded between any pair of locations depends only on the transportation cost between them. But whether or not a shortest route goes through any given road depends on the transportation cost on all roads that might be part of alternative routes. It is useful as an approximation sometimes to consider the flow on a given road (resulting from the demands for all trips) as a function of the transportation cost on that road only. In that case it is implicitly assumed that transportation costs on all other roads are unchanged, and in particular, that they remain unaffected by any shifts of flow from the road in question to alternative routes. This is a plausible assumption only if the flows on the road considered are relatively small.

The fact that there may be several shortest routes, and that a small change in transportation cost on the road may alter its flow by the whole amount of flow on a route, shows that the demand function for road use is discontinuous under our assumption that route selection depends only on relative transportation costs.

2.4. Demand for Transportation

A certain amount of driving on a particular road may of course be for pleasure's sake, in which case it represents ultimate consumption. Typically, however, the demand by drivers for the use of a particular road is not immediate but arises out of the demand for transportation from one location to another.

This need for transportation arises from the divergent locations of economic activities. In personnel transportation, the obvious cause is locational separation of residence, places of work, commodity markets, and cultural facilities. Commodity transportation is promoted ultimately by the geographical division of labor. This in turn is based on differences in the resource endowments of regions and on the greater economies of production on a large scale. Descriptive details on the locational distribution of economic activities fall into the domain of economic geography, and theoretical discussion of these phenomena is the subject matter of location theory.

However, our understanding of locational phenomena is far from sufficient for an accurate prediction of the demand pattern for transportation, given the general economic structure of a city or region. A formula has been advanced by some authors, e.g. Stewart (1950), for the intensity of intercity and interregional relations which is modeled after Newton's law of gravitation. Economic relations according to this formula are directly proportional to the algebraic product of population figures and inversely proportional to distance, suitably measured. By implication this formula should also describe the demand for intercity and interregional transportation. This, however, seems unlikely, for no account is taken of the specific economic structure of cities or regions.

Some interesting theoretical suggestions concerning the demand for transportation in cities are also advanced in the recent monograph by Mitchell and Rapkin (1954). Total origination or termination in an area is related to the character of the residential and commercial establishments in the area. An important observation is, for instance, that origination tends to be proportional to the total floor space devoted to commercial enterprises in a given district. Emphasis is given to the "linkage" in originations of people and of commodities between establishments located in one area.

2.4.1. Demand for Trips

In a model which attempts to set forth the interdependence of flows in a network, recognition must be given to the fact that the amount of traffic that originates at a given point for a particular destination per unit of time is in general not independent of the traffic conditions on the relevant route or routes.

This obvious principle needs careful limitation. It does not imply that the pattern of originations and destinations could not show considerable rigidity in the short run. In particular it does not dispense with the necessity of studying actual typical patterns. It implies caution, however, in the causal interpretation of such origin-destination patterns. Although such and such a ratio of floor space to truck trips prevails in a certain area (Mitchell and Rapkin, 1954, p. 172), this ratio may not be invariant under changes affecting traffic conditions. If the output levels of a plant closely determine its origination and termination intensity for a given technology, traffic conditions may force a change of technology or of location to maintain profits. A point often emphasized is that the central business districts of cities may experience a reduction of their levels of activity to the point where the demand for traffic can be accommodated by their available road capacity (and parking facilities).

In line with our approach to traffic in terms of its economic motivation, we shall consider the demand for transportation between a given origin and destination to be a function of average trip cost between these locations.

Demand must be defined with reference to a time period. Now on each road traffic shows a characteristic variation over time. This is a reflection of the fact that the demand for transportation between

locations fluctuates in various ways. For instance, intercity traffic has
a pronounced weekly pattern of fluctuation, while commuter traffic
shows extreme daily fluctuations as well. Depending on which types of
roads and of road use one is primarily interested in, a different period
is thus appropriate for the definition of demand. In any case it is a
simplification to regard demand in terms of an average flow per period
of given type, as the case may be. It is an even cruder approximation
to have this demand depend on the average traffic conditions during that
period only. However, simplification is the price of analysis.

Let the curve representing the number of trips per period between
two locations which are undertaken at various average cost levels be
called the demand curve for travel between these locations. The curve
in Figure 2.3 is one example.[2] We assume here that the general price
level and the income distribution are fixed. By its nature the demand
curve has an upward slope nowhere. In certain circumstances, when the
number of trips is independent of traffic conditions, the curve is vertical, and demand can then be described completely by fixed origin-
destination figures.

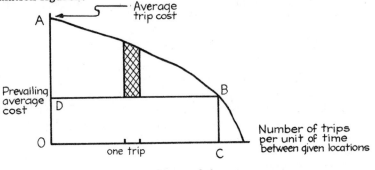

Figure 2.3

The notion of average trip cost requires some attention here because the population of road users changes along the demand curve. To
be consistent, the average should always be taken over the population of
actual road users at any point of the demand curve.

The demand curve may also be interpreted as a ranking of trips,
where each trip is labeled by its urgency, that is, by the "critical" cost
level at which it would still have been undertaken.

The excess of this critical average cost for only one trip over the
prevailing average cost represents a clear gain to the road user in
question. It appears in the form of a saving in money cost and corresponds to what is known in the economic theory of market demand as a
consumer's surplus. Geometrically it is represented (approximately)
by a strip extending from a horizontal line denoting the prevailing average cost to the demand curve with a width corresponding to one trip

---

2. In economics, price or cost is conventionally placed on the vertical axis, even
though in many cases, as in this one, cost is the independent variable.

(crosshatched in Figure 2.3). While the actual cost for a trip need not be the prevailing average cost— so that the area of the strip may be different from the gain of the particular road user in question — nevertheless the total area between the demand curve and the horizontal line of prevailing average cost indicates exactly the cost saving to *all* road users at that level of average transportation cost. Here the benefits in money terms enjoyed by various road users have been added up tacitly as homogeneous and commensurable. In particular it is implied that there are no effects of income differences which would render a dollar saved at a high level of cost worth more, or less, than a dollar saved at a low cost level. However, the equilibrium analysis which follows will do without this or any other value judgment. We will refer again to the road user's benefit in Section 4.1.2.

The form of the demand function is dependent, among other things, on the alternative means of transportation available and their rate structure. In general the demand for transportation between a given pair of locations would depend also on the costs or travel times to and from other locations. It has been shown, for instance (Mitchell and Rapkin, 1954, pp. 39-53), that most automobile trips within cities are round trips with more than one destination. However, this applies to the movement of the persons rather than to those of the vehicle, which appears often to partake in only the initial and final phase of the journey. If intercity traffic is taken into consideration, a merger of the possibly plural destinations into one would not seem to be a bad approximation.

Similarly in the long run when locational changes are admitted, a case can be made for the dependence of demand on transportation cost from or to various alternative locations. But since our interest is in the short-run phenomena, this complication may be disregarded here.

2.4.2*. Demand Functions and Capacity Functions

Let us now introduce a mathematical notation for demand. The number of trips per unit of time from origin i to destination k will be called $x_{i,k}$ for i not equal to k. We shall define the symbol - $x_{k,k}$ to be the termination at destination k. Since terminations at k must match the sum of originations for k, we have $\sum_i x_{i,k} = 0$. The number of trips as a function of trip cost will be written $x_{i,k} = f_{i,k}(y_{i,k})$. We shall make frequent use of the inverse relationship $y_{i,k} = g_{i,k}(x_{i,k})$. This inverse function $g_{i,k}$ exists because the demand function $f_{i,k}$ is monotonic; as the trip cost goes up, the number of trips decreases, if anything.[3] Stationarity of $g_{i,k}$ over some interval would mean that demand is perfectly elastic there; a small rise in the prevailing transportation cost would induce a substantial decrease in demand. This is not to be expected even in the presence of alternative means of transportation. Without

---

3. While the demand for certain commodities may increase with price in particular circumstances involving income effects, this is not likely to be the case with the demand for road transportation.

restricting ourselves we may therefore assume $g_{i,k}$ to be strictly decreasing, that is

(2.10) $$\frac{dg_{i,k}}{dx_{i,k}} < 0 \quad,$$

wherever $g_{i,k}$ is differentiable. The case of fixed origin-destination figures (perfect inelasticity) means that the graph of $g_{i,k}$ is a vertical line and that the derivative is minus infinity.

We shall now give the notation and summarize the relevant properties of road capacity functions. Let x_{ij} denote flow on road ij. The order of subscripts is immaterial here and in what follows: $x_{ij} = x_{ji}$, $y_{ij} = y_{ji}$, and $h_{ij} = h_{ji}$ (notice the absence of a separating comma in the designation of roads). The capacity function $y_{ij} = h_{ij}(x_{ij})$ is never decreasing:

(2.11) $$\frac{dh_{ij}}{dx_{ij}} \geqq 0 \quad.$$

The "=" sign can hold when flow levels are small enough to make interference between elements of traffic negligible. From the considerations in Section 1.4 it appears that delays and hence costs increase indefinitely as a certain flow level c_{ij}, the absolute capacity limit, is approached:

(2.12) $$\lim_{x_{ij} \to c_{ij}} h_{ij}(x_{ij}) = \infty \quad.$$

The most obvious differences between these two types of elementary data functions, the demand function, and the capacity function, are (1) that in the capacity function, flow is the cause and transportation cost the effect, while in the demand function, trip cost is the cause and trips (constituting the flows) are the effect; (2) that demand is defined with reference to any pair of locations while capacity refers only to roads; and (3) that demand decreases as cost increases, whereas in the capacity curve, cost increases or remains constant as flow increases.

From the economic point of view, capacity and demand appear to be pairs of opposites similar to supply and demand. Capacity is the "supply of trip opportunities at various costs." The analogy, however, is a loose one. In particular, while under perfectly competitive conditions the supply function in a market for ordinary commodities tends to be the same as the incremental cost function, here the capacity function corresponds more nearly to an average cost function.

Chapter 3

EQUILIBRIUM

The discussion of capacity and demand in the two preceding chapters has supplied us with some fundamental notions on traffic flow. In this chapter we propose to explain the pattern of traffic in a network from the interaction of the demand for transportation between many pairs of locations and the capacities of roads in the network. This demand is distributed over various routes and, on each road, over various free speeds. It thereby affects the traffic conditions on the roads, and these react again on the demand for traffic. In an attempt to unravel these relationships of mutual determination, it is useful to have reference to a situation of equilibrium.

With regard to a road in isolation, equilibrium means the following. At every level of traffic conditions, as measured by the average cost of transportation, a certain demand for the use of this road is forthcoming. If this demand is larger than the prevailing flow, the traffic conditions get worse and the average cost of transportation increases. This tends to curb the demand, perhaps to the extent that flows fall below the initially prevailing level. Then traffic conditions improve again and at the reduced level of transportation cost an increased demand is forthcoming. There is however one level of flow at which traffic conditions give rise to a demand just equal to the prevailing flow. This is what we shall call the equilibrium flow.

One might think of equilibrium in a network as simply a state in which flows on every road are in equilibrium. But as we have pointed out, the notion of the demand for use of any particular road as a function of transportation cost on that road only involves a simplification that seems inadmissible in the analysis of flows in a network. Such a demand function could be defined only on the assumption of *ceteris paribus,* namely, of unchanged transportation costs on all other roads. But a change of flow on one road is bound to affect flows and hence costs on some other roads. Therefore a somewhat broader approach is called for.

Demand refers to trips and capacity refers to flows on roads. The connecting link is found in the distribution of trips over the network according to the principle that traffic follows shortest routes in terms of average cost. The idea of equilibrium in a network can then be described as follows. The prevailing demand for transportation, that is, the existing pattern of originations and terminations, gives rise to traffic conditions that will maintain that same demand. Or, starting at the other end, the existing traffic conditions are such as to call forth the demand that will sustain the flows that create these conditions.

States of equilibrium may be defined for a short period such as the peak hour in daily traffic, or, if finer fluctuations of demand are disregarded, for a longer period such as a day or a week. In the last case road users presumably go through their routines repeatedly and at regular intervals. The maintenance of the pattern of road use under given demand conditions therefore implies that drivers have not been dissatisfied with their choices. Put another way, this says that the anticipated cost of the various alternative routes or modes of travel on which demand for transportation, choice of route, and choice of free speed are based corresponds to the realized cost.

3.1. Equilibrium in a Network

Suppose that between two points there are two highways, one of which is broad enough to accommodate without crowding all the traffic which may care to use it, but is poorly graded and surfaced, while the other is a much better road, but narrow and quite limited in capacity. If a large number of trucks operate between the two termini and are free to choose either of the two routes, they will tend to distribute themselves between the roads in such proportions that the cost per unit of transportation, or effective return per unit of investment, will be the same for every truck on both routes. As more trucks use the narrower and better road, congestion develops, until at a certain point it becomes equally profitable to use the broader but poorer highway [Knight, 1924, p. 162].

This example demonstrates the principle of traffic distribution among alternative routes in equilibrium. (1) If between a given origin and a given destination more than one route is actually traveled, the cost of transportation to the average road user, as indicated by the average-cost capacity curves, must be equal on all these routes. (2) Since the routes used are the "shortest" ones under prevailing traffic conditions, average cost on all other possible routes cannot be less than that on the route or routes traveled. (3) The amount of traffic originated per unit of time must equal the demand for transportation at the trip cost which prevails.

It is useful to reformulate these conditions in terms of traffic on roads rather than on routes. Making use of the relationship between shortest routes and trip costs we may restate the three principles as follows. At each location there is a well defined trip cost to any destination for the average road user. (1) It decreases toward the destination by the full (average) amount of transportation cost along all roads on which some traffic flows to that destination; (2) along any other road it decreases by less than or at most the same as (average) transportation cost; (3) the amount of traffic originating at any point for any destination is determined by the demand for transportation arising in response to the (average) trip cost to that destination. This origination then equals the excess of outgoing traffic over incoming traffic (to this destination). The amount terminated at a location is, of course, the sum over all origins of traffic flows with this destination.

Total traffic on the various roads fixes the transportation cost on each road and this again determines the trip cost from each origin to the various destinations. Through the demand function this cost regulates the traffic flow between pairs of locations. The distribution of these flows over the various roads follows by means of the relationship between costs on roads and trip costs. Thus the circle of the equilibrium conditions is closed.

But can we be sure that this circular definition is meaningful? Will there always be a well determined equilibrium if demand and capacity curves have the usual properties, that demand decreases as trip costs increase and that transportation costs increase as flows increase on any given road? Is it possible to compute and predict the equilibrium distribution of flows once the demand and capacity data are given? And finally, is the equilibrium stable or will it be thrown off balance by the slightest deviation?

These are all questions that we shall gradually seek answers to in the following sections, not all of them mathematical ones. In these sections we show that the relations described determine an equilibrium, that an equilibrium always exists if demand is a decreasing function of trip cost and transportation cost is a constant or increasing function of traffic flow, and that the equilibrium is unique whenever the shortest routes between all pairs of locations are unique and cost is strictly increasing with increasing flow. These statements are also true in the less obvious case of commodity transportation.

3.1.1*. Formulation of the Equilibrium Conditions

The number of vehicles entering road ij from either end per unit of time, briefly called the flow on that road, was denoted by x_{ij}. However, our elementary variable will be the flow on a road in a given direction to a particular destination, written $x_{ij,k}$, where the ordered pair of subscripts ij denotes the direction from i to j on road ij, and k denotes the destination. This flow is distinct from that in the opposite direction and it does not admit of negative values:

$$(3.1) \qquad x_{ij,k} \geqq 0 \qquad \text{for all } ij,k .$$

By our previous definition total flow on a road equals

$$(3.2) \qquad x_{ij} = x_{ji} = \sum_k (x_{ij,k} + x_{ji,k}) ,$$

and, of course, (3.1) implies

$$(3.3) \qquad x_{ij} \geqq 0 .$$

We have already encountered a third flow variable, namely the number of vehicles originating at location i with destination k per unit of time, $x_{i,k}$. Since this rate of origination is indicated at i by the excess of flow to k on outgoing roads over that on incoming roads we have

$$(3.4) \qquad x_{i,k} = \sum_j (x_{ij,k} - x_{ji,k}) \quad .$$

In Section 2.3.2* the relationship between transportation cost on roads and trip costs was formulated. We can now express the fact that traffic uses shortest routes by saying that on roads not in a shortest route to a location k flow to that destination is zero:

$$(3.5) \qquad x_{ij,k} = 0 \quad \text{if } y_{i,k} - y_{j,k} < y_{ij} \quad .$$

The second relationship between flows and costs is that expressed by the capacity function

$$(3.6) \qquad y_{ij} = h_{ij}(x_{ij}) \quad .$$

Our third flow variable is related to trip cost through the (inverse) demand function for transportation:

$$(3.7) \qquad y_{i,k} = g_{i,k}(x_{i,k}) \quad .$$

Finally we restate the definition of $y_{i,k}$ given in Section 2.3.2:*

$$(3.8) \qquad y_{i,k} - y_{j,k} \leq y_{ij} \text{ and "=" for some j, } y_{k,k} = 0 \quad .$$

We now have for each of the variables y_{ij}, $y_{i,k}$, x_{ij}, $x_{ij,k}$, $x_{i,k}$ at least one relation in which it is "explained" in terms of some other variable(s). Is this a complete system of conditions which under suitable assumptions about the functions involved -- $g_{i,k}(y_{i,k})$ and $h_{ij}(x_{ij})$ -- has a unique solution?

To answer this question our system must be brought into a more concise form. As a direct consequence of (3.5) and (3.8) we have

$$(3.9) \qquad y_{i,k} - y_{j,k} \begin{Bmatrix} = \\ \leq \end{Bmatrix} y_{ij} \text{ if } x_{ij,k} \begin{Bmatrix} > \\ = \end{Bmatrix} 0 \quad , \quad y_{k,k} = 0 \quad .$$

In all cases where the flow between a pair of points is zero, the second alternative of (3.9), which then holds, does not fully determine the values $y_{i,k}$ of trip costs. It merely imposes an upper bound on them. At the same time equation (3.7) affords a lower bound, for it restricts the $y_{i,k}$ to levels above which demand is zero. The slack which is thus introduced whenever flow between two points is zero does no harm, for then the exact value of trip cost is irrelevant, economically. Since the notation in the first line of (3.9) will be used frequently in what follows we shall at this first occurrence write out in full the statements involved: $y_{i,k} - y_{j,k} \leq y_{ij}$, $x_{ij,k} \geq 0$, and $y_{i,k} - y_{j,k} = y_{ij}$ if $x_{ij,k} > 0$. In particular, (3.9) implies the absence of "cross hauling": if $x_{ij,k} > 0$ then

$x_{ji,k} = 0$. As a next step we can substitute for the cost variables the corresponding functions of the flow variables. Our system then reduces to the inequalities

$$(3.10) \qquad g_{i,k}(x_{i,k}) - g_{j,k}(x_{j,k}) \begin{Bmatrix} = \\ \leq \end{Bmatrix} h_{ij}(x_{ij}) \text{ if } x_{ij,k} \begin{Bmatrix} > \\ = \end{Bmatrix} 0$$

plus the defining equations (3.2) and (3.4).

Incidentally, (3.10) may be used to find two expressions for the prevailing total cost of transportation. Multiplication on both sides by $x_{ij,k}$ and addition yields

$$(3.11) \qquad \sum_{ij,k} [g_{i,k}(x_{i,k}) - g_{j,k}(x_{j,k})] \, x_{ij,k} = \sum_{ij,k} h_{ij} \cdot x_{ij,k} \ .$$

Rearranging terms and using (3.4) and (3.2) we obtain

$$(3.12) \qquad \sum_{i,k} g_{i,k}(x_{i,k}) \cdot x_{i,k} = \frac{1}{2} \sum_{ij} h_{ij}(x_{ij}) \cdot x_{ij} \ .$$

The left-hand side represents the sum of all trip costs, the right-hand side the sum of all transportation costs on roads.

3.1.2*. *Existence of Solutions to the Equilibrium Conditions*

A well known characteristic of the equilibria encountered in theoretical mechanics is that they may be regarded as solutions to certain extremum problems, a fact which has occasionally given rise to some speculation about nature's grand design. Whatever the merits of teleological interpretations, the possibility of formulating an equilibrium in terms of maximization is a useful piece of mathematical information. For instance, the fact that there is a maximum problem associated with the present equilibrium system (as there are extremum problems for many other economic equilibria cf. Samuelson, 1948, pp. 21-23), will give us a proof that there exist solutions to our system. Consider the function

$$(3.13) \qquad H(\dots, x_{ij,k}, \dots) = \sum_{i,k} \int_0^{x_{i,k}} g_{i,k}(x) \, dx - \frac{1}{2} \sum_{ij} \int_0^{x_{ij}} h_{ij}(x) \, dx \ .$$

(Economists are warned that this is not to be interpreted as consumers' surplus! The term on the right has as its kernel the *average*, rather than the *incremental* cost to users collectively.) Here the factor $\frac{1}{2}$ comes in because we wish to sum over every road but once, while each road is denoted by two pairs of indices, ij and ji. Differentiate with respect to $x_{ij,k}$ after substituting for $x_{i,k}$ and x_{ij} from (3.4) and (3.2).

The result is

$$(3.14) \qquad \frac{\partial H}{\partial x_{ij,k}} = g_{i,k}(x_{i,k}) - g_{j,k}(x_{j,k}) - h_{ij}(x_{ij}) \quad .$$

The necessary first order conditions for a maximum are that the derivatives of H be nonpositive in all directions in which $x_{ij,k}$ can change without becoming negative. In the interior of the positive orthant $(x_{ij,k} > 0$ for all ij,k) we therefore have the usual conditions that the derivatives shall vanish, while at a point of the boundary where some $x_{ij,k} = 0$ the derivative with respect to any vanishing $x_{ij,k}$ must be nonpositive:

$$(3.15) \qquad \frac{\partial H}{\partial x_{ij,k}} = 0 \text{ if } x_{ij,k} > 0 \text{ and } \frac{\partial H}{\partial x_{ij,k}} \leq 0 \text{ if } x_{ij,k} = 0 \quad .$$

We now recall the existence of absolute capacity limits c_{ij} as expressed in relation (2.12). In the closed set defined by the two conditions, $0 \leq x_{ij,k}$ and $x_{ij} \leq d_{ij} < c_{ij}$ for some suitable d_{ij}, the function $H(\dots, x_{ij,k}, \dots)$ is continuous since it is a sum of indefinite integrals of Riemann integrable (because sectionally continuous) functions. We conclude that H assumes its maximum at some point. While this point may still depend on the d_{ij}, it will not do so if d_{ij} is sufficiently close to c_{ij}, because of (2.12). At that point of maximum the necessary conditions (3.13) must be satisfied. But these conditions are identical with (3.10). Therefore there must exist a solution to inequalities (3.10) and the supplementary defining equations (3.2) and (3.4). Of course, H was just so constructed that the first order conditions for a maximum (3.15) become identical with the equilibrium condition (3.10).

3.1.3*. Uniqueness of the Solutions

In preparation for the question of when a solution to our equilibrium conditions is unique, we shall first show that the function H is concave, as defined below.

Consider the quadratic form of its second derivatives (sometimes known as the *Hessian*) at a point $x_{ij,k}$, with $z_{ij,k}$ denoting the arguments in place of the former $x_{ij,k}$. We shall use the obvious abbreviations

$$z_{ij} = \sum_k (z_{ij,k} + z_{ji,k}), \quad z_{i,k} = \sum_j (z_{ij,k} - z_{ji,k}) ,$$

$$(3.16)$$

$$g'_{i,k} = \frac{dg_{i,k}}{dx_{i,k}} , \quad \text{and} \quad h'_{ij} = \frac{dh_{ij}}{dx_{ij}} \quad .$$

We have

$$\sum_{\substack{ij,k \\ lm,n}} z_{ij,k} \frac{\partial^2 H}{\partial x_{ij,k} \, \partial x_{lm,n}} z_{lm,n}$$

(3.17)
$$= \sum_{ij,k} z_{ij,k}(g'_{i,k} \cdot z_{i,k} - g'_{j,k} \cdot z_{j,k})$$

$$- \sum_{ij,k} (z_{ij,k} + z_{ji,k})h'_{ij} \cdot z_{ij} \quad .$$

$$i < j$$

After rearranging of terms in the first sum, this becomes the left-hand member of

(3.18)
$$\sum_{i,k} g'_{i,k} \cdot z^2_{i,k} - \frac{1}{2} \sum_{ij} h'_{ij} \cdot z^2_{ij} \leqq 0 \quad .$$

The inequality holds identically in the $z_{ij,k}$ and $x_{ij,k}$ because inverse demand $g_{i,k}$ is a decreasing function and capacity h_{ij} an increasing function. This shows that the Hessian is negative semidefinite for all A differentiable function whose Hessian is negative semidefinite is known to be a concave function (Bonnesen and Fenchel, 1934, pp. 18-19). By this, one means the following: for every a, $0 < a < 1$, and every two sets of variables $(x_{ij,k}) = x$, $(\bar{x}_{ij,k}) = \bar{x}$,

(3.19)
$$H \left[ax + (1 - a) \, \bar{x} \right] \geqq a \, H(x) + (1 - a) \, H \, (\bar{x}) \quad .$$

Incidentally, a function is called *convex* if its negative is concave.
Next we prove the following useful lemma.

Lemma: Let $F(u)$ be a concave function of a set of variables $u = (u_1, \ldots, u_r, \ldots, u_n)$. Sufficient for $F(u^0) = \max\limits_{u_r \geqq 0} F(u)$ is that F be differentiable at $u = u^0$ and that

(3.20)
$$\left(\frac{\partial F}{\partial u_r} \right)_{u=u^0} \begin{Bmatrix} = \\ \leqq \end{Bmatrix} 0 \text{ if } u^0_r \begin{Bmatrix} > \\ = \end{Bmatrix} 0 \quad .$$

Proof: Borrowing directly from Kuhn and Tucker [1951], we first prove that for every concave function $F(u)$, differentiable at u^0,

(3.21)
$$F(u) \leqq F(u^0) + \sum_r F^0_r \cdot (u_r - u^0_r) \quad ,$$

where F^0_r denotes $\dfrac{\partial F(u^0)}{\partial u^0_r}$. For any a, $0 < a < 1$, we have

(3.22)
$$F(u) - F(u^0) \leqq \frac{F[u^0 + a(u - u^0)] - F(u^0)}{a}$$

by the definition of a concave function. Hence in the limit, as $a \to 0$,

$$(3.23) \qquad F(u) - F(u^0) \leqq \sum_r F^0_r \cdot (u_r - u^0_r)$$

We proceed to the proof of the lemma proper. By (3.23) and (3.20), in that order, we have for all $u_r \geqq 0$

$$(3.24) \qquad F(u^0) \geqq F(u) - \sum_r F^0_r \cdot (u_r - u^0_r) \geqq F(u).$$

It follows that $F(u^0) = \underset{u_r \geqq 0}{\text{Max}} \ F(u)$, which proves the lemma.

It is easily verified that (3.20) with F and u_r corresponding to H and $x_{ij,k}$, respectively, is nothing but our old equilibrium condition (3.10). We conclude that every solution of the equilibrium conditions yields a maximum of H. The converse fact, that every maximum (in fact every extremum) of H yields a solution to the equilibrium condition (3.10) is already known to us. From this and the concavity of H it is now seen that for every two solutions $x_{ij,k}$ and $\bar{x}_{ij,k}$ of (3.10) the linear combinations

$$ax_{ij,k} + (1 - a) \ \bar{x}_{ij,k} \qquad \text{for } 0 < a < 1$$

are likewise solutions of the equilibrium condition (3.10), a fact which is not immediately obvious.

The possibility of a plurality of solutions is inherent in certain properties of the equilibrium. Suppose that two routes are equally attractive between two locations that are transit points for flows from several origins or to several destinations (a so-called neutral circuit — cf. end of Section 2.3.1). Then it is of course arbitrary in what proportions these flows are allocated to each route as long as the total flows on each route have the proper magnitudes (so as to maintain equality of average cost over the two routes).

On the other hand, one expects equilibrium flows x_{ij} on all roads to be unique when demand functions are strictly decreasing with trip cost and all transportation cost functions are strictly increasing with flow. We are now in a position to prove this assertion. Suppose that there exist two solutions x and $\bar{x}$. By what was said before there must then exist, on the line segment connecting x and $\bar{x}$, a maximum which is located arbitrarily close to x. Call it $x + \delta x$. Expanding H at x

$$(3.25) \qquad H (x + \delta x) = H(x) + \sum_{ij,k} \frac{\partial H}{\partial x_{ij,k}} \delta x_{ij,k}$$

$$+ \sum_{\substack{ij,k \\ lm,n}} \frac{\partial^2 H}{\partial x_{ij,k} \partial x_{lm,n}} \ \delta x_{ij,k} \ \delta x_{lm,n} + \ldots \quad .$$

Because x is a point of maximum the second term at the right vanishes.

Since $x + \delta x$ is also a maximizer, $H(x + \delta x) = H(x)$, so that the last term of (3.25) must vanish. But this term was shown to be equal to

$$(3.26) \qquad \sum_{i,k} g'_{i,k} \cdot (\delta x_{i,k})^2 - \sum_{ij} h'_{ij}(\delta x_{ij})^2 \quad .$$

Our assumptions were

$$(3.27) \qquad g'_{i,k} < 0 \text{ and } h'_{ij} > 0 \quad \text{for all } i,k, ij \quad .$$

Therefore $\delta x_{i,k} = 0$ and $\delta x_{ij} = 0$ for all i,k,ij. That is, the originations and flows on roads are uniquely determined.[1]

Under what conditions does the uniqueness of these variables imply that flows $x_{ij,k}$ distinguished by destinations are also uniquely determined? This is the case when no neutral circuits are present — that is, when the network layout and flow conditions are such that no two routes between any single pair of locations are equally attractive (cf. Section 2.3.1).

3.2. Effects of Changes in Capacity and in Demand

How do the equilibrium flows change in response to shifts in capacity functions or in demand functions? An increase of capacity, brought about by construction or improvement of roads, is understood here to be reflected in a lowering of the capacity curve: to every flow there corresponds a smaller average cost than before. An increase in demand means that the demand curve has shifted upward, so that a given flow comes forth at a higher transportation cost. To be specific, let us assume that all capacity functions are strictly increasing and all demand functions strictly decreasing. Then the following assertions can be made, which are plausible in themselves.

An increase in the capacity on only one road either has no effect on flows at all, or leads to a positive increase of traffic at least on this road. Simultaneous changes in the capacities of several roads either leave all traffic unchanged, or cause a growth of traffic on at least one road of increased capacity, or a decline of traffic on at least one road of decreased capacity. More generally, one can say that traffic growth tends to accompany capacity increases in the sense that a certain weighted sum of the algebraic products of capacity change and traffic change is positive whenever any change in traffic takes place at all.

With respect to demand, similar statements, obtained by appropriate substitutions, are valid. Although these remarks on changes in equilibrium flows appear quite obvious, they have been mentioned here because they hold equally in the less trivial case of commodity transportation, and also because they illustrate a mathematical principle which will be useful later on.

---

1. This proof can easily be extended to show that the two components $\sum_{k} x_{ij,k}$ and $\sum_{k} x_{ji,k}$ of each flow are uniquely determined.

The next section presents the mathematical theorem whose economic content has been given in this section.

3.2.1*. *An Inequality on the Effect of Data Changes*

In order that capacity and demand be characterized by definite parameters, let us assume both to be given in terms of linear functions. For simplicity it will also be assumed that the absolute capacity limits are nowhere attained. Denote the capacity functions by

$$(3.28) \qquad h_{ij}(x_{ij}) = a_{ij}\, x_{ij} + b_{ij}$$

and the inverse demand functions by

$$(3.29) \qquad g_{i,k}(x_{i,k}) = e_{i,k}\, x_{i,k} + f_{i,k} \quad .$$

The maximand H of Section 3.1.2* thereby becomes

$$(3.30) \qquad \begin{aligned} &\sum_{i,k} \left[\frac{1}{2} e_{i,k}\, x_{i,k}^2 + f_{i,k}\, x_{i,k} \right] \\ &- \sum_{ij} \left[\frac{1}{4} a_{ij}\, x_{ij}^2 + \frac{1}{2} b_{ij}\, x_{ij} \right] \quad . \end{aligned}$$

In order to evaluate the effect of finite changes δa_{ij}, δb_{ij}, $\delta e_{i,k}$, and $\delta f_{i,k}$ in the corresponding parameters of capacity and demand, recourse is had to the following general theorem, which in economic theory falls under the heading of the Le Chatelier Principle (Samuelson, 1946–47; 1948, pp. 36–39).

Theorem: Let q_{nr} be the coefficients of a negative semidefinite quadratic form, $q_{nr} = q_{rn}$. Consider the problem

$$(3.31) \qquad \operatorname*{Max}_{x_r \geq 0} \left[\sum_{n,r} x_n\, q_{nr}\, x_r + \sum_r a_r\, x_r \right]$$

$$\text{subject to} \quad \sum_r b_{sr}\, x_r \leq c_s \quad .$$

The solution equations are

$$(3.32) \qquad 2 \sum_n q_{nr}\, x_n + a_r - \sum_s l_s\, b_{sr} \begin{Bmatrix} = \\ \leq \end{Bmatrix} 0 \quad \text{if} \quad x_r \begin{Bmatrix} > \\ = \end{Bmatrix} 0$$

$$\text{where} \qquad l_s \begin{Bmatrix} = \\ \geq \end{Bmatrix} 0 \quad \text{if} \quad \sum_r b_{sr}\, x_r \begin{Bmatrix} < \\ = \end{Bmatrix} c_s \quad .$$

Let finite changes in the parameters and variables be denoted $\delta q_{nr}, \ldots$ $\ldots, \delta l_s$, δx_r, respectively. We shall show that

$$\text{(3.33)} \quad \sum_r \left\{ \sum_n \left[x_n (\delta q_{nr} + \delta q_{rn}) + \delta x_n q_{nr} + \delta a_r \right. \right.$$
$$\left. \left. - \sum_s l_s \delta b_{sr} \right] \delta x_r \right\} - \sum_s \delta l_s (\delta c_s$$
$$- \sum_{sr} \delta b_{sr} x_r) \geq 0 \quad .$$

If q_{nr} represents a negative *definite* form, then $\delta x_r \neq 0$ for some r implies "$>$" in (3.33).

Abstract of Proof: The Kuhn-Tucker Theorem for concave maximands and linear inequalities as constraints (derived below, Section 4.3.1*) asserts that the solution x_r^0 and the Lagrangean multipliers l_s^0 can be obtained in terms of unconstrained extremum problems. For shortness, write

$$\text{(3.34)} \quad \sum_{n,r} x_n q_{nr} x_r + \sum_r a_r x_r$$
$$+ \sum_s l_s (c_s - \sum_r b_{sr} x_r) = M(x,l) \quad .$$

According to the theorem quoted,

$$\text{(3.35)} \quad M(x_r^0, l^0) = \underset{x_r \geq 0}{\text{Max}} \ M(x, l^0) = \underset{l_s \geq 0}{\text{Min}} \ M(x^0, l) \quad .$$

Denote the same function in terms of the modified parameters by $\overline{M}(x,l)$. Then

$$\text{(3.36)} \quad M(x^0, l^0 + \delta l^0) - M(x^0 + \delta x^0, l^0) \geq 0$$

because, by (3.35), the first term is greater than and the second term less than $M(x^0, l^0)$. The "$>$" sign applies if some $\delta x_r^0 > 0$ and q_{nr} is negative definite, because M is then strictly concave in x_r. In a similar way we find that

$$\text{(3.37)} \quad \overline{M}(x^0 + \delta x^0, l^0) - \overline{M}(x^0, l^0 + \delta l^0) \geq 0$$

because, $(x^0 + \delta x^0, l^0 + \delta l^0)$ being the solution to the problem when the parameters are modified, the first term is greater than and the second term less than $\overline{M}(x^0 + \delta x^0, l^0 + \delta l^0)$. The sum (3.36) and (3.37) yields the desired inequality (3.33).

In the present case constraints (other than the restriction to positive values) do not occur, so the l_s in (3.33) are zero. Therefore the inequality (3.33) when applied to the function H of (3.30) becomes simply

$$\text{(3.38)} \quad \frac{1}{2} \sum_{i,k} (2x_{i,k} + \delta x_{i,k}) \ \delta e_{i,k} \ \delta x_{i,k}$$
$$- \frac{1}{4} \sum_{ij} (2x_{ij} + \delta x_{ij}) \ \delta a_{ij} \ \delta x_{ij}$$
$$+ \sum_{i,k} \delta f_{i,k} \ \delta x_{i,k} - \frac{1}{2} \sum_{ij} \delta b_{ij} \ \delta x_{ij} \geq 0$$

where $\sum_{i,k}$ corresponds to $\sum_{r}$, and we can omit $\sum_{n}$ and put n = r, since now q_{nr} is zero whenever $n \neq r$. The "$>$" alternative holds if some $\delta x_{ij} \neq 0$ or some $\delta x_{i,k} \neq 0$, provided that all $e_{i,k} < 0$.

If only one capacity is changed and demand remains unchanged, then all the $\delta e_{i,k}$, $\delta f_{i,k}$ are zero and all the δa_{ij} and δb_{ij} are zero except those for some particular ij. In this case (3.38) becomes

$$(3.39) \qquad \left[-\frac{1}{4} (2x_{ij} + \delta x_{ij}) \; \delta a_{ij} - \frac{1}{2} \delta b_{ij} \right] \delta x_{ij} \geqq 0 \quad .$$

Suppose we have a single capacity increase; a capacity change will be unequivocally an increase only if

$$(3.40) \qquad \delta a_{ij} \leqq 0, \quad \delta b_{ij} \leqq 0, \quad \delta a_{ij} + \delta b_{ij} < 0 \quad .$$

Otherwise the traffic required to bring about some particular level of cost would be less than before. Since x_{ij} and $x_{ij} + \delta x_{ij}$ are non-negative, the bracketed expression in (3.39) is non-negative, and positive when $\delta x_{ij} \neq 0$. We conclude that $\delta x_{ij} \geqq 0$. (Equality occurs when $x_{ij} = 0$, that is, when the road was useless to begin with.) Thus the reactions of flows to changes in capacity follow in all cases the pattern that one would expect.

3.3. Stability

An equilibrium would be just an extreme state of rare occurrence if it were not stable — that is, if there were no forces which tended to restore equilibrium as soon as small deviations from it occurred.

Besides this stability "in the small" one may consider stability "in the large" — that is, the ability of the system to reach an equilibrium from any initial position. This latter type of stability is interesting not only because it concerns the capacity of the system to reach a new equilibrium position after some big change, but also because one may want to use an analogue of the adjustment process as a method of computing an equilibrium solution by successive approximations.

3.3.1. Adjustments of Road Users

The study of stability hinges ultimately on the question of how road users adjust themselves to changes — that is, how they adapt the extent of their travel by road and their choice of routes to varying traffic conditions. This, however, is one of the big unknowns of road-user behavior, so that at the present stage only conjectures are possible. Through a simple and plausible model one can get a rough picture of the minimum of conditions that must be met in order that the adjustment process should converge.

In our model we shall assume simply that those road users who do not just continue in their previous choices will choose their routes and the number of trips by road on the basis of the traffic conditions that prevailed in the preceding period. (Nothing need be assumed about the length of these periods, but this type of behavior is most plausible when the periods are fairly long.) These road users who have or can obtain adequate knowledge of the traffic conditions, even if not by first-hand experience, choose a route which is optimal at the transportation cost of the last period and set their demand for transportation at levels corresponding to the average costs of trips during the last period.

The responsive fraction of road users in each period will be regarded as an independent random sample drawn from the total population of road users. Its size is assumed to decrease as time proceeds, until a new occasion for adjustment arises with another change in the network. Traffic which is actually experimenting to find optimal routes will be disregarded as just a random disturbance, whose size also decreases in the course of time.

As an extreme case, consider first a single road on which *all* road users decide about travel on the basis of the traffic conditions in the preceding period. This is but an instance of the well known cobweb phenomenon which occurs in terms of price fluctuation in certain markets (hogs, shipbuilding) where the production decisions are made considerably in advance of the marketing period (Tinbergen, 1951, pp. 143-148). When prices are high, production is expanded. After the increased output becomes available, prices drop and as a result production is curtailed. When as a consequence prices go up again, the whole cycle is repeated. Whether these fluctuations continue at a steady level, grow increasingly violent, or ultimately die down depends altogether on the relative slopes of the supply and the demand curves in question. In the present example Figures 3.1 and 3.2 show that a damping of the oscillations takes place whenever the slope of the demand curve is greater

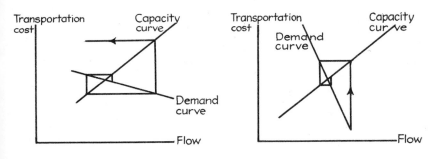

Figure 3.1. Unstable Case   Figure 3.2. Stable Case

in absolute terms than the slope of the capacity curve. This condition is likely to be met in reality, since the demand for road transportation presumably does not respond in a highly elastic way to transportation cost. At any rate the effective demand curve will have a rather steep slope whenever the responsive fraction of road users is small.

By way of contrast consider next a network of two roads between two locations and a fixed demand. To be definite let us assume that just one-fifth of the road users adjust their routes to the last prevailing traffic conditions. Figure 3.3 gives a graphical description of what happens. Let the entire line segment represent total flow and the numbered points the distribution of flow among the two roads during successive periods. Let 0 be the equilibrium distribution. Consider an

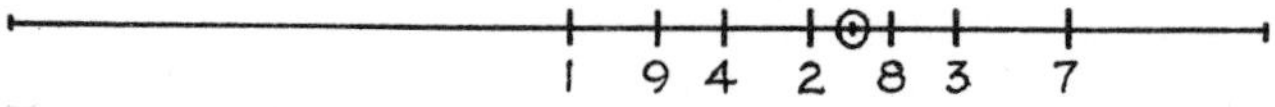

Figure 3.3

arbitrary initial distribution, say point 1. Since the equilibrium point is to its right, the cost on the road whose flow is measured by the interval from 1 to the right end point is larger. Therefore one-fifth of its flow will shift to the other road. The next distribution point is therefore the point which marks one-fifth of the interval to the right of 1 as measured from 1 on. This is point 2. It still is to the left of 0. And so we obtain 3 from 2 in the same way as 2 was obtained from 1. Point 4 will now fall to the left of 0. Continuing in this way the following becomes apparent. Points keep oscillating around 0 for a while with odd-numbered points to the right of 0, even-numbered points to the left. At the same time there is a steady drift of even and odd points among themselves to the right. (This is due to the fact that 0 is situated to the right of the center.) Finally an even numbered point will fall to the right of and rather close to 0. Say, that this is point 8. But then the next step will carry an odd point (9) rather far to the left, but obviously not more than one-fifth of the distance between the left end point and 0. It emerges that oscillations will continue to range over one-fifth of the entire flow. Only by an extremely slight chance can a distribution point ever coincide with 0 and thereby arrest any further oscillation.

It may seem paradoxical that equilibrium is approached to within the same proportion of total flow as that which designates the responsive fraction of road users. The smaller the fraction of drivers who take notice of changes in traffic conditions, the better is the approximation in the end. Emphasis here is on the phrase "in the end." For each step by itself in the movement toward equilibrium carries one so much less far.

The adjustment processes in a network may be understood as a superposition of these two basic types of movement. We have computed two examples which will demonstrate the approach to equilibrium and the extent and persistence of fluctuations that our model describes for a network with flexible demand.

3.3.2. *Numerical Examples of Approach to Equilibrium*

In the following pages two hypothetical examples are presented, solely for purposes of illustration. They are intended to show a possible method of computation and to exhibit the process of convergence toward a stable equilibrium discussed in the preceding section. The parameters were chosen arbitrarily and any resemblance to an actual road network is accidental. An attempt was made to select parameters which would result in relatively inelastic demand functions and significantly different costs on alternative routes.

Both examples are based on the same road network, which is represented in Figure 3.4. All traffic is assumed to move in an eastbound direction (i.e. from lower-numbered points to higher-numbered points);

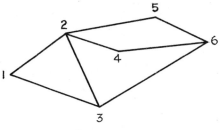

Figure 3.4

or, at any rate, westbound traffic is ignored. Functional relationships between flow and cost and between cost and demand are taken as linear.

In the first example (see below) no flows $x_{i,k}$ were assumed between adjacent points. This example was worked first with the fraction a of

Example 1

$$y_{12} = 2 + \frac{1}{2} x_{12}$$

$$y_{13} = 2 + \frac{2}{3} x_{13}$$

$$y_{23} = 2 + \frac{1}{5} x_{23}$$

$$y_{24} = 2 + \frac{1}{2} x_{24}$$

$$y_{25} = 3 + \frac{1}{4} x_{25}$$

$$y_{36} = 3 + \frac{1}{2} x_{36}$$

$$y_{46} = 2 + \frac{1}{2} x_{46}$$

$$y_{56} = 3 + \frac{1}{3} x_{56}$$

$$y_{1,4} = y_{12} + y_{24}$$

$$y_{1,5} = y_{12} + y_{25}$$

$$y_{2,6} = \text{Min}(y_{24}+y_{46}, y_{25} + y_{56}, y_{23}+y_{36})$$

$$y_{1,6} = \text{Min}(y_{13} + y_{36}, y_{12} + y_{26})$$

$$g_{1,4} = 5 - .4y_{1,4}$$

$$g_{1,5} = 6 - .5y_{1,5}$$

$$g_{1,6} = 8 - .3y_{1,6}$$

$$g_{2,6} = 7 - .6y_{2,6}$$

responsive road users equal to one, and zero flows initially on all roads. With the parameters used, there was no sign of convergence. The example was worked a second time with $a = \frac{1}{2}$, again starting with zero flows on all roads, but there was still little or no indication of convergence. The third attempt was made with $a = \frac{1}{10}$, and beginning flows equal to estimates of the equilibrium flows based on the range of the oscillations observed in the second trial. This approach resulted in apparent convergence.

In the second example some of the parameters were altered, and flows between adjacent points were included. In this case there was already a tendency to converge with $a = \frac{1}{2}$, starting from zero flow on all roads, but some oscillations persisted. The value of a was then decreased by stages first to $\frac{1}{5}$ and then to $\frac{1}{10}$. The amplitude of the remaining oscillations was thereby decreased.

Example 2

$$y_{12} = 5 + .5 \; x_{12} \qquad\qquad g_{1,2} = 16 - .3 \; y_{12}$$

$$y_{13} = 15 + .2 \; x_{13} \qquad\qquad g_{1,3} = 14 - .2 \; y_{13}$$

$$y_{23} = 9 + .6 \; x_{23} \qquad\qquad g_{2,3} = 24 - .2 \; y_{23}$$

$$y_{24} = 10 + .2 \; x_{24} \qquad\qquad g_{2,4} = 30 - .1 \; y_{24}$$

$$y_{25} = 11 + .4 \; x_{25} \qquad\qquad g_{2,5} = 28 - .3 \; y_{25}$$

$$y_{36} = 8 + .3 \; x_{36} \qquad\qquad g_{3,6} = 20 - .6 \; y_{36}$$

$$y_{46} = 6 + .4 \; x_{46} \qquad\qquad g_{4,6} = 18 - .2 \; y_{46}$$

$$y_{56} = 7 + .5 \; x_{56} \qquad\qquad g_{5,6} = 12 - .1 \; y_{56}$$

$$y_{1,4} = y_{12} + y_{24} \qquad\qquad g_{1,4} = 50 - .4 \; y_{1,4}$$

$$y_{1,5} = y_{12} + y_{25} \qquad\qquad g_{1,5} = 60 - .5 \; y_{1,5}$$

$$y_{2,6} = \text{Min} \; (y_{24} + y_{46},\; y_{25} + y_{56},\; y_{23} + y_{36}) \qquad\qquad g_{2,6} = 70 - .6 \; y_{2,6}$$

$$y_{1,6} = \text{Min} \; (y_{13} + y_{36},\; y_{12} + y_{2,6}) \qquad\qquad g_{1,6} = 80 - .3 \; y_{1,6}$$

In both examples it was found that flows from 1 to 6 settled down rapidly to a single route, over which the flows converged asymptotically (if at all). Flow from 2 to 6 oscillated between two routes, namely 2 - 4 - 6 and 2 - 5 - 6. The oscillations were of fairly constant amplitude and period, although the oscillation was asymmetric, as can be seen from the graphs (Figures 3.5-3.8). In the first example there was some indication of longer "waves" superimposed on the oscillations, but these were not apparent in the second example.

It can be assumed that oscillations would die out faster if the fraction a of responsive road users were a decreasing function of the cost difference between the alternatives being compared, with a tending to zero as the cost difference tends to zero. Another factor leading to the same result is the fact that some weight may be given to experience of the more remote past, especially where oscillations have already been experienced.

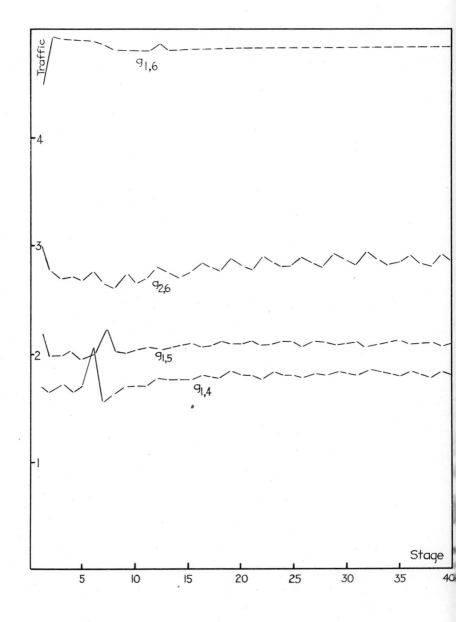

Figure 3.5. Example 1, Demand

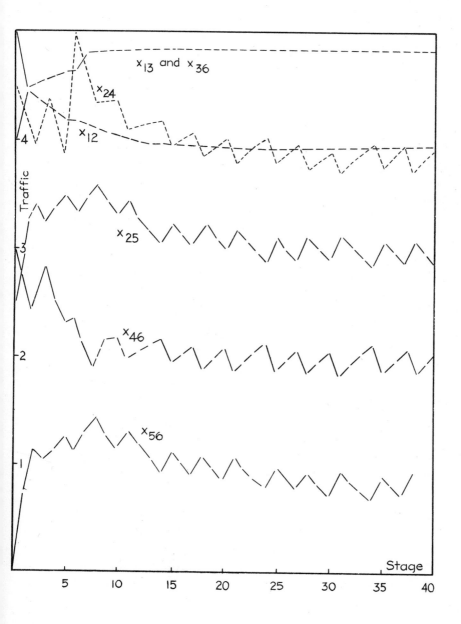

Figure 3.6. Example 1, Flows ($x_{23} = 0$ throughout)

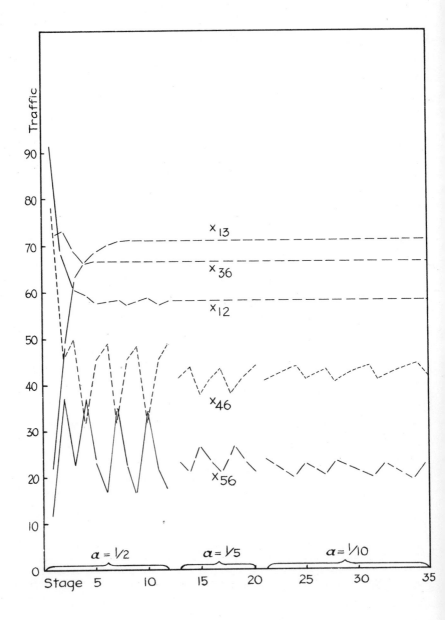

Figure 3.7. Example 2, Flows

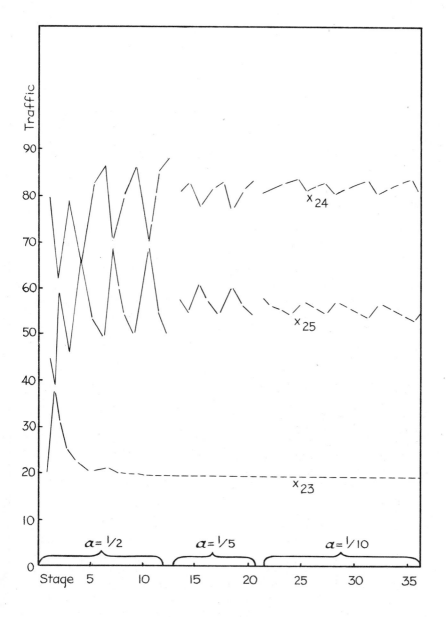

Figure 3.8. Example 2, Flows (second trial)

Chapter 4

EFFICIENCY

4.1. The Problem

An economic approach to traffic analysis should not only explain the interaction of many individual decisions in some state of equilibrium, but also provide criteria by which to judge the performance of the system. Since roads are scarce means, their best utilization is an important concern to the community. In the present chapter we attempt to clarify the economic meaning of "best utilization" and to evaluate traffic equilibrium in the light of this interpretation.

4.1.1. Allocation of Road Capacity

The rules of the road, by determining which traffic is to have priority in crossing an intersection or passing an obstacle, achieve an allocation of the available road capacity to those competing for its use. A similar function is exercised by speed limits and passing restrictions, even if the lawmakers' concern may have been primarily that of safety. Thus a slow vehicle proceeding on a road where traffic conditions afford little opportunity to pass in effect exercises a power to exclude faster vehicles for extended periods from the road space available in front of it. This allocation of capacity necessarily involves a distribution of time losses and hence of cost.

An allocation of road space also takes place in a more subtle way through the adjustment of route selection to traffic conditions. In the case of two roads between a pair of locations traffic distributes itself so that average transportation cost becomes the same on either road. If one road is shorter but of small capacity, the delays at equilibrium due to the more crowded conditions on the shorter road would just compensate for the greater operating cost on the longer road. Congestion on the short road, by discouraging further traffic there, has led to a diversion of some traffic to the long road. This too may be called an allocation of road space.

There is nothing inevitable about this particular allocation; a different distribution could have been achieved by arbitrarily assigning all vehicles with odd-numbered license plates to the longer route, say. In the case of the equilibrium distribution, as Pigou has pointed out, it would be possible, by shifting a few cars from one road to the other, greatly to lessen the trouble of driving for those left on the congested road, while only slightly increasing the trouble of driving along the less congested road. "In these circumstances a rightly chosen measure of differential taxation against [the congested road] would create an 'artificial' situation superior to the 'natural' one. But the measure of differentiation must be rightly chosen" (Pigou, 1920, p. 194). What is the basis of this economic value judgment?

4.1.2. Meaning of Efficiency

As long as the demand for transportation between given points or the demand for net transportation of commodities from each location is fixed independently of flow conditions, the choice of a criterion of efficiency seems obvious: the minimization of the aggregate cost to all road users. But the very notion of aggregate cost involves an evaluation of the time losses and dollars spent by various classes of road users. The way in which we have defined our demand and capacity functions implies, however,that we shall treat everyone like the average road user. There is no scope in this model for a differential evaluation of the costs and benefits to classes of road users. A single exception is to be found at the end of this chapter, in Section 4.5, which explains some of the consequences of differential time valuation.

For our analysis it makes no difference, however, what the relative weights are that we attach to the money cost, time, and risk of the average road user. For, as we shall see, these weights do not affect the relevant properties of the cost function we use, so that the principle of our conclusion holds quite independently of the valuations involved.

At this point it may be remarked that an economic valuation of risk is implied in many decisions that a road user must make and is equally indispensable in an efficiency analysis from the point of view of society as a whole. Now any valuation of risk implies in effect the setting of money values upon human life and health. This is indeed unavoidable whenever economic activities involve danger to human life and health. Since a strict adherence to the principle of safety first would mean the standstill of many economic activities without which modern industrial societies could not exist, everybody makes a compromise, consciously or unconsciously, which implies certain high but finite valuations of human life and health. Highway transportation is no exception to this. In each selection of a free speed, a choice of the probability of fatal accidents is implied. Since operating cost and time cost also vary with free speed, and since presumably the individual seeks his optimum, the increase of the probability of fatal accidents with an increase in free speed must be at least compensated by the simultaneous decrease of other cost. Knowing how this probability depends on free speed permits us, in principle, to estimate an upper bound to the value of life as implied in the individual's driving behavior. There can be no question that individuals are only vaguely aware of the value implications of their behavior regarding risk, and that the values revealed by some types of driving appear socially unacceptable.

Let us consider first the case where transportation cost is identified with travel time. We have mentioned in Section 2.2.2 the fact that for every road user, except possibly the slowest vehicle, travel time increases with flow. This statement can be sharpened with regard to the rate of increase, and we shall need the property we are about to observe as a prerequisite for the applicability of our mathematical analysis. It is clear that the time (per vehicle) spent waiting in queues behind slower cars increases at an increasing rate with flow, at least if the composition of flow by free-speed classes remains reasonably constant. It follows that the weighted sum of all travel times, the aggregate travel time, must increase with flow at a rate which is itself increasing. A function whose rate of increase is itself increasing or constant is called convex.[1] So we may state that aggregate time cost is an increasing and convex function of flow, regardless of the weights used in the aggregation.

Now whatever the form of the operating cost and risk function, this result remains valid so long as time is valued highly relative to money and risk. But in fact both operating cost and risk cost tend to be increasing and convex functions themselves. For small flows both money cost and risk per vehicle increase approximately in proportion to the increase in the number of passings per vehicle per mile. Risk is, except for a fixed component, mainly associated with proximity to other cars, and passing maneuvers involve the closest and most frequent physical approximation of vehicles to each other. For a straight road with very light traffic passing may take place without any substantial variation in speed. However, where passing maneuvers are more numerous, operating cost often goes up because of the fluctuations in speed usually required in their execution, and the consequent increase in fuel consumption over the level required at an equivalent steady speed. At small flows this rate of passing is a convex function of flow. At large flows on the other hand, the money equivalent of the increase of travel time with respect to flow is of a much higher order of magnitude than any variation of money cost and risk. Therefore, even if in an intermediate range of flows the rate of net increase of cost with flow may drop slightly, we should not commit any serious error in assuming that the aggregate transportation cost on a road (per mile or for its entire length) is an increasing and convex function of flow throughout the whole range of flows.

If demand is flexible, that is, if traffic generation depends on traffic conditions, then cost minimization is not the whole story of efficiency, for it leaves undetermined the level of demand at which cost is minimized. What is needed therefore is some measure of the benefits that arise from the satisfaction of a demand for road use.

In our first discussion of demand, attention was drawn to the meaning of the area under a demand curve and bounded by the horizontal at the prevailing level of trip cost (Figure 2.3). This area measures the excess of the maximal cost that road users would have been willing to spend on the current transportation activities over the amount of cost that is actually incurred. This expression seems to be an adequate representation of the advantages (often different for different trips between

---

1. Convexity so defined is the same thing as the convexity concept defined in Section 3.1.3* if the latter is applied to a function of one variable.

the same points) that accrue to road users expressed in comparable terms, money. It is further recommended by the fact that it is of long standing in economic theory as a measure of consumers' benefit or "surplus" and has been put forward repeatedly in the context of discussions on the utility of transportation facilities.[2]

All of this is not to say that the consumers' surplus would be easy to measure in practice, but rather that it is adequate from a conceptual point of view. However, mention should be made again of an implicit assumption on which its applicability rests, namely that there should be no effects on income which would render the costs saved at various levels of spending of unequal (per unit) value to the road users.

4.2. Cost Minimization on Two Roads

4.2.1. Pigou's Problem

The principles of cost minimization in a network may be illustrated by a reconsideration, in terms of a graphical analysis, of the two-road case with fixed total flow. In Figure 4.1 let AB represent the total flow

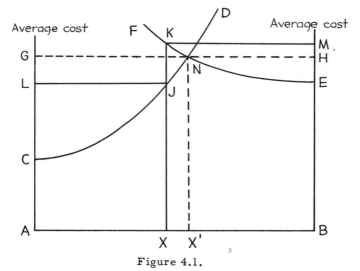

Figure 4.1.

from a certain origin to a certain destination, and let the way this flow is apportioned to the two roads connecting origin and destination be indicated by some point on the line AB such as X, or X'. Now let the functions relating average cost and flow be represented by the two curves CD and EF. If X represents the particular division of traffic under

2. E.g. Hotelling (1938). We shall not recite here the various distinctions possible between consumers' surpluses depending on the assumptions about the income situation before and after. The fact that we have an "average" curve renders such subtleties irrelevant here.

consideration, then AX is the flow on one road and BX the flow on the other; AL (=XJ) and BM (=XK) are the respective average costs. The total cost of transportation corresponding to the division X is therefore represented by the sum of the areas of the two rectangles AXJL and BXKM. As we have seen earlier, the equilibrium division of traffic will be that which results in equal average costs on the two roads. In this case therefore the point X′ with average costs AG and BH (both equal to X′N) represents the equilibrium division; total cost is represented by the sum of the areas AX′NG and BX′NH, which in this case is simply the area ABHG.

Can anything general be said about the division of traffic which results in minimal total cost? This division can be characterized geometrically as that pair of adjacent rectangles with corners on the two cost curves which possesses the smallest joint area. In order to see that in general this will not be the pair of rectangles that have the same height, we may look at a particularly simple pair of average-cost curves, namely a pair of straight lines (CD and EF in Figure 4.2). The problem of minimizing the area of adjacent rectangles with corners sliding along two straight lines boils down to finding the rates of change of their areas with respect to small shifts of the common edge.

Consider for instance the left-hand rectangle, designated AXJL in Figure 4.2. Its area equals that of the trapezoid ACGX which is obtained by drawing a straight line CG which bisects LJ and every other similar horizontal from the vertical axis to the average-cost curve CD. The two triangles, I and II, above and below the bisector CG are congruent. As the rectangle is expanded along the given line CJ, this bisector CG retains its position and the area change is given by a vertical strip extending between the bisector and the horizontal axis (the cross-hatched area in Figure 4.3). For a narrow strip the area is approximately equal to its width times the ordinate XG. At X the rate of increase of the rectangular area AXJL with respect to displacements of the point X therefore equals the length of the vertical XG.

Let the two bisectors CP and EQ be drawn for both cost curves in Figure 4.2. At a point such as X″ or X′ (the equilibrium point) where one bisector lies above the other, a reduction of the area representing total cost can be achieved by diminishing the base of the rectangle for which the corresponding bisector reaches higher. The minimum is therefore realized by letting the common edge of the two rectangles be that verticle line XG which passes through the intersection of the two bisectors in Figure 4.3.

It may happen that there is no such intersection but that one bisector reaches the outer edge below the origin of the other bisectors. In that case all the area is allotted to this one rectangle.

In the linear case just described XG will not pass through the intersection of the average-cost curves unless their intercepts with the vertical axes are equal. This means that, in general, the equilibrium distribution of flows is not the one that minimizes total costs.

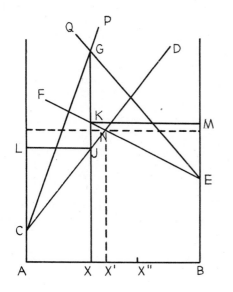

Figure 4.2

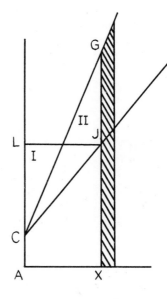

Figure 4.3

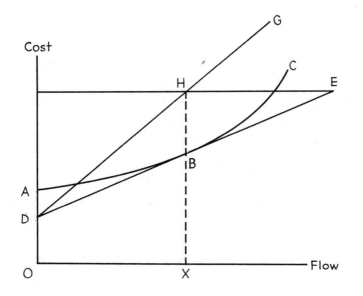

Figure 4.4

The bisector we have constructed for an average-cost curve represents the rate of increase of total cost with flow. The economic name is an "incremental"- or "marginal"-cost curve. These curves can also be constructed for the case of curvilinear average-cost functions as follows. In order to obtain the point of the incremental curve above the point X in Figure 4.4, draw the tangent to the average-cost curve ABC at the point B, where XB represents the average cost when flow is equal to OX. Extend this tangent DBE to a point E selected so as to make DB and BE the same length. Now if in fact DBE were the average-cost curve, the rate of increase of total cost when flow was OX would be given us by the bisector DG, which by definition bisects FE at a point H directly above X (note that FH = HE because DB = BE). But since the true average-cost curve and this hypothetical one are tangent at B, the rates of growth of total cost at X must be equal. Therefore the true incremental-cost curve must also pass through the point H. XH then is the incremental cost when the flow is OX. The curve generated in this way will not generally be a straight line. Nevertheless, with incremental-cost curves our assertions in the previous paragraphs remain valid.

4.2.2. *Private Cost and Social Cost*

Let us turn back from the geometrical argument to the economic phenomena. What accounts for the failure of an equilibrium brought about by free individual decisions to achieve minimization of total cost? Since every individual minimizes his own cost, the failure must lie with the allocation of total cost to the individual road users. To pinpoint the question: does a road user's share of the cost match his contribution to the total cost incurred by traffic in the road system?

The answer very simply is no, if we look at the average cost of transportation on a road before and after addition of a vehicle. From a certain flow on, each additional vehicle causes some delay and risk to the others present for which it does not bear the cost. To be sure, in his own turn this road user will suffer delays and costs from any further vehicles that might be added. But to the marginal road user, who does not care whether he uses this road or an alternative one, his own cost is not a sufficient deterrent, because it does not contain the costs he inflicts on the other road users if he should choose the more congested road. As Professor Frank Knight has put it for the case of two alternative highways,

> The congestion and interference resulting from the addition of any particular truck to the stream of traffic on the narrow but good road affects in the same way the cost and output of all the trucks using that road. It is evident that if, after equilibrium is established, a few trucks should be arbitrarily transferred to the broad road, the reduction in cost or increase in output to those remaining

on the narrow road would be a clear gain[3] to the traffic as a whole. The trucks so transferred would incur no loss, for any one of them on the narrow road is a marginal truck, subject to the same relation between cost and output as any truck using the broad road. Yet whenever there is a difference in the cost, to an additional truck, of using the two roads, the driver of any truck has an incentive to use the narrow road, until the advantage is reduced to zero for all the trucks [Knight, 1952, p. 162].

This situation may also be described in terms of a distinction between "private" and "social" incremental cost. At a given level of traffic the private incremental cost of road use is the operating cost, time, risk, and possibly the toll charges incurred by an additional road user per vehicle mile. Against this one may set the total cost of an extra vehicle mile regardless of who is bearing it, and this will be called the social incremental cost of a vehicle mile. If traffic flow is so small that the interference of vehicles with each other is negligible and if traffic does not cause any annoyance to the public at large — a possibility which we are disregarding on the whole — the social and the private incremental costs of a vehicle mile are identical. In general, however, the presence of an extra vehicle causes delays and risks to other road users, so that the social incremental cost of a vehicle mile exceeds its private incremental cost.

In terms of the capacity function this fact appears as follows. Since average cost increases with flow, the cost of a vehicle mile, as averaged over all road users, is raised by an extra vehicle. This increase of the average cost level times the traffic flow equals the excess of social incremental cost over private incremental cost. If the road user were to bear his full share of cost, he would pay a tax or toll equal to this excess. This would make him realize the cost he causes to others and thus provide an incentive to keep social cost down by making the proper choices. This is indeed Pigou's "rightly chosen measure of differential taxation."

4.3. Efficient Transportation in Networks

In the two-road model there was no serious problem of determining which roads would be used under efficient utilization. Traffic on one or the other road was zero whenever the incremental cost of transportation on that road was greater than that on the other road even with all the traffic on it. In a more involved network the answer is less obvious. Which routes must be considered as possible alternatives to a congested route is part of the problem. Also, a single origin-to-destination flow cannot be looked at in isolation, since it competes with other traffic over some or all of its route. (This is clear when it is remembered that a given road can be a part of several routes.) If the analysis were to be

---

3. The gain is a clear gain in this case because Professor Knight has assumed that on the broad road an increase of flow will not reduce average speeds. Capacity, that is to say, is very high.

in terms of routes, it would thus appear vastly complicated. Fortunately an approach in terms of flows on roads rather than routes is possible. The problem of this chapter thus becomes one of determining for each road the levels of flow in each direction which are compatible with the fixed net originations and which result in the smallest aggregate transportation cost. Since graphical analysis is unpromising in a problem of such complexity, it becomes necessary to apply the formal mathematical apparatus for minimization of a function of many variables that are subject to constraints. Economic intuition may, however, be called upon in terms of an analogous problem in the theory of the firm.

Let us consider a chemical or metallurgical material which is capable of various stages or modifications, and a firm which undertakes to transform it from certain stages to certain other stages. Not all conceivable transformations may be possible, of course, and it may be that various stages can be reached from a given one only via certain other intermediate stages. Let this firm be given some fixed amounts of this material in various stages and be asked to produce certain fixed amounts of the material in other stages. How should the firm choose the transformation processes which will achieve the production goal at minimal cost if the further assumption is made that each transformation is subject to per unit costs which increase with volume?

Here the stages of the material correspond to locations, the transitions correspond to roads, and sequences of transformation processes which lead from a given stage to a desired stage of the material — that is, the production methods — correspond to routes.

With reference to the production problem economic intuition has been crystallized in the so-called principle of incremental cost. According to this principle, the last unit of the material at any particular stage should cost the same in any production method that is used. Also, an additional unit would cost more if it were produced by one of the production methods that is not used. To spell out the principle in the present case we may have recourse to an internal price system for the firm. Even though the production task did not specify any prices of the original or desired stages of the material, the principle of incremental cost asserts that it should be possible to associate a suitable price with each of the various stages. A cost-minimizing selection of production methods is then one where the incremental cost of every transformation process — that is, the cost occasioned by the last unit so transformed — is just covered by the price difference between the two stages. In particular, when nothing is transformed by a particular process, the cost of the first unit transformed by that process would already exceed the price difference. These internal prices, also called opportunity costs, have a distinct intuitive appeal. But is their existence really so obvious, and can one be sure in all cases that the incremental cost conditions, in terms of opportunity costs, ensure the minimization of total cost?

A substitution of one production method for another changes the costs of all the transformation processes involved in the two methods. But these same processes may also be part of other sequences of processes. In that case their cost structure would be upset, too. Is it always possible to satisfy the incremental cost conditions with respect to all methods simultaneously? Moreover, might not the far-reaching cost changes involved in any substitution of methods permit the possibility that the incremental cost conditions will be satisfied before and after a change, while the total costs will be different? In such a case the incremental cost conditions might still be necessary but would certainly not be sufficient for cost minimization.

What these questions amount to is really this: can the choice of the best production methods and of the extent of their application always be reduced to comparisons "in the small," that is, to considerations of the effect that the shift of one unit produced in this or that way will have on cost? Or in ascertaining the optimality of a certain combination of processes, are comparisons with combinations very different from the one under consideration indispensable?

To meet these and similar objections that might be raised, a mathematical analysis is called for. Such an analysis will be presented in the next section. In Section 4.4 we shall return to the economic interpretation of the incremental cost conditions for the road allocation problem, which in that context are called the efficiency conditions.

4.3.1*. Maximization Subject to Linear Inequalities as Constraints

The fact that the constraints of our maximum problem include inequalities makes it different from the standard extremization problems in the calculus. Fortunately, the theory of linear inequalities has been well developed, and in recent years several theorems for convenient use in so-called *linear* and *nonlinear programming* have been advanced. For our purposes the following theorem from Kuhn and Tucker (1951) is adequate.

Theorem: Let f(u) be differentiable and concave.[4] Necessary and sufficient that u^0 be a solution of

$$(4.1) \qquad \underset{u}{\text{Max}} \ f(u) \text{ subject to } u_r \geq 0 \text{ and } \sum_r b_{sr} \, u_r \leq c_s$$

is the existence of multipliers v_s such that

$$(4.2) \qquad v_s \geq 0 \text{ and } \text{``=''} \text{ if } \sum_r b_{sr} \, u_r^0 < c_s \ ,$$

and such that

$$(4.3) \qquad \frac{\partial}{\partial u_r} \left[f(u) + \sum_s v_s \left(c_s - \sum_r b_{sr} \, u_r \right) \right]_{u=u^0} \begin{Bmatrix} = \\ \leq \end{Bmatrix} 0$$

$$\text{if } u_r^0 \begin{Bmatrix} > \\ = \end{Bmatrix} 0.$$

---

4. Concavity is defined in (3.17), Section 3.1.3*.

Proof: Necessity. Let u^0 be a point where a constrained maximum of $f(u)$ is reached. At this point some of the constraints are effective (i.e. the limits are reached) and some are not. Without loss of generality we can suppose that $u_r^0 = 0$ for $r = 1, \ldots, R'$ and $u_r^0 > 0$ for $r = R' + 1, \ldots, R$; and similarly that $\sum_r b_{sr} u_r^0 = c_s$ for $s = 1, \ldots, S'$ and $\sum_r b_{sr} u_r^0 < c_s$ for $s = S' + 1, \ldots, S$. Let u be any other point such that

$$
\begin{aligned}
\sum_r b_{sr} u_r &\leq c_s && \text{for } s = 1, \ldots, S' \\
u_r &\geq 0 && \text{for } r = 1, \ldots, R' \quad .
\end{aligned}
$$
(4.4)

Then $(1 - a) u^0 + a u, \ 0 \leq a \leq 1$, satisfies the same constraints and for sufficiently small a leaves all those constraints ineffective that are ineffective for u^0. Define $z_r = u_r - u_r^0$ and

(4.5)
$$
\beta_{jr} = \begin{cases}
b_{jr} & \text{for} & j = 1, \ldots, S' \\
0 & \text{for} & j = S' + 1, \ldots, S \\
-1 & \text{for} & j = S + r \text{ and } r = 1, \ldots, R' \\
0 & \text{otherwise.}
\end{cases}
$$

Then $u^0 + az$ satisfies the original constraints, provided that

(4.6)
$$
\sum_r \beta_{jr} z_r \leq 0 \qquad \text{for } j = 1, \ldots, S + R
$$

and $0 < a < 1$, a sufficiently small. Because $f(u)$ is maximized at u^0 subject to the constraints in (4.1) we have therefore that

(4.7)
$$
\frac{f[u^0 + a(u - u^0)] - f(u^0)}{a} \leq 0
$$

for all z satisfying (4.6) and for sufficiently small a. But the limit of this expression as $a \rightarrow 0$ is

(4.8)
$$
\sum_r \left(\frac{\partial f}{\partial u_r} \right)_{u=u_0} \cdot (u_r - u_r^0) \quad .
$$

Writing f_r for $\left(\dfrac{\partial f}{\partial u_r} \right)_{u=u_0}$ and z_r for $u_r - u_r^0$ we obtain that $\sum_r f_r z_r \leq 0$ for all z_r such that $\sum_r \beta_{jr} z_r \leq 0, \ j = 1, \ldots, S + R$. We now have

recourse to the fundamental *Farkas lemma* (Farkas, 1901): In order that $\sum_r a_r u_r \leq 0$ for all u_r such that $\sum_r b_{jr} u_r \leq 0$ it is necessary and sufficient that

(4.9)
$$
a_r = \sum_j b_{jr} v_j \qquad \text{with some } v_j \geq 0 \quad .
$$

The Farkas lemma now tells us that there exist $v_j \geq 0$, $j = 1, \ldots, S + R$, such that

(4.10) $f_r = \sum\limits_j v_j \, \beta_{jr}$.

Since $\beta_{jr} \equiv 0$ for $j = S' + 1, \ldots, S$ and $S + R' + 1, \ldots, S + R$ the corresponding v_j can take on arbitrary non-negative values. Let us set these v_j equal to zero. Then, translating back into the b_{sr} we have

(4.11) $f_r = \sum\limits_s v_s b_{sr} - v_{S+r}$ for $r = 1, \ldots, R$.

By the definition of v_{S+r} it follows that

(4.12) $f_r - \sum\limits_s v_s b_{sr} \begin{Bmatrix} = \\ \leq \end{Bmatrix} 0$ if $u_r^0 \begin{Bmatrix} > \\ = \end{Bmatrix} 0$.

In other words

(4.13)

$$\left(\frac{\partial}{\partial u_r} \right) \left[f(u^0) + \sum\limits_{s=1}^{S} v_s \left(c_s - \sum\limits_r b_{sr} u_r^0 \right) \right] \begin{Bmatrix} = \\ \leq \end{Bmatrix} 0$$

$$\text{if } u_r^0 \begin{Bmatrix} > \\ = \end{Bmatrix} 0 \ .$$

Sufficiency. Suppose that there exist v_s for which (4.2) and (4.3) are satisfied. Then, since $f(u)$ is concave, we have by the lemma of Section 3.1.3*

(4.14) $f(u^0) \geq f(u) + \sum\limits_s v_s \left(c_s - \sum\limits_r b_{sr} u_r \right)$

for all u with $u_r \geq 0$. By (4.2), for all u with $\sum\limits_r b_{sr} u_r \leq c_s$,

$\sum\limits_s v_s \left(c_r - \sum\limits_r b_{sr} u_r \right) \geq 0$, so that

(4.15) $f(u^0) \geq f(u)$ for all u with $\sum\limits_r b_{sr} u_r \leq c_s$.

4.3.2*. Minimization of Transportation Cost Subject to a Fixed Program

We now apply the theorem of the last section to the problem of minimizing transportation cost. In the case of fixed originations $f_{i,k}$ and terminations $-f_{k,k}$ the maximand is the negative of total cost:

(4.16) $-\frac{1}{2} \sum\limits_{ij} h_{ij}(x_{ij}) \, x_{ij}$.

The factor $\frac{1}{2}$ is needed because every road appears twice in the sum, once as ij and once as ji, while x_{ij} already denotes the total flow in both directions. Applying the sufficient criterion for concavity, used in Section 3.1.3*, that the Hessian be negative semidefinite, we see that every term $-\frac{1}{2} h_{ij}(x_{ij}) \, x_{ij}$ is concave in x_{ij} provided

$$(4.17) \qquad \frac{d^2}{dx_{ij}{}^2} \left[h_{ij}(x_{ij}) \, x_{ij} \right] \geqq 0 \quad .$$

The left hand side equals

$$(4.18) \qquad \frac{d^2 h_{ij}}{dx_{ij}{}^2} x_{ij} + 2 \frac{dh_{ij}}{dx_{ij}}$$

and each of the two terms is non-negative as already argued in Section 4.1.2. It follows that the maximand (4.16) is concave in x.

As constraints of the minimum problem we have the "program conditions"

$$(4.19) \qquad \sum_j (x_{ij,k} - x_{ji,k}) = f_{i,k}$$

and

$$(4.20) \qquad x_{ij,k} \geqq 0 \quad .$$

Since consistency of the program implies $\sum_i f_{i,k} = 0$, we can replace the "=" sign in (4.19) by "$\geqq$", for the "$>$" sign cannot be attained. Labeling the multipliers $l_{i,k}$ we obtain the solution equation (4.3) in the form

$$(4.21) \qquad \frac{\partial}{\partial x_{ij,k}} \left[-\frac{1}{2} \sum_{ij} h_{ij}(x_{ij}) x_{ij} + \sum_{i,k} h_{i,k} \left(\sum_j [x_{ij,k} - x_{ji,k}] - f_{i,k} \right) \right] \begin{Bmatrix} = \\ \leqq \\ = \end{Bmatrix} 0 \quad \text{if} \quad x_{ij,k} \begin{Bmatrix} > \\ \\ = \end{Bmatrix} 0 \quad .$$

In explicit form,

$$(4.22) \qquad l_{i,k} - l_{j,k} \begin{Bmatrix} = \\ \leqq \\ = \end{Bmatrix} h_{ij} + h'_{ij} x_{ij} \quad \text{if} \quad x_{ij,k} \begin{Bmatrix} > \\ \\ = \end{Bmatrix} 0$$

with suitable numbers $l_{i,k}$. We notice that (4.22) leaves the $l_{i,k}$ undetermined up to additive constants c_k. We may fix these such that $l_{k,k} = 0$. The relations (4.22) are then reminiscent of the equilibrium conditions (3.10). They suggest that the $l_{i,k}$ be interpreted as trip costs, based however on transportation charges different from simple transportation costs on roads.

4.3.3*. Maximization of Consumers' Surplus

Before discussing this result it is convenient to derive the corresponding conditions for the case of flexible demand. In Section 2.4.1 the consumers' surplus was defined geometrically as the area between the demand curve and a horizontal line representing the prevailing average cost (Figure 2.3). It is now necessary to find an analytic expression for this. Let $x_{i,k}$ be the prevailing flow between locations. Then the area OABC in Figure 2.3 is given by

$$\int_0^{x_{i,k}} g_{i,k}(x) \, dx \, .$$

The area OCBD representing the prevailing trip cost equals

$$g_{i,k}(x_{i,k}) \cdot x_{i,k} \, .$$

The sum of all consumers' surpluses would seem to be therefore

$$(4.23) \qquad \sum_{i,k} \left[\int_0^{x_{i,k}} g_{i,k}(x) \, dx - g_{i,k}(x_{i,k}) \cdot x_{i,k} \right] \, .$$

However the sum of all trip costs to road users need not be identical with the total transportation costs. An equality of the two, as it was derived in equation (3.12) at the end of Section 3.1.1*, depends on the particular incidence of cost that we have under conditions of ordinary traffic equilibrium. If, for instance, tolls are charged, then these are part of trip costs, but they should not be included in total transportation costs, since they become available again and can be used for such purposes as tax reduction. On the other hand public expenditures for highway control and maintenance may depend on traffic, but as this is a further variable it will be excluded by making the analysis a "short-run" one in which such public expenditures are held constant. Under these assumptions we arrive at the proper expression for the consumers' surplus if we replace the sum of trip costs to individuals,

$$\sum_{i,k} g_{i,k}(x_{i,k}) \cdot x_{i,k} \, , \quad \text{by} \quad \frac{1}{2} \sum_{ij} h_{ij}(x_{ij}) \cdot x_{ij} \, ,$$

the sum of operating cost, risk costs, and time costs on roads.

$$(4.24) \qquad \text{Consumers' Surplus} = \sum_{i,k} \int_0^{x_{i,k}} g_{i,k}(x) \, dx \\ - \frac{1}{2} \sum_{ij} h_{ij}(x_{ij}) \cdot x_{ij} \, .$$

It differs from the function H of (3.11) in the second term only.

In Section 3.1.3* we have shown that the first term represents a concave function of the $x_{ij,k}$. In Section 4.3.2* the same was proved for the second term. Therefore the expression (4.24) is a concave function. Its maximum over the positive orthant $x_{ij,k} \geq 0$ is therefore characterized, according to the theorem proved in Section 4.3.1*, by the necessary and sufficient condition

(4.25)
$$g_{i,k}(x_{i,k}) - g_{j,k}(x_{j,k}) - h_{ij}(x_{ij}) - h'_{ij}(x_{ij}) x_{ij} \left. \begin{cases} = \\ \lessgtr \\ \leq \end{cases} \right\} 0$$

$$\text{if } x_{ij,k} \left. \begin{cases} > \\ = \end{cases} \right\} 0 \quad .$$

This may be written out in terms of two relations

(4.26)
$$y_{i,k} - y_{j,k} \left. \begin{cases} = \\ \lessgtr \\ \leq \end{cases} \right\} h_{ij}(x_{ij}) + h'_{ij}(x_{ij}) x_{ij} \text{ if } x_{ij} \left. \begin{cases} > \\ = \end{cases} \right\} 0 \quad ;$$

$$x_{i,k} = f_{i,k}(y_{i,k}) \quad .$$

We thus obtain an efficiency condition of the same form as that in (4.22) which related to a fixed program.

4.4. Efficiency Tolls

4.4.1. Interpretation of the Efficiency Conditions

The efficiency conditions suggest that efficient utilization can, at least in theory, be achieved through a state of equilibrium in which suitable taxes or tolls are levied on the use of all congested roads. These tolls are to express the excess of social over private cost caused by an additional road user. The "toll" term added in (4.22) to the private cost of transportation equals the increase in the private cost to the average road user caused by a unit increase in traffic, multiplied by the total flow of traffic. If this term is added to the private cost of transportation, one obtains what was called in Section 4.2.2 the social cost of transportation at the prevailing flow on a road. In the absence of congestion, as indicated by constant average cost independent of the amount of traffic, no toll would arise.

If such "efficiency tolls" could be levied, they would restore the power of competitive equilibrium to achieve an efficient utilization of resources. By charging everyone a toll equal to his contribution to the total cost of others, road users can be induced to make an efficient use of the available capacity. It is clear that this toll or tax does not discriminate between destinations or commodities. On the other hand, for accurate effects it would have to vary with the traffic conditions and hence be different at different times. In a more detailed analysis based on a model which (unlike the one given above) takes more aspects of traffic into account, it would also turn out that the best charges are different for vehicles of different free speeds and of different congestion characteristics, e.g. trucks as compared with passenger vehicles. We will not pursue this possibility here.

Under present conditions congestion is the main obstacle to more traffic. While traffic is not an end in itself, cheap transportation is a contributing factor to the economic division of labor. Ready accessibility of centrally located markets is of particular importance, because it determines the size of markets and the extent to which economies of large scale production and distribution can be reaped. Congestion, by setting a limit and a premium upon the movement of persons and commodities, restricts the effectiveness with which the functions of centrally located markets can be performed. It seems a paradoxical conclusion then that the answer to congestion should be less traffic — even less, that is, than the existence of congestion at present permits.

The point to be made is that traffic becomes uneconomical if its social cost exceeds the value of the advantages. And if a full charge were made for the social cost caused by each road user, traffic would keep by itself within the economically warranted limits. There is no avoiding the conclusion that, in the short run at least, free access to congested roads just permits too much traffic. Congestion is not selective in any proper way, because it spreads the cost of the least important or marginal traffic over all other traffic. It may still seem odd that every individual should pay more for transportation, as must be the case when demand is reduced on the whole. The clue is of course that since transportation costs other than tolls tend to go down with a decrease in flow, they decrease as a result of the imposition of tolls. The remaining part of the expense becomes available again as toll revenue; so that the community can gain where every individual seems to lose.

The preceding analysis of efficiency in the case of elastic demand has been based on an equal weighting of everyone's money cost and on uniform money equivalents for time and risk. This is of course only a special way of evaluating the costs and benefits to various classes of road users, but one which has the distinction of simplicity and of *prima facie* egalitarianism.

One can convince himself that the charging of suitable, discriminatory tolls, depending either on the free speed or the destination or any other characteristic of road users, if feasible would result in an efficient utilization of roads in terms of certain nonuniform weights assigned to the benefits to various road-user classes. But the proper choice of such tolls is a formidable problem.[5]

By discriminating against the use of congested roads the imposition of efficiency tolls gives rise to additional shortest routes between given origins and destinations. For through the added costs, part of the traffic on these congested routes is diverted. In this way the availability of these uncongested alternative routes has the effect of placing a ceiling on the efficiency tolls.

When demand is elastic, tolls have the obvious additional effect of

---

5. It may be mentioned, incidentally, that almost every distribution of traffic over roads represents a (Pareto) optimum in the sense that it is impossible to make any road user better off without making someone else worse off, as long as no compensation is payable, either directly or via tolls or taxes. For as a result of the change, traffic is almost bound to increase somewhere. It is for this reason that a weighting of benefits becomes indispensable.

reducing not only the demand for the use of roads with heavy tolls but also the total demand for transportation on all roads. This implies that the level of tolls, which rises with increasing flows, must be less than the level that a calculation of social costs at the ordinary equilibrium levels of traffic would suggest. One of the reasons for this is, of course, the utilization of uncongested alternative routes noted above. From the fact that flows are decreased, on the whole, we must conclude that the cost of transportation to road users has risen on the average.

For any particular road, of course, the diversionary effect of tolls on parallel routes may overshadow the decline in the demand for transportation to locations, so that traffic may actually increase there as a result of tolls. This is quite obvious for a two-road network. What can be shown, however, is that flows tend to decrease on roads relatively congested. We shall do this in the next section for the case in which demand and capacity functions are linear and the absolute capacity limits are unattained.

4.4.2*. Equilibrium and Efficiency Flows

With linear demand and capacity functions the expression (4.24) for the consumers' surplus is, using the notation of (3.28) and (3.29),

$$\sum_{i,k} \left[\frac{1}{2} e_{i,k} x_{i,k}^2 + f_{i,k} x_{i,k} \right]$$

(4.27)

$$- \sum_{ij} \left[\frac{1}{2} a_{ij} x_{ij}^2 + \frac{1}{2} b_{ij} x_{ij} \right] \quad .$$

This is less than the function H of (3.30) by an amount $\sum_{ij} \frac{1}{4} a_{ij} x_{ij}^2$. Viewing this difference as one brought about by parameter changes $\delta q_{nr} \equiv - \frac{1}{4} a_{ij}$ we can apply the inequality (3.33) of Section 3.2.1* in order to learn something about the differences between the ordinary equilibrium flows and the efficient flows. In this case the inequality assumes the simple form

(4.28) $$- \frac{1}{4} \sum_{ij} a_{ij} (2x_{ij} + \delta x_{ij}) \, \delta x_{ij} \geqq 0 \quad .$$

Since $a_{ij} > 0$, $x_{ij} \geqq 0$, and $x_{ij} + \delta x_{ij} \geqq 0$, we conclude that δx_{ij} tends to be negative for those ij with relatively high values of a_{ij} or x_{ij}. In other words on congested roads, efficient flows tend to be smaller than flows at ordinary equilibrium. Changing the sign of (4.28) and adding $\sum_{ij} a_{ij} x_{ij}^2$ to both sides we have

(4.29) $$\sum_{ij} a_{ij} (x_{ij} + \delta x_{ij})^2 \leqq \sum_{ij} a_{ij} x_{ij}^2 \quad .$$

Since the $a_{ij}(x_{ij} + \delta x_{ij})$ are the toll rates when flows are efficient, and

the a_{ij} x_{ij} the efficiency toll rates indicated by conditions at ordinary
equilibrium, we see that equilibrium flows and the corresponding cost
and demand conditions tend, if used naively, to produce an overestimate
of the revenues that would be collected from efficient flows at efficiency-
toll rates.

4.4.3. A Limited Toll System

At the present state of technology it is impractical to charge tolls
on every congested road. However, ways other than the present ones of
collecting tolls may be found which at the same time are cheap and do
not add to congestion. Or it may be found possible to levy the corresponding toll charges in indirect ways. While there are psychological
resistances against out-of-pocket charges even where the price paid is
less than the cost incurred for alternative means to the same end, the
case for toll charges to relieve congestion is economically unassailable.
The problem of how to make the road user sensitive to the social cost he
causes is a real one and the means to achieve it are worth further attention on the technological level.

But even when there are only a limited number of toll roads or
bridges, the question arises how the tolls on these should be set so as to
achieve, with the obtainable means, a maximum of economic benefit to
all road users. In discussing this problem we shall assume that pay-
ment of the construction cost from the toll revenue is no consideration.
A situation like this may be found in practice after the debt on a toll
road has been paid off.

This limited efficiency problem can be approached in terms of the
maximization of our consumers' surplus function subject to the additional constraints that on each free road the difference of trip costs
between the two end points of the road should not exceed the average
transportation cost on the road. Solution of this modified problem shows
that best tolls on the toll roads are different from what they would be
for the same roads in a general toll-road system in which efficiency
tolls are charged on *each* congested road. They are higher where congested free roads are predominant as feeder roads, and are less where
free roads compete with a toll road as alternatives.

4.4.4. Value of a Road

The fact shown in Section 3.2 that an upward shift of the cost schedule for one road decreases traffic on that road implies that road use decreases or at most remains constant with added fixed costs (independent
of flow) such as tolls. The demand for use of a road as a function of
tolls on that road alone has thus a normal (downward or level) slope,
whatever the capacities of or flows on other roads. This demand function is really a description of the path followed by the equilibrium as
one particular constant (the toll on the road under consideration) is
varied. Its steepness is of course dependent primarily on the number

and capacities of alternative roads and on the demand for transportation to locations reached via this road.

This demand function also defines the amount of toll revenue forthcoming at different toll levels. Obviously the maximum amount of tolls collectable is not above the value of the road to its users. Therefore any road which can be paid for by tolls (at the market rate of interest) is worth its construction cost under given road and traffic conditions on all other roads. We also obtain a lower-bound estimate of the value of a road in the amount of toll that is actually collected or that should be collected in order to achieve efficient utilization.

However there may still be a wide margin between what the road user pays in tolls and what the trip is actually worth to him over and above other transportation costs. Therefore a road will have a higher value in general than what its possible toll income amounts to. It follows that the "pay for itself" criterion of the usefulness of a toll road is too conservative for determination of the proper extent of a highway network.

4.5. Toll Roads Reconsidered

The analysis of an efficient allocation of flows to routes has led in its own course to the notion of a road toll as an instrument of controlling access to roads. The common meaning of a toll road is, however, that of a special route (an expressway) which offers superior roadway and traffic conditions at an extra charge. Inherent here is an element of economic discrimination in making extra service available at a price. To bring out this significant feature of toll roads, as understood in contemporary discussion, let us resort again to our two-road example. Suppose that the alternative roads are of equal capacity and are equivalent also as far as all other roadway conditions are concerned. Deviating now from our previous notion of aggregate transportation cost (Section 4.1.2) let the per-unit value of time vary between the various road users. If the total amount of flow is again taken to be fixed, the ordinary equilibrium distribution of equal flows on the two roads is also the efficient distribution, and there is no place for any compensating tolls in our previous sense. It may be asked, however, whether total welfare could not be improved by the creation of an artificial difference between the two roads through the levying of a toll on one of them. To the extent that this discourages traffic, it improves the traffic conditions on that road, and in particular it reduces delays to faster vehicles. Is it possible that the time saving to road users who value time highly more than compensates for the toll paid, and that conversely the money collected is worth more than the added inconvenience to drivers unwilling to pay the toll? Other things equal, a high money value of time goes with a high free speed. But of course, other things are never equal; road users differ in their operating cost at given speeds and in their valuation of risk. Differences in the free speed on a long-distance highway tend to be relatively small. Therefore in a first formulation of the problem we may disregard any correlation between money value of time and free speed and use the same average-speed capacity curve for both roads regardless of whether or not the traffic with a high valuation of time has been separated out.

In the following mathematical note it is shown that the total benefits to road users can in fact be improved by giving them, through a suitable toll, a choice between faster travel at higher money cost and slower travel at smaller money cost. This is still on the assumption that everybody's dollar is valued the same by the community. If the roadway conditions differ also between the two roads the case for a separation of high and low speed traffic by a toll on one road is even stronger.[6] For simplicity we shall disregard the dependence of operating cost and risk on speed and consider time and toll costs only.

4.5.1*. Analysis

Let there be N road users entering the two roads per unit of time. We shall consider them arranged in decreasing order of the money value which they assign to time. Thus let

$m(n)$ be the money value of time to the nth road user;

x the index of the road user with the smallest money value of time who still uses the toll road (at the same time x is a measure of flow);

$t_1(x)$ the average travel time on the toll road;

$t_2(N-x)$ the average travel time on the free road;

p the toll rate.

For the user x of the toll road who does not care which of the two alternatives he chooses (the marginal road user)

$$(4.30) \qquad m(x) \, t_1(x) + p = m(x) \, t_2(N-x) \; .$$

This may be considered a definition of toll as a function of the flow called forth by it on the toll road (the inverse of the demand function for use of the toll road);

$$(4.31) \qquad p(x) = m(x) \, [t_2(N-x) - t_1(x)] \; .$$

Total cost of transportation to road users is now (using the integral notation for convenience)

$$(4.32) \qquad t_1(x) \int_0^x m(n) \, dn + xp(x) + t_2(N-x) \int_x^N m(n) \, dn \; .$$

---

6. If the effect on demand for transportation is taken into consideration, the case for toll roads emerges even better, but the determination of the optimal toll becomes more involved. An integrated network raises problems of still greater complexity. The two-road example presented here gives, however, a rough idea of the considerations involved.

From the point of view of the community the tolls do not constitute costs but are available again for redistribution or use in road construction and maintenance. The object of minimization is therefore

$$(4.33) \qquad t_1(x) \int_0^x m(n) \; dn + t_2(N-x) \int_x^N m(n) \; dn \quad .$$

In our example of two roads of equal length and capacity this minimand is

$$(4.34) \qquad G \equiv t(x) \int_0^x m(n) \; dn + t(N-x) \int_x^N m(n) \; dn \quad .$$

All we shall show is that the minimizing flow x must lie in the open interval $0 < x < \dfrac{N}{2}$. Let $x = \dfrac{N}{2} + z$ with $z > 0$. Now

$$(4.35) \qquad \left[t \left(\frac{N}{2} + z\right) - t\left(\frac{N}{2} - z\right) \right] \cdot \left[\int_0^{\frac{N}{2}+z} m \; dn - \int_{\frac{N}{2}+z}^N m \; dn \right] > 0,$$

since by assumption t is an increasing and m is a decreasing function. Multiplying out and substituting for z,

$$(4.36) \qquad \begin{aligned} & t(x) \int_0^x m \; dn + t(N-x) \int_x^N m \; dn \\ & \qquad > t(N-x) \int_0^x m \; dn + t(x) \int_x^N m \; dn \quad . \end{aligned}$$

This means that $G(N-x) < G(x)$ for $x > \dfrac{N}{2}$. Therefore the minimizing x must be contained in the interval $0 \leqq x \leqq \dfrac{N}{2}$. That it does not fall into an interval end point is seen from

$$(4.37) \qquad G'\left(\frac{N}{2}\right) = t'\left(\frac{N}{2}\right) \left(\int_0^{\frac{N}{2}} m \; dn - \int_{\frac{N}{2}}^N m \; dn \right) > 0$$

and

$$(4.38) \qquad G'(0) = [t(0) - t(N)] \; m(0) - t'(N) \int_0^N m \; dn < 0 \quad .$$

The first-order minimum conditions are

$$(4.39) \qquad \begin{aligned} & t'(x) \int_0^x m(n) \; dn + t(x) \; m(x) \\ & \qquad - t'(N-x) \int_x^N m(n) \; dn - t(N-x) \; m(x) = 0 \quad . \end{aligned}$$

But for $x = \frac{N}{2}$,

(4.40) $$t'(\frac{N}{2}) \int_0^{\frac{N}{2}} m(n) \ dn > t'(\frac{N}{2}) \int_{\frac{N}{2}}^{N} m(n) \ dn \quad .$$

As this shows, the derivative of the minimand at $x = \frac{N}{2}$ is positive. We conclude that the minimum is obtained for a flow $x < \frac{N}{2}$ on the toll road.

If different weights are attached to the economic benefits for various road user classes, say $w(n)$ to the value of money benefits of the nth class and w_0 to the availability of public funds, the minimand is

(4.41)
$$\int_0^x [t_1(x) \ m(n) + p(x)] \ w(n) \ dn$$
$$+ \int_x^N t_2(N-x) \ m(n) \ w(n) \ dn - w_0 \ p(x) \ x \quad ,$$

which after substitution for $p(x)$ becomes

(4.42)
$$t_1(x) \int_0^x m(n) \ w(n) \ dn + t_2 \ (N-x) \int_0^N m(n) \ w(n) \ dn$$
$$+ m(x) \left[t_1(x) - t_2 \ (N-x) \ (w_0 - \int_0^x w(n) \ dn) \right] \quad .$$

Except for rather special weight functions w our conclusion remains valid.

Chapter 5

SOME UNSOLVED PROBLEMS

The preceding models had to employ many simplifications. Some of the more obvious shortcomings will be pointed out in this chapter on unsolved problems.

5.1. *Theoretical Capacity Functions*

Although one has come to rely more on empirical capacity measurement, the study of theoretical capacity functions can still be useful. For the design, the interpretation, and the use of measurements always presuppose some theoretical model, however simple.

The regression line of average speed on flow — that is, the empirical capacity function — cannot be held to give a universal relationship valid for all roads with the same roadway conditions, because the influence of the driver population is disregarded.

The effect of the driver population and in particular the free-speed distribution on capacity raises many problems for both theory and measurement. The outstanding mathematical problem is perhaps that of deriving the mean delays on a road to vehicles of a given free speed from the free-speed distribution, from the arrival sequences of cars at entrances to the road, and from other features (such as the timing of traffic lights) which may have a bearing on it. Such a model, if it were not to run into unmanageable complications, would have to use some average concepts again, although it should allow for a distinction between classes of road users. The possibility and fruitfulness of such an analysis is intimately tied up with the question of whether an equilibrium in the particular sense of queuing theory can be realized on a road or even in a network. Equilibrium of this kind on a road implies that the flow remains constant and that the free-speed distribution is preserved. The question arises whether these two traffic characteristics together will always maintain the same traffic conditions, i.e. the same mean delays to vehicles of given free speeds.

Delays to traffic may be understood in terms of queuing as shown in Section 1.2. Now a queue of vehicles behind a slower vehicle may show two kinds of behavior. After an initial phase of building up, it may either fluctuate around a fixed mean value or continue to grow indefinitely, according as the mean time between passing opportunities for successive cars in a queue is or is not less than the mean time between arrivals at the queue. It is the first case that is labeled the stationary case in queue theory. However, on a road of finite length the second process may take place to some extent, even without ultimately causing a tie-up at the entrance of the road. The effect would merely be to slow down traffic more and more as it proceeds along the road. As this is compensated by a higher density of traffic, the same flow can be maintained throughout. In this case a stationary flow does not imply a constant free-speed distribution along the length of the road; the queues that grow as they move on absorb an increasing share of high-speed traffic. Therefore, the number of road users with high free speeds represents a larger and larger fraction of the total number of road users per mile as one moves down the road.

Considering both types of queuing process at the same time, a more interesting question is the behavior of queue lengths over time. Is there any tendency for queue lengths in a particular road section to approach a fixed distribution after a sufficient lapse of time? An affirmative answer would imply that the travel times for each speed class also would approach a definite probability distribution. Such a situation could represent a maximum of predictability. For it would mean that the past history of delays is irrelevant for the mean delay which prevails after a sufficiently long period, when the system has settled down to equilibrium.

The attainment of such an equilibrium does not exclude altogether the occurrence of fluctuations around the equilibrium points. These persist in all queuing processes. All that equilibrium means is that there is some constant time average of delays, and that this mean value is all one can predict about traffic conditions in the future.

For instance, there may under some conditions arise prolonged deviations in the average queue lengths of the two lanes of a two-lane road even when a steady and balanced total flow prevails. The reason for this is as follows. To the extent that queues are built up from a given flow, passing opportunities for traffic in the opposite direction increase. This in turn leads to a more dispersed distribution of cars over that lane, thus reducing again the passing opportunities for traffic in the first lane. In this way traffic in the second lane can gain the advantage of the bunched-up condition in the first lane and maintain or even aggravate this condition. Thus an even distribution of queuing between the two directions may be an unstable situation tending to break away in one direction or the other. After a given time has elapsed from a given initial state, the average queue length may therefore have a bimodal distribution. Once the situation has shifted to the neighborhood of one mode, the probability of it shifting to the other may in some cases be large enough to produce frequent shifting back and forth, or in other cases so small as to lock the situation almost completely at one mode or the other.

The *Highway Capacity Manual* refers to a related but slightly different cause of fluctuations in the following illuminating passage: "At this traffic volume [1,000 passenger cars per hour] spaces occur ahead of the slow-moving vehicles which cannot be filled by other vehicles performing passing maneuvers. In effect, traffic in both directions tends to form in queues which continue to increase in length until the spaces between the queues become sufficiently long to permit the performance of passing maneuvers. As soon as a few passing maneuvers are performed the spaces between the queues become partially occupied and are no longer of sufficient length for the performance of passing maneuvers, and the queues immediately start forming again. This accordion effect, with all but a very limited number of vehicles traveling at the same speed as the vehicle immediately ahead, occurs at the same total traffic volume regardless of the distribution by directions" (Normann and Walker, 1949, p. 37).

While it is clear that on a road of finite length the possible fluctuations are definitely limited in magnitude, they may be significant enough to constitute a qualification to an analysis that ignores them. In some cases these fluctuations may warrant a study of the desirability and means of controlling them.

Any treatment in terms of probability of the delays caused by passing runs up against the problem of repeated queues discussed in Section 1.6. Since this problem requires (except for the trivial case of service times with exponential distributions) some new theoretical ideas, it may provide a challenge to statisticians and mathematicians.

5.2. Alternative Notions of Capacity for Economic Analysis

The average-cost capacity function as used in Chapters 3 and 4 gives only an approximate expression of the impact of traffic conditions on transportation cost. Under any given conditions a vehicle causes a different amount of delay and affects various classes of road users differently depending on its free speed and the direction in which it uses the road. A more detailed model would specify a set of capacity functions, one for each class of users of the given road, which gives the average cost to this class as a function of the traffic that falls into every single class. We notice that in this way some account would be taken of the effect of the driver population on capacity.

Disaggregation of the capacity concept in this way would also permit a refinement of the analysis of traffic distribution over alternative routes — the problem of "shortest routes." Two routes that appear to be of equal transportation cost in terms of averages may in fact have different attractions to high- and low-speed traffic. If one route once has a certain advantage over an alternative for high-speed traffic, this will in itself lead to a relative concentration of high-speed traffic on this route and in this way further encourage the differentiation of traffic by speeds. Segregation of high- from low-speed traffic seems to have some advantages for both, and an efficiency analysis should determine whether this segregation goes far enough under conditions of ordinary spontaneous equilibrium.

Whether the demand function should also be disaggregated by free-speed classes is less obvious, for it may turn out that there is no essential difference in the flexibility of the demand of high-speed or low-speed road users. Some other differences in user characteristics, such as risk preferences, are perhaps more relevant here.

5.3*. Commodity Transportation Models

The principal difference between passenger transportation as discussed in this study and commodity transportation lies in the substitutability of commodity shipments from different origins to a given destination. This makes the demand for trips between two given points a function not only of the cost of this particular trip but also of all the costs of other trips that might compete with the one considered. These other trips would include those from the given supply point to other markets, and those from other supply points to the given market. A convenient framework for dealing with this type of demand for transportation is provided by the introduction at each point of a function relating price and net or excess supply of the commodity in question. For any given price the excess supply of a commodity at a certain location is the amount locally supplied at that price minus the amount locally demanded at that price. Excess supply, which of course can be negative, may therefore be regarded as a function of the local price of the commodity.

For a proper explanation of the demand for commodity transportation it is fundamental that these local prices should not themselves be treated as predetermined data but should be regarded as interdependent and are so balanced against each other that all markets of a commodity taken together are in equilibrium. This means that no profits should be possible through arbitraging commodity movements between any pair of locations. Prices of the same commodity in different locations cannot differ by more than the transportation cost. The price differences are exactly equal to transportation cost for all pairs of markets between which shipments of the commodity take place.

The mathematical formulation of equilibrium in a model of commodity transportation is now obvious. Let a subscript m in lieu of the previous k denote a commodity.

Let $x_{ij,m}$ be the flow of commodity m from point i to point j on road ij;

$p_{i,m}$ the price of m at point i; and

$q_{i,m}(p_{i,m})$ the excess supply of m at point i.

Then $q_{i,m}$ is a non-decreasing function,

$$(5.1) \qquad \frac{dq_{i,m}}{dp_{i,m}} \geq 0 \qquad \text{wherever it is differentiable.}$$

We assume for the moment that all traffic flows are of commodities:

$$(5.2) \qquad x_{ij} = \sum_{m} (x_{ij,m} + x_{ji,m}) \; .$$

Also we shall again use the notation

$$(5.3) \qquad \sum_{j} (x_{ij,m} - x_{ji,m}) = x_{i,m} \; .$$

The equilibrium conditions, in addition to the identities (5.2) and (5.3), are

(5.4)
$$p_{j,m} - p_{i,m} \begin{Bmatrix} = \\ \leqq \end{Bmatrix} h_{ij}(x_{ij}), \quad \text{if} \quad x_{ij,m} \begin{Bmatrix} > \\ = \end{Bmatrix} 0 \; ;$$

and

(5.5)
$$x_{i,m} = q_{i,m}(p_{i,m}) \; .$$

Notice that the prices increase along routes of transportation by the amount of transportation cost, while trip costs decrease by the same amount.

Passenger transportation may in fact be included as a special case of commodity transportation. This is the case of a "commodity" whose subscript is really a substitute for two indices, the origin and the destination, and for which the excess supply and demand are localized, respectively, in these two points. Here the prices are determined only up to an additive constant and may be set equal to zero at the destination, thus making trip cost appear to be simply a negative commodity price.

The system (5.2) - (5.5) may be regarded as a more general formulation of the equilibrium conditions (3.2), (3.4), and (3.10). It turns out that our analysis of equilibrium in terms of an associated maximand carries over to this more general model. It follows that the inequality (3.33) on changes in the data applies and that the assertion about the adjustments of flows to changes in capacity remains valid.

We also obtain the efficiency conditions in a form corresponding to (4.11):

$$p_{j,m} - p_{i,m} \begin{Bmatrix} = \\ \leq \end{Bmatrix} h_{ij}(x_{ij}) + h'_{ij}(x_{ij}) \, x_{ij}$$

$$\text{if} \quad x_{ij,m} \begin{Bmatrix} > \\ = \end{Bmatrix} 0 \; ;$$

(5.6)   and

$$x_{i,m} = q_{i,k}(p_{i,k}) \; .$$

Nothing is changed in the role of efficiency tolls, the relation between equilibrium and efficient flows, and the relationship between tolls and the value of a road. In short, our analysis can be repeated with appropriate changes and some increase in analytical complexity for a model of commodity transportation.

The unsolved problems concern the application of this model to particular cases. A one-commodity network would be of special interest. In particular, the problem of the generation and distribution of electric energy in a network comes to mind. The task of verifying the

assumptions or modifying the model might be rewarding, but would call
for considerable technical knowledge of electrical engineering.

5.4. Dynamic Equilibrium Models

The notion of a static equilibrium of flow in a network may be
thought somewhat limited because of the noted periodicity of traffic during the day, week, year, and perhaps the business cycle. While the
equilibrium mechanism is operative during the relatively short periods
of a constant load, one would like to see a more comprehensive model
which contributes to our understanding of the time pattern itself. For
instance, there are certain forces which tend to smooth the fluctuations.
Since the off-peak hours offer better traffic conditions, some of the demand which is flexible with regard to time is diverted to these periods.
On the other hand, the availability of parking space depends on the accumulation and dispersal of stocks of cars at various locations. This
puts a premium on early arrival during rush hour periods and might
either aggravate, merely advance, or even spread the peaks of traffic.
The generation and the economics of traffic peaks are subjects for
further inquiry.

While it is not difficult, by attaching time subscripts to the flow
variables, to write down formally the equilibrium conditions of Chapter
4 for a dynamic model, this merely makes the analysis more complicated without explaining much that is new. An understanding of the dynamic aspects of traffic really depends on an understanding of demand
substitution over time. To what extent are traffic conditions and parking opportunities the effective considerations? Is differential pricing of
parking in response to the daily fluctuations of traffic an equilibrating
factor? Are there any economic forces at work or could any such
forces be made operative which would induce a staggering of working
hours while preserving the essential economies of the simultaneous
availability of personnel in business activities depending on mutual con-
tacts? This last problem has also arisen with respect to the proper
pricing of transportation services of the New York subway system
(Vickrey, 1952).

5.5. Problems of the Long Run

In assuming the capacities of roads as given, this study has taken
the short-run point of view. Interesting and important problems of a
long-run character are met if one recognizes that demand functions will
shift and that road capacity will be adjusted to demand to some extent.
One of the objectives of a short-run analysis is precisely to supply some
of the prerequisites for the study of long-run problems. Still the utilization of capacity by traffic is in large part a short-run phenomenon, for
the economic advantages of road construction can be appraised only in
the light of the uses to which this capacity is put at various times of the
day, week, and year, and of the rates of growth of these uses.

Some of the difficulties of a long-run analysis lie in the long-run responses of demand through locational decisions. The problem here is to determine and explain how the location of economic activities is influenced by traffic conditions. Location theory tells us in general terms how transportation costs affect the locational pattern. But further insights could be gained from an analysis of the differential impact of time losses through congestion on various industries. Most important perhaps is the question of how the location of people (their residential distribution) depends on traffic conditions. Without a clearer insight into the factors determining residential choices, the prediction of long-run traffic trends on urban expressways, for instance, must be hazardous.

In the long run the network layout does not remain fixed, and this calls for consideration of construction and maintenance costs as functions of capacity created and maintained. It would be important to derive capacity-cost schedules of broad applicability from the technological information available. This would help answer questions as to how the (publicly incurred) cost of construction and maintenance can best be balanced against the (privately sustained) costs of congestion.

Here we encounter what is perhaps the most fundamental problem in traffic economics: determining the proper extent and layout of a road network. The difficulty of this problem springs from the fact that choices between a great number of all-or-nothing alternatives are involved. Adding a particular road to a network may not be remotely worth while unless it is built to at least some reasonably good standard, which would involve a considerable fixed cost. But the flows needed to justify this investment depend on what other roads may also have been added to the network. Thus to get the most out of an integrated program of road construction one would have to compare a huge number of possible combinations of road capacities that might be added. The principles of economics have not been developed far enough to permit shortcutting such a vast analytical problem. In the economics of indivisible resources we touch one of the problem areas in economic theory where results of a general character are urgently needed but seem very hard to come by.

Still other problems arise in situations where the predominant part of transportation cost is delay at intersections. To give an indication of this kind of problem, let us consider an example of two alternative roads intersecting with two other alternative roads. The efficiency problem reduces to the question of which is more efficient, to cross the entire cross traffic at once, or to cross one-half of it at each of two consecutive intersections? Suppose that the cross traffic has priority in each case. Since delays increase more than proportionally with cross flows, crossing one-half of the traffic on two occasions involves less total waiting. In the case that the one road to be crossed has twice the width of each of the two alternative roads, the result is plausible on physical grounds, for crossing one-half of the traffic twice amounts to finding a safety island in the middle of the road. The economics and technology of the synchronization of traffic lights is still another problem area in its own right, which we can only just mention here.

5.6. Tolls and Finance

Finally, the problem of benefit evaluation is important for the assessment of the financial burden to be borne by various classes of road users. This is again illustrated by the case of toll roads. The necessity of financing the construction and maintenance of a toll road largely or entirely from toll revenue imposes a lower bound on the toll charges, which we have not taken into account here.

From the point of view of the best over-all expansion and utilization of a network the constraint that each toll road should pay for itself must be dropped. Instead, the problem becomes one of finding the most "equitable" allocation of road costs to sources of tax revenue. To what extent should finance be sought in the form of taxes on vehicle ownership at particular locations, on gasoline consumption (and hence total mileage, approximately), and on the use of particular roads (tolls)? Although congestion is incident on particular roads at particular times, of course, charges which tend to alleviate traffic need not always be levied in the form of tolls. For instance, a general tax on gasoline consumption renders traffic in general more expensive and thus tends to reduce the total amount of traffic. On the other hand it puts a premium on the use of the geographically shortest routes and therefore induces congestion there. The net effect may therefore be an increase in congestion losses.

It may also be possible to relieve congestion by taxes on business activities, or on car ownership at residences, of which the locations are such as to be mainly responsible for the congestion. However, a charge in this form will discourage traffic along any roads from these locations, congested or not, so that the welfare of road-user classes who are not responsible for congestion on the routes in question is affected. Only a road toll proper is specific enough to be free from this objection. On the other hand, the mere collection of a road toll may itself add to congestion. It is therefore an interesting problem to what extent efficiency can be approximated by other forms of taxation.

Even a specific toll of one of the types currently in use is subject to the drawback that it is usually thought necessary to keep the toll charge constant for considerable periods of time. The best that can then be done is to set the rate at some average level, even though congestion may fluctuate widely. In many cases it would be markedly more efficient to reduce the toll during certain periods of lower traffic or even to suspend it entirely. (This problem has an obvious analogue in electricity tariffs.) In addition there are differences between various classes of road users in their contribution to delays and to the deterioration of the road. Thus slow or heavy vehicles tend to contribute more heavily. To some extent this may be allowed for by differentiating between tolls on trucks and passenger cars, for example, and by requiring vehicles to be at least capable of maintaining a certain minimum speed, especially in climbing long grades.

However, the difficulties of toll collection as well as a general desire for "freedom of the roads" limit the amount of revenue that can be collected in the form of tolls. Indeed, toll facilities are often such a bottleneck to the flow of traffic at peak periods that in some cases efficiency would be best served by suspending the collection of tolls at such peak periods, thus eliminating excessive queues at toll booths. Other taxes are likely to be needed to sustain the roads. While a case can be made for some use of general funds for this purpose, since an efficient road system contributes to the general welfare, the intensity of communication, and the speed of emergency help, etc., it would seem to be a point of justice that the bulk of the money should come from the road users in a form connected with road use. This would leave a considerable share to both general vehicle and gasoline taxes. The optimal apportionment — optimal, that is, with respect to the combined standards of equity and efficiency — poses an interesting problem which will be the subject of discussion for a long time to come.

PART II

A STUDY OF

RAILROAD TRANSPORTATION

Chapter 6

THE TIME ELEMENT IN RAILROAD TRANSPORTATION

In our study of highway transportation we emphasized the importance of including time as a dimension of the output of a transportation system. In assessing the capacity of a system of highways, it did not suffice to talk simply about the traffic flows that did, or could conceivably, take place. It was also necessary to have some information about the speeds at which these flows did, or could, take place. We found that these time considerations were all the more important because there existed interactions between flows and speeds. Greater flows could usually occur only with reductions in speed and, conversely, speed increases had to be paid for in lesser flows unless the road system was improved.

The factor of time is no less important a consideration in a study of railway transportation. As far as passenger traffic goes, the parallel with road traffic is clear. Despite the current advertising slogan, "Getting there is half the fun!" it is probably safe to say that travelers on the whole prefer fast transportation to slow, other things being equal. Thus from this point of view a given distribution of passenger traffic over a railway system represents a more valuable product when the average time of travel is less.

For freight traffic the parallel with passenger traffic on roads is not quite so clear. How important is the time consumed in carrying out a freight shipment? In the chapters that follow we shall quite often have occasion to refer to the delays a freight shipment encounters at various stages in its journey. We shall attempt to determine some of the factors influencing these delays, and also show how delays and other kinds of costs are related. In this chapter we shall try to justify our concern with time costs in freight transportation. First, we shall discuss the transit time of a shipment from the point of view of the consumer of railway services. The later discussion will be concerned with the relation between transit time and the stock of freight cars. While the stock of cars has, through this relationship, an important influence on the capacity of a railway system, we shall not, except in this chapter, deal with it explicitly but rather focus our attention on factors affecting transit time itself. In addition, it is hoped that in the process of this brief discussion the reader will get some idea of the magnitudes of the various kinds of delays involved.

6.1. *Transit Time and Inventory Costs*

One obvious advantage of faster freight transportation is the resulting reduction of in-transit inventories that it makes possible. That this phenomenon is a familiar one is evidenced in the popular use of a transportation term in discussion of inventories of another sort. "Filling the pipelines" has come to mean the building up of inventories of many kinds to some required level. The implication is that the inventories made necessary by the time lag involved in transportation are more easily explained in an intuitive way than other kinds of inventories.

The pipeline analogy is worth carrying another step to make clear the relation between speed and inventory requirements. A pipeline half as big in cross-section area as another could carry the same flow of, say, gasoline only if its pumps were capable of sending the liquid through the pipe at twice the speed. The gasoline inventory required to fill the smaller pipeline is just half that required to fill the larger, and this reduction of inventory is permitted by the higher speed of transport. Approximately the same phenomenon takes place in any other form of transportation.

So far we have only discussed the effect of speed on the levels of inventories of goods in transit. There is still another effect of speed on inventory requirements in general. First we must ask why inventories, aside from the in-transit type just described, are desired at all. One reason is that commodity price fluctuations cause buyers to stock up beyond their immediate needs when they believe the price to be a favorable one. Another reason is that commodity traffic flows in practice seldom occur smoothly, but rather in lumps. It is more practicable to send a carload of wheat once a day, say, than to send a ton of wheat every hour. This lumpiness occurs even in the one case where one might not expect it, that of pipeline transportation, where one pipe often serves for the transmission of several different liquids. Since these cannot be pumped through simultaneously and still preserve their identity, the pipe is given over to each liquid alone for a certain period of time.

Still another reason for inventories, and perhaps one of the most important from our point of view, lies in the uncertainty involved in predicting just how much of a commodity will be needed in a particular place at some future date. This uncertainty on the part of a consumer of a commodity (or a producer who uses this commodity as an input), together with the time involved in transportation oblige this consumer or his merchant to keep on hand stocks sufficient to cover errors in predicting his needs.[1] If transportation took no time at all, no prediction would be necessary; he could order more of the commodity as the need arose. The slower the transportation is, however, the greater the range of time that the prediction must cover; consequently, the greater the errors are likely to be and the greater the inventories that are required to ensure against these errors.

It is clear, therefore, that the time involved in transportation affects the levels both of inventories of goods in transit and of other inventories. To the extent that inventory holding is costly, the people

---

1. Where costs of storage are high relative to costs of short supply, this rule must be modified.

concerned, sometimes shippers, sometimes consignees, are better off with faster and more dependable freight transportation.

For a few special commodities the advantages of fast transportation are especially clear. Livestock requires special handling (watering, etc.) every few hours by federal law. This treatment is expensive and especially so if performed at locations without the proper facilities. The faster this livestock movement can be made, the less of this costly unloading and reloading procedure will there be.

Perishable commodities, such as fresh fruit and vegetables, must be shipped in refrigerator cars. These perishable shipments are commonly made over long distances, and call for re-icing along the way. Fast shipment reduces the number of such treatments that are necessary, and, as in the livestock case, reduces the investment in special facilities required to provide this service.

The data we might examine to see how far the foregoing considerations go in explaining the relative transit times for various commodities are very sparse indeed. For 1933, however, we do have the results of one very small sample of traffic. In the *Freight Traffic Report* of the Federal Coordinator of Transportation an extensive tabulation of information on all traffic terminating in the U.S. on December 13, 1933, is given. Figure 6.1 is derived from this report (Federal Coordinator of Transportation, 1933, Appendix I, pp. 120-173). On the vertical axis is measured the average transit time. This includes all the time from the moment a car is given to a shipper for loading until it is returned empty from the consignee. On the horizontal axis is measured the average length of haul. Points are plotted for several of the commodity groups

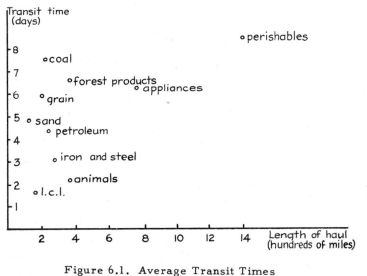

Figure 6.1. Average Transit Times
for Several Commodities

in the *Report*. While we see from the figure that perishables take the longest time for shipment and l.c.l. ("less-than-carload lots") the shortest time, we also see that their relative hauls bear the same relationship. If for each commodity we divide haul by time we get an estimate of the miles traveled per loaded-car day on the average. Since "time" here includes loading and unloading time, these figures should not be though of as measuring the distances traveled per day when actually moving in trains.

Live Animals	188
Perishables	159
Appliances	119
L.c.l.	113
Iron and Steel	104
Petroleum	61
Forest Products	57
Bulk Grain	38
Coal and Coke	33
Sand and Gravel	27

This ranking does seem to give some support to the hypothesis that the effect of speed on inventories in turn influences the speed of railway services provided. The more valuable a commodity is (per ton) the higher the cost of keeping idle stocks of it; in the list we find, as we should expect, the higher priced commodities near the top. There are of course many qualifications to such a conclusion. The relative values of carloads of different commodities are quite different from their relative prices per ton, because cars are loaded heavily with some commodities and lightly with others. Unfortunately for our argument the last two on the list, coal and coke, and sand and gravel, are among the heavy loaders. Nevertheless, it is difficult to believe that this difference would alter our conclusion. The ranking by "miles per day" rather than simply "days," although obvious enough, requires some explanation in order to show more clearly the shortcomings of such a procedure. In a railroad system ideally organized from the economic point of view we should expect the transit time of a particular service to be cut down whenever the consequent reduction of inventory costs exceeds the costs of providing this faster service. One of the reasons that on the average a carload of appliances requires almost two more days (see Figure 6.1) in shipment than a carload of sand and gravel, even though we believe the first carload to represent a greater investment than the second, is that it costs *very* much more to provide four-day service for appliances than it does to provide four-day service for sand and gravel. The difference in lengths of haul is of course the obvious reason for these cost discrepancies, and it is the one we have taken account of in our ranking of the various commodities by "miles per day." However, there are other and perhaps just as important reasons for these differences in the costs of providing fast service for particular goods. Our ranking, accordingly, must be viewed with some suspicion for this reason. We shall say no more at this point about these other influences on cost, since much of the rest of this study is devoted to them. Our purpose here has only been to demonstrate the fact that speed of shipment is a valuable characteristic of freight transportation.

6.2. Transit Time and the Stock of Freight Cars

So far we have shown that just as in passenger travel on highways the time used up in rail transportation of freight must be considered part of the cost of a railway system because time is a costly commodity to the consumers of railway services. It remains to be shown that speed (understood in the general sense of being the inverse of transit time) is costly to produce. There are obvious costs associated with speed increases if we think of these increases as requiring more or better equipment and physical facilities. Of more interest to us at present, however, are the increases of speed brought about as a matter of choice by different use of a given physical plant. In the case of highways both these types of speed increase also exist. Roads can be straightened and overpasses built to replace intersections, or, on the other hand, traffic flows at certain points can be reduced, and traffic regulations and signals can be changed. Both procedures can lead to speed increases, the one by a change of the physical facilities and the other by a change in operating procedures alone.

Is this second method of reducing the time of freight shipments costly? Without a careful investigation, it is by no means clear that it is. In our highway investigations we found that the penalty paid for an increase of speed on a given road was a reduction of flow on that road and perhaps a decrease of speed on the competing road to which this excluded flow was forced to turn. The road capacity curves discussed were the relationships which gave us quantitative estimates of these effects. Somewhat similar relationships between traffic flow and speed of service will be discussed in the chapters to come.

There is, however, an important type of relationship between speed and traffic flow in railroad transportation which was relatively uninteresting in the case of passenger traffic on highways. It arises from the fact that the longer the average shipment takes to complete, the greater is the supply of freight cars necessary to carry out a given program of transportation. Putting this another way we can say that if the stock of freight cars is fixed, the traffic flows that can take place are limited in size by the transit times of shipments. Considerations such as these help to explain why it is the case, as we shall see below, that a freight car is idle so much of the time, and also why the stock of freight cars is what it is. This relation between the stock of cars, the transit times of shipments, and the number of carloadings in a year is sometimes summed up in a railroad rule of thumb: "To find the number of cars necessary to protect loading, multiply weekly carloadings by two" (Parmelee, 1940, p. 635). The number two in this case represents an opinion that the average time of transit, including the time spent in empty movement, is two weeks.

The most interesting aspect of this relationship presents itself when peak traffic periods are examined. Rail carloadings are by no means even over the year, a high peak usually occurring between May and October, with very sharp dips taking place on the Fourth of July and Labor Day. To meet these midyear peaks without severe car shortages a much greater number of freight cars is needed than would be if the same level of annual carloadings were spread out evenly over the year. This means that when the relationship connecting the freight car stock with carloadings and transit times is applied to a period of a year it appears to represent a constraint which is unimportant because it never seems to pinch. In this context an increase of speed would seem to provide no saving in the number of freight cars necessary. As we shall see below, an examination of peak periods dispels this illusion.

Returning to the case of road transportation for a moment, it is instructive to ask how the same considerations apply there. To start with let us suppose that we know how many automobile trips are to take place in a certain year, and we also know the average distance of each trip and the average time necessary to complete it. If these trips are spread out evenly over the year a very simple calculation will tell us how many serviceable vehicles are necessary to accomplish the job. If this minimum number of vehicles were the number actually in use, it would mean that every serviceable vehicle was being used at every moment. The nationwide system of car pools represented by this description has little correspondence to the real situation in transportation by automobile, for we know that most automobiles stand idle a great part of the time. The fact that the actual stock of vehicles is so much greater than the minimum number derived above can in part be explained by the great variations in the number of trips in process at different times. While it has been suggested that a careful examination of peak traffic periods for railroads is worth while, it is not as likely to be so in the case of auto transportation for several reasons. First, since the average length of trip by automobile is short, the periods we must examine to find a peak period are also short. The information requirements are therefore great. Second, the peak periods in different locations will surely occur at different times. While this is also true of rail traffic the trouble can be at least partly eliminated there by taking explicit account of the time spent in empty travel. In the absence of this shortcut it would be necessary to do a separate analysis of each location. Third, we already know to a large degree what the result of such an analysis would be in the case of passenger automobiles. The cost of automobiles appears to be such that people are quite willing to pay to rid themselves of the inconveniences of part ownership in a car pool. Where this institution does exist (taxicabs are one example) it is always surrounded by special conditions such as the use of a chauffeur, the identity of trips, or the common residence of members of the pool (family cars). In any case it is clear that many more considerations enter than in the case of rail transportation.

Table I

Average Number of Days Spent by a Car between Delivery for Loading and Release from Unloading — Cars Terminated December 13, 1933*

	All Commodities	LCL	Coal & Coke	Perishables	Live Animals	Sand, Stone, & Gravel	Appliances	Petroleum & Products	Forest Products	Iron & Steel	Bulk Grain & Beets	All Carload Commodities
Loading-unloading	2.21	.36	3.96	3.08	.54	2.52	2.49	2.09	2.99	1.53	2.33	2.84
Interchange	.29	.05	.42	.71	.16	.23	.51	.34	.33	.20	.20	.37
Intermediate handling	.61	.17	1.02	1.29	.36	.51	.80	.53	.86	.36	.75	.75
Carrier termini	1.02	.73	1.25	.83	.26	.90	.87	.80	1.39	.56	2.01	1.10
Carrier road	.83	.45	.81	2.88	.84	.49	1.57	.71	1.04	.40	.65	.96
Total	4.95	1.77	7.47	8.79	2.16	4.64	6.25	4.47	6.60	3.05	5.94	6.02
No. of cars in sample	65769	16664	14804	2199	2696	1592	840	5180	3448	2432	3085	49105
Average haul	331	201	249	1400	405	127	746	272	376	316	224	376
Miles per loaded car day	74	113	33	159	188	27	119	61	57	104	38	63

* Source: Federal Coordinator of Transportation, *Freight Traffic Report, Appendix I*, pp. 120–173.

Table II

Distribution of Active Car Time — Cars Terminated December 13, 1933*

	All Commodities	LCL	Coal & Coke	Perishables	Live Animals	Sand, Stone, & Gravel	Appliances	Petroleum Products	Forest Products	Iron & Steel	Bulk Grain & Beets	All Carload Commodities
Loading-unloading	44.8%	20.5%	53.1%	35.1%	25.2%	54.2%	39.9%	46.8%	45.3%	50.2%	39.3%	47.3%
Interchange	5.8	2.8	5.6	8.1	7.4	5.0	8.2	7.6	5.0	6.5	3.3	6.1
Intermediate handling	12.3	9.7	13.7	14.7	16.7	11.0	12.8	11.8	13.0	11.8	12.6	12.5
Carrier termini	20.5	41.9	16.7	9.5	11.8	19.4	14.0	18.0	21.1	18.4	33.8	18.3
Carrier road	16.8	25.2	10.9	32.7	38.9	10.4	25.1	15.8	15.7	13.2	11.0	15.9
Total	100.0%	100.0%	100.0%	100.0%	100.0%	100.0%	100.0%	100.0%	100.0%	100.0%	100.0%	100.0%

* Source: Federal Coordinator of Transportation, *Freight Traffic Report, Appendix I,* pp. 120-173.

Before we enter into a more detailed examination of the influence of speed on the freight car supply required, it will be useful to discuss first the available information on the time per shipment actually used at various stages of the transportation operation.

For this purpose we refer again to the 1933 *Freight Traffic Report* of the Federal Coordinator of Transportation. This material covers the 65,769 cars that terminated on December 13, 1933. From it can be derived, for several commodity groups and for the group as a whole, the average times spent by a car at various stages in its journey from shipper to consignee. Table I presents these averages and Table II translates them into percentages of total time of shipment for each commodity group. The labels along the left edges of both tables require some explanation. *Loading-unloading* time represents the time a car spends in the hands of its shipper plus the time in the hands of its consignee. *Carrier termini* time measures the delay a car suffers at both ends of its journey while still in the hands of the carrier. *Carrier road* time tells us how long a car is in a train during its trip. This time is not necessarily consecutive, for the car may leave one train, spend some time in a classification yard, and then join another train for more road time. It should also be pointed out that road time is not quite the same as time spent rolling. Trains are subject to many kinds of delays; these also count as road time for the cars of a delayed train. *Intermediate handling* and *interchange* times cover the period a car spends waiting in classification yards along the way. Interchange time represents that part of this wait which occurs at points where the car is transferred from one railroad to another, that is, "interchanged." Total time therefore represents the time from the moment an empty car is supplied to the shipper until the time the car is returned empty by the consignee (perhaps, of course, to a different railroad).

One of the striking things about the entries in these two tables is the relatively small amount of time a car spends in trains. Thus carrier road time amounts to only about a sixth of the total time of shipment, or about a third of the shipment time less the loading-unloading period. Also, if these carrier road times for the different commodities are plotted against lengths of haul, we notice that there is a fairly good straight-line relationship between the two (Figure 6.2).

Of the 4.95 days average transit time, 1.92 days or 38.6 per cent are used up at the three stages, interchange, intermediate handling, and carrier termini. This is 70 per cent of the total shipment time less loading-unloading time. We throw these three types of delay together for reasons that will be better understood in later chapters; it is the time used at these three stages with which we shall be most concerned. In Figure 6.2 we saw that road time could be fairly well explained in terms of the length of haul of a shipment. In Figure 6.3, where the vertical axis now measures the sum of interchange, intermediate handling, and carrier termini times, we find that no such simple explanation of the variation suffices in this case. There seems to be little if any relationship between the two variables plotted.

Except in this chapter we shall not say any more about loading-unloading time despite its very substantial magnitude. Part of the reason for the size of this component of transit time undoubtedly lies in the fact

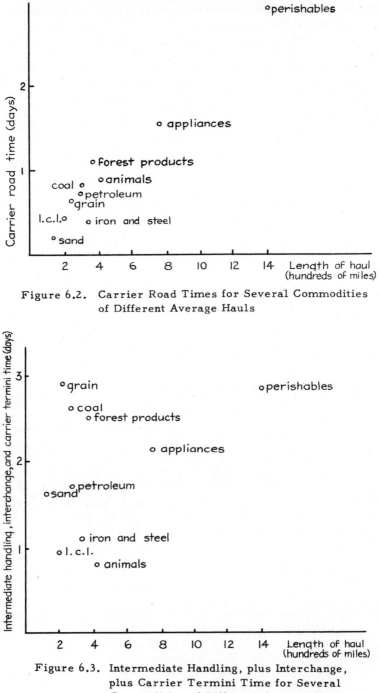

Figure 6.2.   Carrier Road Times for Several Commodities
of Different Average Hauls

Figure 6.3.   Intermediate Handling, plus Interchange,
plus Carrier Termini Time for Several
Commodities of Different Average Hauls

that at current rates of demurrage consignees find it cheaper to use freight cars instead of warehouses for storage purposes.

These time estimates from a single day in 1933 seem to be about the only publicly available source of such information. Individual railroads, it is true, have conducted investigations of the transit times of various shipments over their own lines, but we do not know how extensive these have been, nor quite how the results compare with those of the *Freight Traffic Report*. Since we have so few other data with which to compare these figures, it is difficult to estimate the changes that have taken place in them since 1933. The regular statistics of the ICC bear on only one of these components of transit time — carrier road time. By making some rather daring assumptions we shall attempt to use these latter statistics, together with the results of the *Freight Traffic Report*, to estimate the transit times for years other than 1933. We shall then try to extend this attempt to cover the time consumed in the average empty trip. Finally a comparison of the sum of these two times will be made with the actual freight car time available in each of several years, in order to see to what degree the stock of freight cars is utilized.[2]

If for each year we knew the average length of haul of freight cars and their average speed when in trains, the average time in trains during a trip could be found by dividing haul by speed. The result could be compared with the estimate of carrier time derived from the 1933 data. While we are not quite so fortunate as this, some very closely related data are regularly reported by the ICC and the Association of American Railroads. Using these we have the ratios $\dfrac{\text{car-miles}}{\text{carloadings}}$ and $\dfrac{\text{train-miles}}{\text{train-hours}}$ as estimates,[3] respectively, of the average length of haul of a car and the average speed of a train. If now we assume that the average speed of a train is the same as the average speed of a car, we have the relation

$$(6.1) \quad \frac{\text{car-miles x train-hours}}{\text{carloadings x train-miles}} = \frac{\text{average carrier road time}}{\text{of a car.}}$$

For the year 1933 this estimate of carrier road time is 23.4 hours as compared with the estimate of (.83 x 24 =) 19.8 hours in the *Freight Traffic Report* (Table I). These new estimates of carrier road time will err on the low side if, on the average, longer trains are slower than shorter trains, and on the high side if longer trains are faster than shorter trains.

To obtain estimates of transit times for the different years we have assumed that carrier road time comprises a constant proportion of transit time from year to year, so that for 1940 for instance

$$(6.2) \quad \frac{\text{transit time}}{\text{for 1940}} = \frac{\text{transit time}}{\text{for 1933}} \times \frac{\text{carrier road time for 1940}}{\text{carrier road time for 1933}} ,$$

---

2. The discussion that follows has been greatly stimulated by a reading of Chapter 4 of Hultgren (1948).

3. For *car-miles* see ICC, *Statistics of Railways in the U. S.*, Table 158, Item 457; for *train-miles* see *ibid.*, Item 429; for *train-hours*, *ibid.*, Item 488. For *car loadings* see Association of American Railroads, *Revenue Freight Loaded and Received from Connections*, Statement CS-54A.

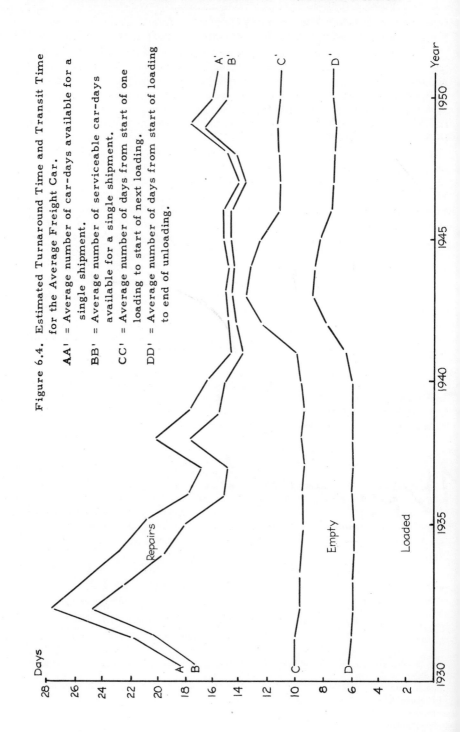

Figure 6.4. Estimated Turnaround Time and Transit Time for the Average Freight Car.

AA' = Average number of car-days available for a single shipment.

BB' = Average number of serviceable car-days available for a single shipment.

CC' = Average number of days from start of one loading to start of next loading.

DD' = Average number of days from start of loading to end of unloading.

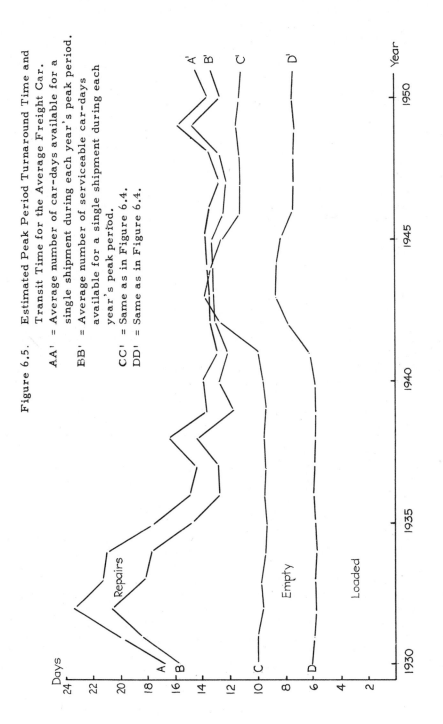

Figure 6.5.   Estimated Peak Period Turnaround Time and Transit Time for the Average Freight Car.

AA' = Average number of car-days available for a single shipment during each year's peak period.

BB' = Average number of serviceable car-days available for a single shipment during each year's peak period.

CC' = Same as in Figure 6.4.

DD' = Same as in Figure 6.4.

where, on the right hand side, the 1933 figures are from Table I and the 1940 figure is derived from the relation (6.1). The resulting graph is shown as the curve DD' in Figures 6.4 and 6.5.

The curve CC' in Figures 6.4 and 6.5 graphs for the different years our estimates of the total transit time *plus* the average time spent by a car in completing its empty trip to the next shipper. The distance between the two curves is simply

$$(6.3) \quad \text{time of empty trip} = \text{transit time} \times \frac{\text{empty car-miles}}{\text{loaded car-miles}} .$$

The curve CC' therefore represents the number of days on the average that a car uses to complete a whole cycle from one loading to another.

The average time that is available for this cycle depends on the level of traffic and on the stock of freight cars in serviceable condition. Curve AA' in Figure 6.4 represents

$$(6.4) \quad \frac{365 \text{ days}}{\dfrac{\text{annual carloadings}}{\text{stock of freight cars}}}$$

and tells us the length in days of the average turnaround period of a freight car. Curve BB' is derived in the same way except that stock of serviceable cars is substituted for stock of cars. The difference between AA' and BB' tells us what part of each cycle is devoted to repair work on the average. Notice that in the early thirties this difference is markedly higher than in other years. This does not mean that more repairs had to be made, but rather that, since business was slack, "bad-order" cars were not repaired immediately.

The difference between curves BB' and CC' represents freight-car time so far unaccounted for. The size of this unexplained part is surprising until we recall the fact that peak traffic periods have not entered the analysis. In Figure 6.5 the Curve BB' has been changed to represent only the two-week period of each year with the highest average number of carloadings. If every year's two-week peak persisted throughout the whole twelve months Figure 6.5 would tell us what proportion of a freight car's time was utilized. As it is, it refers only to the utilization in these peak periods (which do not always occur on the same, or even nearly the same, date).

Another reason for the unexplained part of a car's time is very similar to the reason, discussed earlier, for holding idle stocks of any commodity. Quite often at some location a number of empty cars larger than that which subsequently turns out to be needed may be kept on hand in order to cover errors in forecasting carloading requirements. To the extent that the movement of empties from one location to another can be speeded up, these empty-car stocks at various places can be reduced, just as the speeding up of commodity movements enables a reduction of ordinary commodity inventories.

Chapter 7

FREIGHT OPERATIONS AND THE CLASSIFICATION POLICY

7.1. *General Description of Freight Operations*

In this section some aspects of railroad operations are sketched. The object is not to give any detailed account of them but rather to focus attention on those aspects of the operations with which we are concerned in later chapters, and to introduce some phrases and definitions which we will find useful. Attention will be concentrated on the workings of a freight system.

It may be useful to follow a carload of freight on a highly simplified railroad system. Figure 7.1 shows such a system. Suppose a load is being dispatched from A to D. At A it will be loaded into an appropriate car. However it may have to wait at A for some time either until a sufficient number of other cars are ready to travel in the same general direction to warrant running a train, or perhaps until a train is scheduled to leave. Delays of this type arise fundamentally because it is not usually considered economical by the railroads to haul trains with only a few cars. It is an example of what we call an *accumulation delay*.

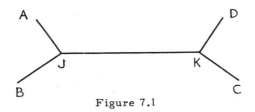

Figure 7.1

After a time enough cars will have collected to go in the direction of J. Some of these may be going to B, C, or K or perhaps only as far as J itself. In any case the order of the cars for all five destinations will probably be well mixed up in the train. Thus at J the cars in the train will have to be uncoupled and sorted. Cars going on to K and beyond will be sorted together. Again they may then have to wait until more cars destined for K or beyond (that is, to C or D) arrive from B; they may therefore suffer more accumulation delay. Then the car we are following will be hauled out in a train to K.

At K the same sequence may be followed. The train will be uncoupled and sorted into cars going to C and to D, and cars remaining at K. Again there may be a wait until the train for D leaves, and the car is taken on the last lap of its journey.

At points such as J and K there must be facilities for *sorting* out the cars, and storing them until they are taken out in a train. Such facilities are called *classification yards*. These yards may be large and complicated, with a considerable amount of expensive equipment. They usually involve a large investment for the railroads.

We have suggested already that there are two principal ways of arranging the times at which trains are dispatched from one yard to a second. One possible method is to wait until enough cars have been collected which are traveling as far as the destination yard or farther. How many cars are considered "enough" to make up a train should presumably depend on a balancing of various economic factors; for example the extra delay involved in waiting for sufficient cars for a long train as against the increased costs in fuel, labor, etc., of running several short trains instead of one long one. Such a method of operation can be flexible, since those responsible for dispatching trains can change their plans to meet different types of flows. However this method is not well adapted to synchronizing the various movements of trains to ensure that they meet at junctions -- the classification yards -- in such a way as to hold down accumulation delays. For this to be accomplished, the trains must be dispatched according to timetable. This method of operation is becoming increasingly common for freight trains on American railroads. The disadvantage is that, on occasions when traffic fluctuates, trains may have to run either very short, or so long that they must be run in two sections in order to keep to the scheduled times, so that the system may not be working most economically. With timetable operation, accumulation delays occur in slightly different ways. After a car has been sorted it has to wait until the train on which it has to travel is scheduled to leave. We still call this an accumulation delay, however, to keep to a single term. For fairly steady flows of traffic, it may be possible to adjust the timetable to ensure that delays and the costs of running trains are properly balanced. This question is taken up in later chapters.

Various modifications of the method of operation outlined above are used. One of these is "maintracking." If sufficient traffic from A is going to K or beyond, it may be a sound policy to allow traffic to accumulate at A for a train to be dispatched from there consisting entirely of this type of traffic. Such a train need not have any work done on it at J; indeed it can pass by J on the main line. But such a policy may cause traffic for J or B to be delayed longer at A, or trains from A to be run shorter. It may also have the same effect on traffic leaving J. Thus the question of whether or not to run a maintracker can be a difficult one. In practice there may be a quite intricate pattern of maintrackers, some trains, for example, running straight from A to C, others from J to C, others from A to K, as well as trains running only between adjacent stations.

Preclassification is another frequently used device. It is primarily a method of transferring the sorting work from one yard to another. Such a transfer may be necessary if one yard gets overloaded, for example, so that delays become too heavy. Or it may be useful if one yard is better equipped than another, so that sorting work can more easily be

carried out there. The idea of preclassification can again be explained
in terms of Figure 7.1. Suppose a train from A arriving at J contains
traffic for all the other stations. At J it will have to be broken up and
sorted. One train is to leave for B, and another, containing traffic for
C, K and D is to leave for K. It would be possible to leave the actual
sorting out of cars for C, K and D from each other until the train
reached K. However, the yard J may do this work for the yard at K. In
that case the train from J to K will have all the cars for J grouped together, all the cars for C grouped together, and all the cars for D
grouped together. It will then be completely preclassified. The only
sorting work left to the yard at K will be the separation of the three
groups associated with the three different destinations. It is also possible to preclassify the train less completely. It may, for example, be decided to sort out only the traffic bound for K at J and leave traffic for C
and D mixed up, to be finally sorted out when the train gets to K. In
later chapters an attempt is made to develop a rational approach to the
problem of how much preclassification should be done in some situations.

7.2. *Classification Policy of a Yard*

In the last section the main functions of a classification yard were
described as the sorting of cars into different groups, the storage of
cars up to the time of departure, and the making up of trains. Clearly
there are many different ways in which these functions can be carried
out. Before entering into a discussion of the advantages and disadvan-
tages of these different methods, it is necessary to have some language
in which to discuss them. In the rest of this chapter we shall try to develop this terminology; having done this we shall devote some time to
describing instances of its use.

"In the early days of railroading," according to E. W. Coughlin,
"freight trains generally were made up of any cars on hand for movement to or beyond the next terminal, without regard to final destination
or class of freight. Thus each successive terminal or yard switched out
from their chance locations in each arriving train the cars belonging in
its environs as well as those ... cars for local stations short of the next
terminal.... The balance, plus such loads and empties as were 'made'
at the terminal or from incoming local movements, were let go in the
same chance order into succeeding trains run to the next terminal"
(Coughlin, 1952, p. 44). If we add to this description some such rule as
"A train will be dispatched when 85 cars are available," we have one
instance of what we shall call a *classification policy*.

More generally, a classification policy is a set of rules, for each
yard, which completely specifies the manner in which incoming traffic is
to be reconstituted into outbound trains. This set of rules need not be
explicit, nor indeed even consciously in the minds of the men responsible
for the various operations involved. The formal itemizing of rules may
be more a theoretical than a practical necessity. In setting out to construct a model of yard operations, we cannot rely as the president of a

railroad does on the expert judgments of yardmasters, division superintendents, dispatchers, etc.; these must be supplanted in our theory by formal rules whose consequences can be studied by logical and mathematical means. This is not to say of course that where in practice such formal rules are found to be lacking, things would necessarily be improved by the application of the same simple rules. Our theory, to be useful, must be a great deal simpler than its real counterpart, and while it may be possible to formulate theoretical rules that are in some sense "good," the same formalization in practice may prove to be difficult. In such a case a combination both of "formal" rules and "informal" judgment will always be used.

Our problem here is to determine what alternative sets of rules adequately describe the range of policies available to a railroad in its conduct of yard operations. We cannot of course say anything as yet about what makes one set of rules better or worse than another; these policy choices will be based on the cost considerations studied in later chapters. At this point we only wish to indicate the different questions relating to methods of operation to which any classification policy, good or bad, must give definite answers.

7.3. Typical Yard Operations

Some of these questions will be made clear by a brief examination of the operations in a typical classification yard. Although yards differ in many important respects, the classification operations carried on in all of them are basically the same. Usually a yard is made up of several sub-yards, each of which has a track pattern essentially like that in Figure 7.2, where the arrows indicate the direction of traffic through the yard. The picture abstracts from several important differences between yards, but for the moment it will serve our purposes. Suppose now we

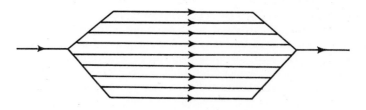

Figure 7.2. The Basic Track Pattern of a Sub-Yard

consider a yard handling only one direction of traffic and consisting of two sub-yards as in Figure 7.3. The first sub-yard the traffic enters is usually called the receiving yard or receiving tracks; the second, the classification yard[1] or classification tracks. Incoming trains, entering

---

1. We shall usually avoid this term, since it is the same as the term for the yard as a whole. The word *sub-yard* is useful but, so far as we know, not popular.

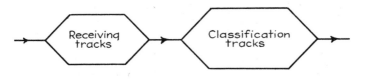

Figure 7.3

Figure 7.3 from the left, are run as a whole into one or another of the receiving tracks to await sorting. Since only one string of cars can be sorted at a time, these receiving tracks are sometimes necessary as storage space for trains that arrive while another is being sorted.

When its turn comes for sorting or classification, this trainload of cars is pushed out of the receiving track, through the neck of the yard between the two sub-yards, and by various means each car of the train is made to run into the classification track to which it is assigned. Usually these classification tracks will already have other cars standing on them, to which the cars of the train we are examining will couple automatically. When the classification process is finished the cars which at the start were all on one track in the receiving yard will generally be scattered over several of the classification tracks. The choice of the classification track into which a particular car is moved will usually be made on the basis of the car's destination and perhaps its contents or condition, the idea being to group similar traffic for departure in outbound trains and to separate out cars needing attention.

As this sorting procedure is being carried on in a fairly continuous manner at one end (the left in Figure 7.3) of the classification tracks, the process of making up outbound trains is also carried on at the other end of the classification tracks. This make-up process consists in drawing the strings of cars out of specified classification tracks and assembling them into trains.

This description of the classification operation leaves out many yard activities that will require our attention at a later point. However, such things as the inspection of cars and the re-icing of refrigerator cars are not essential parts of the classification process even though, for reasons of convenience, they are usually carried out at the same time and place. The description therefore brings out most of the important questions which a classification policy must answer.

7.4. The Requisites of a Policy

7.4.1. Receiving

The first question is one of priority. If the sorting facilities are prepared to receive another string of cars, and if there are several trains waiting on the receiving tracks, which should be handled first? In very small yards this problem may never arise, since only one train at a time will be available. In the usual case, however, the arrivals of incoming traffic are not always spaced out evenly over the day and it is quite likely that at some moment, after a period of bunched arrivals, several trains will be standing on the receiving tracks while an earlier train is being sorted. In some yards the problem is more complicated. If the receiving tracks are not long enough to accommodate the full length of an incoming train, this train will have to be broken up into two or three (usually not more) pieces, and each put onto a separate receiving track. Often, too, it is desired to give high priority to one part of a train and low priority to the other, in which case the question of just how to break up the train for storage on the receiving tracks creates another policy problem. The rule or set of rules dealing with these problems we can designate as the yard's *receiving policy*, which is part of its general classification policy. The simplest possible receiving policy is exemplified by a "first come, first served" rule. This is the one we shall usually assume to exist, since this element of policy is not the one we shall find most interesting.

7.4.2. *Grouping*

The second policy question has to do with the sorting of cars. Into which of the classification tracks is any given car to be switched? Since a given classification track is at some yards used for different kinds of cars at different times, the question is perhaps better phrased as, to which *classification* does a car belong? The latter question is substantially equivalent to the former since at any given time a single classification track is devoted to the cars of only one classification. The practice in larger yards, especially those with an ample number of classification tracks, is to assign one or more tracks to each classification on a permanent basis. Since the number of classifications is a matter of policy, it becomes a maxim of yard operation that the number of classifications should not exceed the number of classification tracks. Departures from this rule are however not uncommon, and if it ever happens that cars of all these classifications are present at the same time, then extra switching is called for.

Destination, contents, type and condition of a car are the most common bases of its classification. Thus among the classifications used by the Southern Pacific's Taylor Yard at Los Angeles we find:

Track		
	2	Fresno to and including Planehaven
	3	Edison to but not including Fresno
	4	San Pedro -- Los Angeles Harbor
	.	.
	.	.
	7	King City to but not including San Jose
	8	San Luis Obispo to but not including King City
	9	Colton to but not including Indio
	10	All points Roseville and beyond including Ogden

Track   .   .
         .   .
12 Weighers
         .   .
         .   .
20 Commodity cars to clean
21 39th St. to and including Firestone Park
22 Empty gondolas, etc.
         .   .
         .   .
24 Dirty reefers
25 Santa Fe R.R.
26 Union Pacific R.R.
         .   .
         .   .
38 Icers
39 Bad order empties

Henceforth we refer to the list of classifications as the *grouping policy,* to signify that cars in a given classification are to be grouped in outbound trains.

7.4.3. Make-Up

The third policy question refers to the make-up of trains. Let us identify each outbound train by some code name, such as "No. 97," etc., and let us suppose that we know its time of departure. Then, calling the string of cars standing on any one classification track a *group,* we ask what groups are to go into any given train. If traffic conditions vary from day to day, the exact number of cars in any one group at any particular moment will not be known in advance. The total of cars in the groups designated to be made up into "No. 97" may therefore be sometimes more than the train can haul; at other times the number may be so small as to render the movement of this train quite unprofitable. Although these matters somewhat encroach upon the discussion of later chapters, their mention is necessary here, because the *make-up* policy described above does not, as it stands, facilitate consideration of train length. One way of avoiding this difficulty is to define the make-up policy to be a set of numbered lists, each one of which ranks the groups that are to go into some outbound train. Each list is to be interpreted as an assignment of priorities to the groups of cars on different classification tracks. An outbound train will be filled by first taking the group at the head of that train's make-up list, next the group second in the list, and so on until the length of train thought in the circumstances to be best has been reached.

7.4.4. *Scheduling*

Before saying any more about make-up, let us go on to the fourth and last policy question we shall examine. This pertains to the scheduling of outbound trains. The *scheduling policy* for a yard may consist simply of a list of trains with a departure time and destination for each, or it may be somewhat more complicated. If the make-up policy is not of the priority-list type, the scheduling must be of a somewhat different form in order to avoid the train-length troubles mentioned earlier. Suppose train "No. 97" is to be made up of groups A, B, and C; *all* of the cars in these three groups are to go in "No. 97," and no other cars are to be allowed in the same train. If traffic in these groups is quite variable from day to day, so that at 10 AM, say, on one day there are 200 cars for "No. 97" and on another day only 25, the schedule for "No. 97" must take one of the following forms:[2]

" No. 97" will depart when (say) 100 cars are avaiable.

or perhaps

" No. 97" will depart at 10 AM if at least 100 cars are available at that time,
at 11 AM if at least   80 cars are available at that time,
at 12 AM if at least   60 cars are available at that time,
at   1 PM if at least   40 cars are available at that time,
at   2 PM if at least   20 cars are available at that time.

This last rule lends itself very conveniently to a graphical representation. The curve DD' in Figure 7.4 represents this rule, with the addition that points of time intermediate between 10 AM and 11 AM, for example, are also assigned numbers of cars between 100 and 80, etc. The curve EE', representing the availability experience of one particular day, shows how many cars of groups A, B, and C, taken together, have accumulated on the classification tracks at any one time. On this day, according to the scheduling rule, "No. 97" will depart at about 11:50 AM with about 64 cars, these figures being the coordinates of the intersection of curves EE' and DD'.

The important point in this discussion is not why the curve DD' should have such a slope but only that it is possible to ensure against absurdly long trains (by making the schedule of departure times dependent on the numbers of cars of the proper kinds which have accumulated), and at the same time not completely abandon the timetable type of scheduling. Notice in Figure 7.4 that if the curve DD' were vertical, we should have a pure timetable schedule; if DD' were horizontal we should have what might be called a "leave when filled" type of scheduling. The curve as drawn represents a scheduling policy for "No. 97" which is intermediate between these two extremes. It must be emphasized of course that a schedule can be represented sensibly by a curve only when the make-up policy for the train specifies certain groups of cars *all* of

---

2. The corresponding rules in actual practice will not of course be capable of such simple representation. It is felt, however, that the scheduling rules presented here do take into account the important considerations upon which practical decisions on this matter are made.

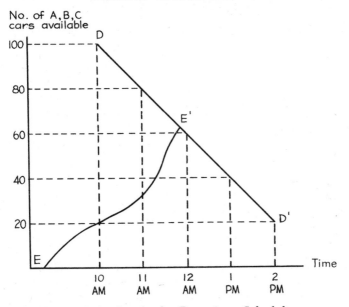

Figure 7.4. Graph of a Departure Schedule

which must go on the train. The make-up policy that assigns priorities
to different groups is not of this kind. Make-up and scheduling policies
which represent mixtures of the two variants we have described are conceivable and probably can be found in practice, but we shall not attempt
to discuss them.

Of the four components of classification policy discussed, we shall
be concerned mainly with the last three: grouping, make-up, and scheduling. Briefly, these tell us, respectively, what cars go into what
groups, what groups go into what trains, and when each train departs.

7.5. Some Examples

To return to Coughlin's description of early railroading practices,
we can now restate in our new terminology the classification policy used
there. In Figure 7.5, let the points denoted by capital letters be what
Coughlin refers to as terminals; at each, we shall assume, there exists
a classification yard. Let the points denoted by lower case letters be
local stations. At Yard A the grouping will be

> Cars for a, a', a"
> All other cars.

At Yard B the grouping will be

> Cars for b, b', b"
> Cars for D and beyond
> Cars for c, c', c"
> Cars for C and beyond

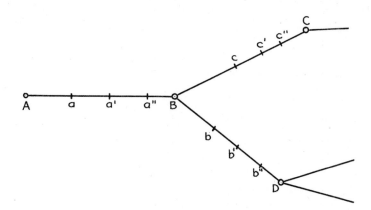

Figure 7.5. Classifications in a Rail Network

The make-up in both cases is particularly simple. Each outbound train
will consist of one group only, local trains from A carrying only the
single group [a, a′, a″] and through trains carrying only the single group
[all other cars].

At B, one local train will be dispatched with the single group
[b, b′, b″], another local with the group [c, c′, c″], a through train with
the group [D and beyond], and another through train with the group
[C and beyond]. Nothing explicit was said in the example about scheduling.

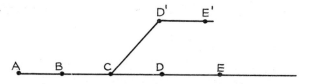

Figure 7.6. Showing Locations of Yards

Another example is provided by a scheme proposed by M. L. Byers
(1908, pp. 539-540). Interesting in itself, it fits in here as the plan next
in order of simplicity to the one described by Coughlin. Since we shall
have occasion to refer to Byers' plan again in Chapter 9 we shall quote
it at length. The reader should be aware that Byers uses the word "cut"
where we have used "group"; we shall reserve the former term for a
somewhat different use. The plan is as follows:

1. Normally, each yard will classify through trains into two cuts
   each, viz.:
   (a) Cars for the first yard in advance, including cars for
        points between the first and second advance yards and
        which consequently are not handled in through trains
        beyond the first advance yard
   (b) All other cars

Example. Yard A (Figure 7.6) will make up through train for yard B with all cars for Yard B (including local cars for points between B and C exclusive) in one cut, and all cars for Yard C and beyond in a second cut.

Yard B will receive this train, remove the first cut and classify the second cut into:

A_1. Cars for Yard D and local beyond D;
A_2. Cars for Yard E and beyond.

It will add any cars held in the yard for these destinations to these cuts, and the train is then ready to proceed to Yard D. In like manner, it will classify other cars of the second cut into:

B_1. Cars for Yard D' and local beyond D';
B_2. Cars for Yard E' and beyond.

It will add any cars held in the yard for these destinations and the branch train is then ready to proceed. Then, at its leisure, it will dispose of the cut set off and switch the cars into the locals, or to points in the yard as the destinations of the cars may indicate.

2. If any yard, after performing the normal work above indicated, has available yard-engine time before the departure time of the through train, it will perform such of the work of the next succeeding yard as may be done without delay or increased cost.

Example. Yard A, having completed its work in time to do further switching on the through train for B, will separate the second cut (for points beyond C) into:

A. Cars for yard D and beyond;
B. Cars for yard D and beyond.

If further time is available, it will separate cut A into cuts A_1 and A_2, and cut B into cuts B_1 and B_2, before mentioned, thus reducing the delay at Yard C.

In spite of the omissions with respect to the disposition of cars bound for C and local points beyond C, the general principle of classification is clear. If we list, one on a line, the groups formed at a yard, and if we use brackets to indicate the groups that are made up together into trains, Byers' policies for the various yards can be written as follows:

For A   { local beyond A   }

          { B and local beyond B   }
          { C and beyond   }

For B^3 { local beyond B   }

          { C and local beyond C   }
          { D and beyond   }

          { D' and beyond   }

---

3. We have altered the grouping at B so as both to bring in the C traffic which Byers inadvertently omitted, and at the same time to make B's policy conform to the principle implied. The C traffic of course could equally well have been put on the third train.

For C   { local between C and D }

{ local between C and D' }

{ D and local beyond D
  E and beyond }

{ D' and local beyond D'
  E' and beyond }

et cetera.

If a yard has spare time at its disposal its policy, according to Byers, is to be modified. The first such modification for Yard A is described as follows:

{ local beyond A   }

{ B and local beyond B
  C and local beyond C
  D and beyond
  D' and beyond }

The second modification, to be carried out if A still has time available, is:

{ local beyond A   }

{ B and local beyond B
  C and local beyond C
  D and local beyond D
  E and beyond
  D' and local beyond D'
  E' and beyond }

et cetera.

Both of the above examples are of course extremely simple ones. The classification policies in actual use today are much more complicated. While each yard's policy is still quite capable of being expressed in our terminology, it is true that the policies of a system of yards cannot be easily expressed in a general form as we have done with the plan of Byers. Indeed, there is little reason to expect such a uniform pattern of policies. For an example of a system of policies the reader is referred to the Baltimore and Ohio's *Working Book No. 19*,[4] which devotes a page to the grouping, make-up, and scheduling of each train.

---

4. Baltimore and Ohio Railroad Company (1951).

Chapter 8

A SINGLE CLASSIFICATION YARD

In this chapter we shall attempt to give some more precise meaning
to the concept of the "work" involved in classification operations. For
the moment we shall confine our discussion to the workings of a single
yard in isolation; we shall ask how costs at this yard depend on the
yard's physical facilities, on the characteristics of the traffic handled,
and on the classification policy. Cost will be thought of as being made
up of two components, money cost and time cost, where the latter represents the delays suffered by cars and freight in undergoing the classification process. Most of the description will be of a qualitative rather
than quantitative nature; that is to say, we shall usually have to be satisfied in knowing whether costs go up or go down with certain changes in
yard facilities, traffic, or policy. The exact extent of these changes, except in a few cases, must remain a subject for further inquiry. It should
also be emphasized that the relationships we shall describe are tentative ones, open to criticism and perhaps refutation by subsequent studies
of a similar nature. While it is felt that most railroad men would be in
agreement with each one of the cost relationships taken singly, many
different opinions can undoubtedly be found on the relative importance of
each.

To begin with, it is convenient to break down yard costs into three
categories -- the cost of handling, the cost of accumulation, and the cost
of congestion. Under the title *handling* are included all those yard operations having to do with the movement and servicing of cars in the yard.
Handling costs will obviously contain both money costs, in the form of
switch-engine and labor costs, and time costs corresponding to the periods of time necessary to carry out the classification operations. *Accumulation* and *congestion* costs are composed entirely of time costs.
The first of these, which we shall usually refer to as accumulation delay,
pertains to the delay suffered by a car waiting either for its scheduled
departure or for a train length of the "right" kind of traffic to accumulate in the yard. What kind of traffic is "right" and what the train length
shall be will of course be specified by the make-up and scheduling policies of the yard. The reason for the name we have given to this element
of delay is clear in the case where the scheduling policy is of the "leave-
when-filled" type but not so clear when it is of the timetable type. As
soon, however, as we realize that one of the ruling considerations in the
selection of a particular timetable is the average train length to which it
leads, we see that the delay involved in waiting for a timetable departure
can also be considered a waiting for cars to accumulate.

Congestion delays refer to the periods during which a car must
stand idle as it waits to be serviced because the handling of cars

serviced ahead of it is not yet finished. It should be pointed out that this definition excludes some delays that are also caused by congestion, such as those brought about by a possible slowing down of handling operations in times of heavy traffic. These latter delays (if they exist) would in our terminology still be classed as handling costs.

We shall now enter into a more detailed discussion of each of these costs.

8.1. Handling Cost

It is perhaps simplest first to discuss handling cost entirely in terms of its time-cost component. We shall usually find in fact that both the time- and the money-cost components respond in the same way to changes in yard facilities, policy, and traffic. On the important question of the degree to which, under different circumstances, the two types of cost are substitutable, something will be said at a later point.

Following the discussion of yard operations in the preceding chapter we shall consider separately the delays arising in each of the several handling operations -- receiving, sorting, and make-up.

8.1.1. In the Receiving Operation

If, in the receiving operation, an incoming train is broken up into two or more pieces to be stored on the receiving tracks, the delays involved are probably greater than when the whole train is treated in a single section. More important at this point of the operation are the delays brought about by the inspection process. It was stated earlier that the condition of a car was one of the classification criteria. The inspection of cars to determine their condition must therefore precede this sorting operation. If a car's need of immediate repair is only discovered after it has been sorted, extra switching will be necessary to remove it from the group with which it has been placed. Such switching will very likely have to be performed at a part of the yard designed for other work. Unless this work can be done at a slack period, the result is delay, not only to the car in question, but also to the cars coupled to this bad-order car. The inspection therefore is usually carried out in the receiving yard.

A small crew of men goes through a routine checklist inspection of each car in the train. The list includes such things as couplings, journals, and brakes, and is quite often very detailed. The time needed to finish the inspection of a train depends partly on its length, of course, but it also may depend on the number of men available for inspection at any one moment. Large classification yards have as many as 100 men, divided among three shifts, who devote full time to inspection. This means that during slack periods the process can be considerably speeded up. In order that the reader might have some idea of the length of this inspection period, we have plotted in Figure 8.1 inspection times (vertical axis) against train lengths (horizontal axis) for one particular

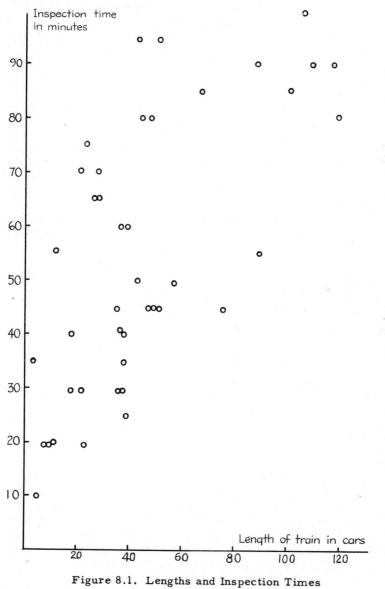

Figure 8.1. Lengths and Inspection Times
of Trains in a Hump Yard

day's traffic through a large classification yard. The preponderance of short "train" lengths is explained when it is recalled that quite often sections of a train are treated separately. While the scatter of the points in Figure 8.1 is large, perhaps reflecting variation in the size of the inspection crew, there does seem to be some indication that, on the average, the time required to inspect a train increases with train length. If inspection time per car is, on the average, a constant independent of train length, as seems most likely, it is still true that the inspection delays incurred by cars will depend on the lengths of the trains (or sections of trains) in which they are stored in the receiving tracks. This is so because no single car can be moved until the inspection of the whole string of cars to which it is coupled has been completed. This is perhaps a roundabout way of stating that the inspection delay attaches to the train (or section of train) rather than to the car. However, since the train loses its identity in the sorting process (its cars may end up in several other trains), we prefer to use the car rather than the train as our base.

Clearly, then, the average inspection delay suffered by cars will vary with yard facilities and with receiving policy. The shorter the sections into which incoming trains are broken up the less will be the average inspection delay of a car. Such savings are offset, however, by the fact, previously mentioned, that a train is more quickly moved in and out of the receiving tracks when it is handled in fewer sections. While the question of how receiving delays are affected by receiving policy is an interesting one, we shall not pursue it further here.

8.1.2. *In the Sorting Operation*

The handling delays arising in the sorting[1] operation are of special interest to us because it is here that the possibility of shifting work from one yard to another is most in evidence. According to the means by which they carry out the sorting procedure we shall distinguish two main types of classification yards -- the *flat yard* and the *hump yard*. In order to explain the difference, the diagram of the classification track pattern will be slightly elaborated for the two cases.

In Figure 8.2 we see a typical pattern of classification tracks for a flat yard together with the leads to and from these tracks. To sort a train of cars a switch engine pushes the train in along the entering "lead track" from the receiving yard. From a previously prepared "switch list" the members of the switching crew know into which classification track each car is to go. *Cut* is the name given to each of the parts into which a train is cut up in the sorting operation; thus a cut is a group of successive cars bound for the same classification track. The switch list therefore defines the cuts to be made. Let us say that the first two cars

---

1. To describe the operation of switching cars into the classification tracks the term "sorting" is used rather than the more commonly used "classification" in order to avoid confusion with the whole yard operation, for which the latter term is reserved.

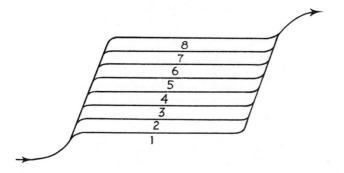

Figure 8.2. A Typical Classification-Track Pattern
for a Flat Yard

of the train are to go into Track 4; cars 1 and 2, that is to say, constitute the first cut. As the string of cars moves toward the switch leading
into Track 4 one man pulls the pin that locks the coupling between the
second and third car. A switchman throws the switch so as to direct the
pair of cars into Track 4, and the engineman brakes the train sharply,
thus "kicking" this cut into the proper track. These two cars roll down
Track 4 until they lose momentum, couple with other cars already
standing there, or in some cases are stopped by a brakeman on the cars.
Meanwhile the switchman restores the switch to Track 4 and sets the
switch for the track appropriate to the next car or cars. The pin-puller
separates this next "cut" of cars, and the engine brakes again, and so
it continues.

   An experienced crew can perform this operation much more
smoothly than it can be described. One who has never watched it would
suppose that, after each kick, the engine would have to back up with its
string of remaining cars to repeat the process. However this is by no
means always the case. Quite often several cuts can be kicked into
their appropriate classification tracks without ever completely halting
the forward progress of the engine. The only requirement is that there
be sufficient space between the cuts to enable the switchman to reach
and operate the proper switches. Suppose three successive cuts are
destined for Tracks 6, 7, and 4 respectively (Figure 8.2). The second
cut must be far enough behind the first to give the switchman time to restore the switch to Track 6 after the first cut has passed over it and
then set the Track 7 switch if he has not already done so. He must then
be able to reach the Track 4 switch before the third cut does. Unless
the train is very short, backing up will often be necessary, for the string
of cars will eventually have passed beyond the turnouts for classification
tracks still to be used.

   In Figure 8.3 a typical classification-track pattern of a hump (or
gravity) yard is shown. It will be noticed that the right-hand half of the
diagram is no different from that for a flat yard. The essential difference between the two types of yard is to be found in the "hump," the

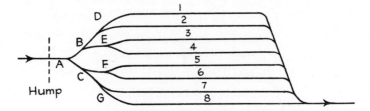

Figure 8.3. Typical Classification-Track Pattern for a Hump Yard

crest of which is indicated in Figure 8.3 by the dotted line. The track from the receiving yard slopes gradually up the left side of this hump, and drops off rather sharply on the right side. The downslope continues through the switches A, B, C, etc., and, almost imperceptibly, well into the body of classification tracks. The crest of the hump is usually 12 to 20 feet above the level. The grade of the tracks varies from as much as 4 per cent just beyond the hump to about 0.2 per cent in the classification tracks (American Railway Engineering Association, 1952, p. 301).

In sorting, or in this case "humping," a train, the switch engine pushes it up the left-hand side of the hump at about walking speed. Just before a cut of cars passes the hump, a pin-puller unlocks the coupling between this cut and the following one. As soon, then, as the cut is pushed over the hump, it breaks away from the rest of the train and starts rolling down the sharp grade toward the switch A in Figure 8.3. The switches A, B, and E are set so as to direct this first cut into, let us say, Track 4. Meanwhile the engine continues pushing the train up the hump, so that perhaps at the moment the first cut is moving through switch E, the second cut is already passing over switch C, and the third over switch A. It is not at all unusual to see three or four cuts rolling down from the hump simultaneously (each, of course, a little behind its predecessor), for the whole operation is a very rapid and continuous one. Except for unusual events, such as jammed couplings or cars requiring special handling, the movement of the train over the hump takes place at an almost constant speed.

In the earliest hump yards the switches were thrown manually, as in a flat yard, and the cars were braked as they rolled off the hump and into the classification tracks by men called "riders," who rode the cars and operated the hand brakes. Today most hump yards are equipped with electrically controlled switches, operated from desks in control towers that give their operators a good view of car movements. Braking is also automatically operated from control towers by means of electrically or pneumatically powered "car retarders." These retarders consist of cast-iron shoes, one on each side of each track, which can be made to pinch the wheels of cars as they pass over. In most yards a skilled operator, having information on the weight of a cut of cars and the classification track it is headed for, applies just enough pressure with the retarders to slow the cut to a speed that will bring about a gentle coupling with the cars already standing on that classification track. There are usually several retarders; in Figure 8.3 there would probably be one between the hump and switch A, another between switches A and B, another between B and D, and others between successive points. In some modern yards, retarders can be set to apply automatically according to the speed and acceleration of the approaching cut.

In discussing the inspection process we assumed quite realistically that the inspection period of a car was not finished until the whole train or section of train to which it was coupled had also been inspected. We shall make exactly the same assumption with respect to the sorting process. That is to say, we shall suppose for simplicity that nothing further can be done with any single car until the whole string of cars containing it has been sorted. Our first concern therefore is with the time necessary to sort a train. Once we have this information we can return to the question of the average delay suffered by a single car.

In both flat yards and hump yards we should expect sorting time to increase with the length of the train being sorted. This is borne out for the case of a hump yard by the observations plotted in Figure 8.4, where the vertical axis measures the time used to sort a train, and the horizontal axis measures the train length. Each point represents a single train or section of train. The scatter of the points cannot be ignored, but it is clear that train length has an important effect.

From the description it is quite obvious that, at least for a flat yard, the number of cuts in the train must also play an important part in determining the sorting time. In flat switching, the number of times the engine will have to back up will almost certainly be higher if the number of cuts is high. In hump sorting the influence of the number of cuts is less obvious and not nearly as great. Nevertheless the number of cuts has a significant effect. In Figure 8.5 we have plotted sorting time per car against cuts per car for the same set of observations as were plotted in Figure 8.4. Because the relationship is not obvious in this case, and because it seems quite reasonable that cuts might have no appreciable effect on sorting time in a hump yard, we have computed the regression of "minutes per car in sorting" on "cuts per car" and "length of train." The resulting equation is

$$(8.1) \qquad \frac{t}{n} = \underset{(.0666)}{.0942} + \underset{(.084)}{.291} \frac{c}{n} + \underset{(.00028)}{.00131} n \quad,$$

where t is the time used in sorting a train, n is the length of the train in cars, c is the number of cuts into which the train is separated in the sorting process, and the figures in the parentheses are the standard errors of the coefficients above them. Since there were 108 observations, it is seen that all coefficients but the constant term are significantly different from zero. The equation is plotted in Figure 8.5 for n = 0 and n = 100. Sorting time per car for train lengths intermediate between zero and 100 can be found by linear interpolation if the cuts-per-car variable is taken to be fixed.

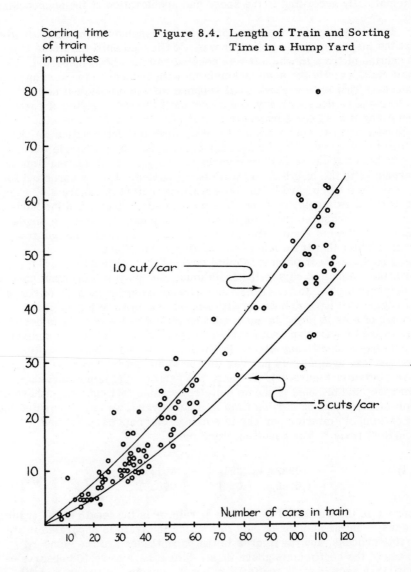

Sorting time
of train
in minutes

Figure 8.4. Length of Train and Sorting
Time in a Hump Yard

1.0 cut/car

.5 cuts/car

Number of cars in train

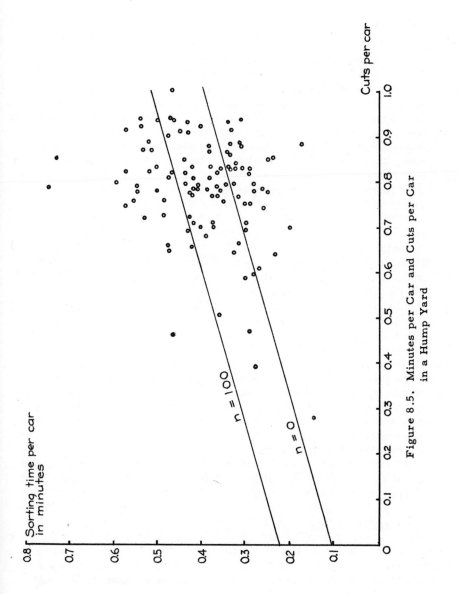

Figure 8.5. Minutes per Car and Cuts per Car
in a Hump Yard

Multiplying through by n, the equation (8.1) can be put in the form

(8.2) $\qquad t = [.0942 + .291 \frac{c}{n}] n + .00131 n^2$,

which is plotted in Figure 8.4 for $\frac{c}{n} = 1$ and $\frac{c}{n} = .5$. It must be emphasized at this point that the figure, "sorting time per car," used in Figure 8.5, is not the same thing as the sorting delay of a car, which, as we have said before is equivalent to the sorting time of the whole train.

Unfortunately we do not have statistics on flat-yard operation that would tell us how sorting time depends on cuts per car. It is clear however from more casual observation than that underlying Figure 8.5, and from the statements of railroad men, that, for a flat yard, the lines corresponding to those in Figure 8.5 would have a much sharper slope upward. This difference in the effect of the number of cuts per car is, in fact, the essential difference between a flat yard and a hump yard. The latter is much better equipped to handle sorting when the number of cuts per car is high.

What makes this relationship interesting is the fact that the variable, cuts per car, is almost completely a matter of policy. In order to concentrate our attention on this effect of cuts alone, let us simplify the discussion by supposing that the lengths of trains as they are sorted are fixed. This need not mean that all trains are of the same length, but only that from day to day, let us suppose, the same pattern of train lengths keeps repeating itself, so that, for instance, the twelfth train through the yard each day is always sorted in two sections of about 50 cars each. We can now examine the effect of grouping policy on sorting time through its influence on the number of cuts per car.

Other things equal, the number of cuts per car will be high if the list of classifications which constitutes the yard's grouping policy has many entries. On the other hand, cuts per car will be low if the grouping policy lists only two or three classifications. Any yard therefore, which wishes to minimize sorting delays incurred in it will maintain as coarse a classification system as possible; local traffic will be sorted into one group, and traffic for the next terminal and beyond will be sorted into another -- nothing more. The minimization of sorting delays at each yard does not at first glance appear to be a foolish aim, and probably goes far toward explaining the early classification practices described by Coughlin (quoted in Section 7.2). Even aside from the fact, however, that sorting delay is only one part of total delay, the minimization of sorting delay at each yard individually is not a wise goal. For it may be possible by way of a judicious choice of grouping policies at the various yards of a system to decrease the delay considerably at one yard by increasing the delay to a lesser degree at another; the aggregate result is then better than that achieved by individual minimization. The way this can take place is as follows.

We have described how the grouping policy influences the number of cuts per car, and how the latter in turn affects the sorting time differently in a flat yard and a hump yard. The third influence on sorting time operates, like grouping policy, through its effect on cuts per car. This is the character of the incoming traffic with respect to the ordering of cars in trains. To the extent to which cars in incoming trains are already grouped, the number of cuts per car will be less and the time consumed in the sorting operation will be diminished. If the preceding yard has exactly the same grouping policy, then in any single train not more than one cut will go into any classification track; cuts per car will have been reduced as far as possible by this means. If no grouping has been done by the previous yard (if, that is to say, it puts all traffic into *one* group) then cuts per car will, on the average, be very high. There will usually still remain some two- and three-car cuts, for no matter how mixed up a train may be, a chance remains that similarly destined cars will be found next to one another in a train. Many-carload shipments will also prevent the number of cuts per car from attaining the level 1.0. To this interesting problem of just how the grouping policy at a preceding yard influences cuts per car we shall return in Chapter 10, where an attempt will be made to take these chance variations into account by means of an explicit mathematical treatment.

At this point we only wish to emphasize that since cuts per car have little effect on sorting delay in a hump yard it becomes, as far as the sorting delays at this yard alone are concerned, almost a matter of indifference how fine the grouping policy is and how mixed up the trains are as they enter the yard. On the other hand, in a flat yard each additional classification in the grouping policy adds noticeably to sorting delays, and whether or not a train has been already grouped to some extent at a previous yard is a matter of considerable importance.

8.1.3. *In the Make-Up Operation*

The third type of handling delay we shall consider is that arising in the make-up operation. The make-up policy as described in the previous chapter specifies which of the classification tracks are to be "pulled" in order to assemble any particular outbound train. Suppose that the cars on Tracks 1, 3, 7, and 14 are to be made up into a train. While there are several different ways of doing this it is perhaps simplest to imagine the switch engine entering Track 1 from the departure end of the classification tracks, coupling on to the group of cars in Track 1, and pulling these out onto the ladder track which connects the classification tracks at this end of the yard. This string of cars is then pushed into Track 3 and a coupling is made with the string of cars standing there. This in-and-out movement is continued to pick up the groups in Tracks 7 and 14, and finally the train as a whole is moved off to a departure track. In large yards there may be several departure tracks side by side forming another subyard much like the receiving subyard.

In a well-designed yard it is quite possible that more than one train can be made up at a time. For this to be the case there must be more than one lead track to the departure end of the classification tracks and the groups to be made up into separate trains must be so located on the classification tracks as to permit carrying on the two operations without interference.

The time consumed in making up a train depends for the most part on the number of groups that go into the train, since each group calls for a movement in and out of a classification track on the part of the switch engine. If the number of cars in a group has an influence on the time necessary to pull this group out of its classification track, perhaps make-up time is best expressed as a function of number of groups and length of train. Notice that this last relationship is formally identical to the one we have proposed for delay in the sorting operation. This should not, of course, surprise us, for make-up is very much like the flat-yard sorting operation in reverse, with the difference that it cannot be performed quite so smoothly. Cuts have been replaced by groups in the relationship; there will usually be only a few groups, but the influence of this number on make-up delay will probably be relatively greater than the influence of the number of cuts on sorting delay, because each group calls for a push-pull action which even in flat-yard sorting was quite often avoidable.

Just as cuts per car was in great part determined by grouping policy, so the number of groups in a train (or perhaps better *groups per car*, if train length by itself proves to have an important effect) is in great part determined by make-up policy.

8.2. Congestion Cost

From the foregoing discussion and the data that have been presented, one might suppose that there is little reason for the average car to spend more than about three hours in any one classification yard. This would allow one hour for inspection (Figure 8.1), one hour for sorting (Figure 8.4), and one hour for make-up. Not all yards, it is true, are like the one for which we have presented data, but it is probably not unrepresentative of a large class of hump yards. In Table III are presented some daily averages of the time spent by *some* cars in undergoing classification at this yard.

The table presents a rather worse picture than it might have, for perishable traffic, which has highest priority in going through the yard, has unfortunately been omitted in calculation of the averages. Granted, however, that Table III describes only the delays to slow traffic, it is still clear that a great part of the total delay suffered by a car in the process of classification remains to be explained. At this point it would be naive indeed to assume that the difference between the three or four "explained" hours and the fifteen hours, say, of Table III, represented waste or inefficiency on the part of railroad management. The remainder of this delay falls into categories we have called congestion delay and accumulation delay. We shall first say a few words about congestion delay and its determinants.

Table III

Some Daily Averages of Delays to Nonpriority Traffic
in a Classification Yard (Hours)

	Northbound Traffic		Southbound Traffic	
	Average Time from Arrival to End of Sorting	Average Time from Arrival to Departure	Average Time from Arrival to End of Sorting	Average Time from Arrival to Departure
June 2	5.88	17.63	2.98	10.42
3	6.67	18.73	4.22	11.80
4	6.20	17.73	4.30	12.65
5	5.37	16.65	4.60	11.48
6	5.23	15.83	5.08	11.70
7	6.62	18.90	5.65	12.67
8	6.73	17.35	4.32	12.53
9	6.80	18.43	4.33	13.88
10	6.33	17.68	5.40	12.88
11	4.82	17.57	4.37	12.07
12	3.18	14.93	5.43	12.18
13	4.60	14.35	5.00	12.10
14	6.22	17.25	4.20	11.75
15	7.85	18.68	4.58	11.95

If every train took exactly one hour to inspect and one hour to sort, the average time from arrival to the end of sorting would still be greater than two hours, unless no train ever arrived until the inspection of the train preceding it had been completed. Where a yard has only one main track leading into it, there is some reason to expect incoming trains to be spaced out in this manner, for the capacity of the main-line track is limited, and the previous yard is not likely to make up and dispatch trains in very close succession. In large yards however, incoming trains will quite often enter from several directions. Bunched arrivals will not be uncommon, with the result that cars will often be forced to stand idle in the receiving yard while another train is being inspected. We shall call the time spent in such "waiting lines" or "queues" a congestion delay. Such delays are also caused by fluctuations in the lengths of inspection and sorting times.

Table IV presents a record of the inspection and sorting operations for part of one particular day. The arrival time of each train is given, along with the beginning and end of the inspection period, and the beginning and end of the sorting period. The numbers in the first column simply denote first train, second train, section a, section b, etc., while the third column shows the lengths in cars of the sections into which each train is broken up for handling purposes. The fourth column, "Paperwork," indicates the time at which the switch lists are completed. Sorting cannot begin until both the inspection and the paperwork are finished.

Hunting through the table one finds that at 12:20 AM, while 6, 8a, and 9a are being inspected, six train sections are standing in the receiving yard awaiting inspection. These are 7a with 28 cars, 7b with 112

Table IV

A Record of the Trains Classified between Midnight and Noon
on March 15, 1953, in a Large Hump Yard

Train	Arrival	Cars	Inspection	Paperwork Finished	Classification
1	3:50 PM	22	6:40-7:10 PM		3:28-3:35 AM
2	5:00 PM	24	5:55-7:10 PM	6:30 PM	12:32-12:38 AM
3	5:55 PM	19	7:10-7:50 PM	7:05 PM	4:27-4:33 AM
4	7:20 PM	53	8:00-9:35 PM	8:25 PM	3:40-3:55 AM
5	9:25 PM	21	10:00-11:10 PM	10:35 PM	3:10-3:22 AM
6	10:00 PM	112	10:35-3:50 AM	11:55 PM	4:42-5:35 AM
7a	11:05 PM	28	1:45-2:50 AM	11:35 PM	6:17-6:25 AM
b		112	3:30-5:00 AM	2:40 AM	6:34-7:25 AM
8a	11:30 PM	60	11:30-12:20 AM	12:35 AM	12:48-1:12 AM
b		4	12:30-12:40 AM	12:57 AM	1:23-1:24 AM
c		46	3:40-5:00 AM	12:57 AM	8:22-8:40 AM
9a	12:10 AM	39	12:10-12:50 AM	1:07 AM	1:25-1:42 AM
b		40	12:50-1:15 AM	1:35 AM	1:46-2:00 AM
c		29	12:40-1:45 AM	1:40 AM	2:08-2:17 AM
10a	1:00 AM	35	1:15-2:00 AM	2:00 AM	2:26-2:40 AM
b		38	2:00-2:30 AM	2:10 AM	2:50-3:03 AM
c		49	5:00-5:45 AM	2:55 AM	9:02-9:17 AM
11a	3:50 AM	10	7:00-7:20 AM	4:00 AM	9:55-9:58 AM
b		118	5:45-7:45 AM	4:50 AM	9:58-10:52 AM
12	5:41 AM	45	5:45-7:20 AM	6:10 AM	9:25-9:42 AM
13	5:50 AM	76	7:15-8:00 AM	6:30 AM	11:17-11:42 AM

cars, 8b with 4 cars, 8c with 46 cars, 9b with 40 cars, and 9c with 29
cars -- a total of 259 cars in the inspection queue. At 1:10 AM six
train sections whose inspection has been completed are waiting to be
sorted: 1, 3, 4, 5, 8b, and 9a with a total of 158 cars. The yard is not
always this congested, but a short study of Table IV does indicate that
queues usually form ahead of the inspection and sorting operations, and
that the resulting congestion delays are fairly substantial. One writer
(Crane, 1953, p. 102) has reported the following average delays to
trains for a one-week period in a hump yard:

Waiting for inspection	65 minutes
Inspection	71 minutes
Waiting for sorting	160 minutes
Sorting	25 minutes

In interpreting both these delays and those in Table IV a word of
caution is in order. Strictly speaking, the time spent waiting in inspection queues and sorting queues can *all* be called congestion delay only
if traffic is pushed through these operations as fast as possible, given

the working force of both labor and switch engines. If, however, the yard manager knows that the cars in a certain inbound train are not scheduled to leave the yard for say twelve hours, then he may very well put off the inspection or the sorting of these cars for eight hours or so, not simply because other traffic is waiting but only because it makes no difference whether the work is done now or later. This difficulty of separating congestion delay and accumulation delay makes the measurement of congestion delay rather difficult and may account in part for the surprisingly large estimates quoted above, as well as the congestion delays in Table IV.

In most queuing situations[2] the average congestion delay increases with the level of traffic. To test whether this is the case in a hump yard, linear regressions of daily average time from arrival to end of sorting on number of cars per day were computed for both northbound and southbound nonperishable traffic through a large hump yard over a period of four weeks. The results fail to tell us very much:

(8.3)   Northbound: $d = 135 + .31n$
                                    $(.11)$
(8.4)   Southbound: $d = 204 + .11n$
                                    $(.11)$

where d = average time in minutes from arrival to end of sorting, n = number of cars per day, and the numbers in parentheses are the standard errors of the coefficients of the n's. For the northbound traffic a significant increase of average delay with number of cars was found; for the southbound traffic the increase was not significant. The validity of these calculations is of course seriously impaired by the omission of the perishable traffic, which, although exact figures are not available, is known to constitute quite a large portion of the total traffic.

Policy choices will affect average congestion delay to the extent that handling times both in inspection and sorting can by this means be made more regular. Such opportunities are probably not very great. Equal in interest to the effect of policy on average congestion delay is the effect of receiving policy on the distribution of congestion delays to different classes of traffic. By assigning high priority in handling to one class of traffic the congestion delay of this class is reduced at the expense of the congestion delays suffered by all other traffic. Notice in Table IV that the first sections of trains 5, 8, 9, and 10 are sorted before trains that arrived earlier. The average delay is unchanged by such priority assignments; only the distribution of the total is affected.

8.3. Accumulation Costs

When the sorting of a train has been completed, the cars that were in it are ready to be made up into new trains. In the case of the usual

---

2. Cf. Section 1.2, especially Figures 1.8, 1.9, 1.10 at the end of that section.

car this make-up operation does not take place immediately, with the result that the car suffers another loss of time which we shall call an *accumulation* delay.

The name is derived from the reason for this delay. Enough similarly bound cars to achieve long-train economies must accumulate before an outbound train can be assembled. The decision as to how long the train is to be, and just how similar the destinations of the cars must be, is implicitly expressed in the make-up and scheduling policies, which state, respectively, what groups go into any particular outbound train and when the train is to be made up. If a whole trainload of low-density traffic is to be assembled, the average accumulation delay to the cars involved will be high; it will be low, on the other hand, if a train carries all traffic bound in its general direction. Considerations as simple as these go far in explaining why traffic bound from New York to Seattle is "yarded" at several intermediate points instead of being hauled in one solid train from origin to destination without interruption.

Speaking more precisely, we define the accumulation delay of a car to be the sum of the periods during which the car is waiting for the arrival or handling (or both) of other cars with which it is to be dispatched.[3] If we assume that the inspection and sorting of cars proceeds as fast as possible, given a certain working force, then the above definition is equivalent to the statement that the accumulation delay of a car is the period of time between the completion of sorting of the train (or section of train) in which it arrived and the beginning of the make-up of the train in which it is to depart. With this assumption, the accumulation delay of a car becomes very nearly the same as the time the car spends on a classification track.

The level of the average accumulation delay suffered by a particular component of traffic will, for the most part, be determined by the make-up and scheduling policies together with the level of flow of that traffic component. To make this clear let us suppose for a moment that the make-up and scheduling policies are of the "leave-when-filled" type (Figure 7.4) rather than the timetable type. Now let us look at the traffic specified by the make-up policy to go out on one particular train, "No. 97." If this traffic flow is high, then the intervals between departures of No. 97 will be short and accumulation delay per car for this traffic will be low. If some of this traffic departs on other trains as well as on No. 97, the description becomes more complicated, but our conclusion is unchanged. If the make-up policy is altered so as to exclude some of this traffic from No. 97, and if no other new traffic enters the make-up of No. 97, then the accumulation delay per car for No. 97 is increased, for it will take a longer time to accumulate a train

---

3. Only in the extreme case of dispatching by timetable will this definition of accumulation delay become somewhat ambiguous; for this one particular case we can define accumulation delay as the waiting time to the beginning of the make-up of the train in which the car is to depart.

load from this smaller traffic flow. To find out what happens to the accumulation delay of the excluded traffic it is of course necessary to look at more than one train at a time. If the scheduling policy is altered so that trains (with the same make-up as before) are dispatched more frequently, accumulation delay is decreased.

The effects on accumulation delay of simultaneous changes in make-up and scheduling may sometimes cancel out. Thus if the make-up of some trains is restricted but trains are scheduled more frequently, accumulation delays may remain the same.

In the case of timetable scheduling, the average accumulation delay per car of each component of traffic is only affected by make-up and scheduling and not by changes in the level of flow of that component, since a train's departure does not depend on the time required to accumulate a train load. In this case, as we shall see in Chapter 11, the influence of flow levels acts through their effect on the total of accumulation delays for all cars.

8.4. Summary

We shall now attempt to sum up in tabular form our discussions of the effect of yard facilities, traffic input, and policy on the various costs at a single yard and on the traffic output from that yard.

Across the top of Table V are listed the various factors influencing costs and output, and along the left margin are listed the various costs and the output. For the sake of completeness we have also included line-haul cost from this yard to whatever yards the departing traffic goes to. The phrase in any one cell of the table is an attempt to describe very briefly the means by which the item at the head of the column influences the item named in the left margin of the row. Where the influence is negligible or indirect, the cell has been blacked out.

Effect of On			Yard Facilities	Traffic Input	Policy			
					Receiving	Grouping	Make-up	Scheduling
Yard Cost	Handling	Receiving	size of inspection crew	/////	length of sections into which incoming trains are broken		/////	/////
		Sorting	hump or flatswitching	order of cars	length of sections into which incoming trains are broken	cuts per car	/////	/////
		Make-up	simultaneous make-up of two trains	/////		/////	number of groups in train	size of groups
	Congestion		through effect on handling time	bunched train arrivals	priority in handling	through effect on handling time	through effect on handling time	through effect on handling time
	Accumulation		/////	level of component flows	substitution of receiving delay for accumulation delay	/////	restrictive make-up means less frequent departures	frequency of departures
Line-haul cost to next yard					/////		length of train	length of train
Traffic output				order of cars within groups	/////	order of cars	number of groups in train	size of groups

Table V

The Influence of Yard Facilities, Traffic Input, and Policy on Cost and Output of a Single Yard

Chapter 9

THE ASSIGNMENT OF CLASSIFICATION WORK
IN A SYSTEM OF YARDS

9.1. Selection of a Set of Policies
That Minimizes System Costs

We have seen that various characteristics of the incoming traffic play a large part in the determination of both money and time costs at any single classification yard. Since many of these characteristics, such as the bunching of trains, the lengths of trains, and the grouping of similarly bound cars are importantly influenced by the classification policies of earlier yards, it is clear that the cost at any one yard is a function not only of its own policy, but also of the policies at all those yards through which the traffic of the yard in question has passed at earlier stages in its journey.

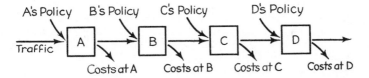

Figure 9 1. Causal Relationships in a System of Yards

Diagrammatically, this causal relationship can be represented as in Figure 9.1, where the boxes represent classification yards, and the arrows represent policies, costs, and the characteristics of various traffic flows. The arrows leading into a yard determine the arrows leading out. Thus C's costs and traffic output are jointly determined by C's policy and traffic input, and the latter, being B's output, is in turn determined by B's policy and the input to B, etc. The arrangement depicted, four yards in line, could easily be extended to more complicated systems.

We see therefore that costs at different yards are closely related to each other. A yard which adjusts its policy so as to reduce costs at a yard farther down the line will usually find that its own costs have increased in the process. If we assume the program of traffic (i.e. the traffic flows between various points of origin and destination) handled by a given system of yards to be fixed, any selection of a set of policies for the different yards is equivalent to a particular assignment to the yards of the classification work involved in handling this program.

The problem of policy selection, therefore, amounts to assigning this work in such a way that, in some sense, the sum of costs over the system is minimized. The system costs to be summed here must include not only the costs at yards but also line-haul costs, in order to bring into the problem recognition of the fact that accumulation delays are incurred to gain the hauling economies of long trains. The hauling operation involves time as well as money costs, of course, but for purposes of simplicity we shall ignore these time costs (by assuming them to be constant) on the grounds that yard policy has little influence on them.

Strictly speaking, it is not, of course, quite correct to refer to the problem as one of simple minimization,[1] since our cost concept, involving both time and money cost, has more than one dimension. Indeed, if delays to different components of traffic are valued differently — and very often they are in practice — our cost concept becomes many dimensional. In such a case the search for the "best" set of policies for the yards of a system takes the following form. First those assignments (substituting this shorter word for "sets of policies") must be found which have the characteristic that if another assignment results in less of one kind of cost, it inevitably results in more of another. An assignment which meets this specification will be called *efficient*. Thus one efficient assignment might result in fast service through the system of yards to AB traffic, but slow service to CD traffic. Since both assignments are efficient there can be no assignment which provides the same fast service to AB traffic *and* the same fast service to CD traffic. In searching for a best assignment we need not consider any inefficient assignment because by definition there is always an efficient assignment which is less costly in all respects.

The next step is to select from among the set of efficient assignments the one (or ones) which most nearly reflects the valuations put on the various time costs. The plural "valuations" is used because of course equal time losses to different components of traffic will not in general be valued equally. If we knew from the start how time was to be valued in terms of money, we should not have had to break down costs into time cost and money cost; instead, we could have treated time just as we have treated labor and fuel, in terms of money cost. With such advance knowledge, the problem of policy selection would simply have consisted in minimizing total money costs, and we should not have needed to trouble ourselves with the intermediate step of searching for efficient assignments.

From the economic point of view, however, knowledge of the set of efficient assignments and the various costs associated with each is of fundamental importance. For the valuations of time eventually decided upon (perhaps only implicitly) will be influenced not only by the diverse demands for speed on the part of shippers, but also by the extent to which a change from one efficient assignment to another enables a reduction of delay to one component of traffic at the expense of an increase of delay to another, or perhaps an increase in money cost. This latter information is precisely what we learn from the set of efficient

---

1. In the mathematician's language the problem is one of vector minimization.

assignments and the costs corresponding to each. The same considerations apply, of course, to labor, fuel, and other inputs, but since markets and prices exist for these commodities we have felt justified in
summing them up in money terms.

In the rest of this chapter and in the next two chapters we shall
attempt to explore the differences in costs between various assignments.
In Chapter 10 we shall examine assignments which differ only in grouping policies, in Chapter 11 those which differ only in scheduling policies. Since it is not immediately apparent that the work assigned to
yards changes with changes in scheduling, it should be recalled that,
not only does scheduling influence yard costs, directly, but also that
some schedules enable grouping and make-up policies not consistent
with other schedules. Only the direct influence will be treated in Chapter 11. In this chapter we shall be concerned with an exploratory, and
consequently rather general, discussion of these differences. In the
next two chapters, simplifying assumptions are made which enable more
rigorous discussions.

9.2. Two Extremes in Assignments

One of the earliest writers to give some attention to the problem of
selecting the classification policies for a system of yards was M. L.
Byers, a Chief Engineer, Maintenance of Way, on the Missouri Pacific
Railway. As early as 1908, he pointed out, as other authors have since
done, that generally speaking there are two extremes among policies:

(1) Where no classification is made until the car has arrived
at the last yard which it enters, it being left to this yard to separate such cars from those going to the yards beyond.

(2) Where each yard brings together all cars for the same
destination and then arranges the groups of cars in the train in the
order in which the yards follow.

For convenience we shall refer to these as the extreme deferment
and extreme anticipation methods. In evaluating the relative virtues of
these two policies, he went on to say that

The effect of [the anticipation] method as compared with the
[deferment method] is especially noticeable where the railroad
system contains one or more very large cities, toward which traffic gravitates from the other points on the system. The work of the
outlying yards is increased over that required of them by the [de-
ferment] method, but the work in each succeeding yard approaching
the final terminal is reduced, owing to part of the work having been
already performed by the outlying yard; the total work performed
by all of the yards is, however, considerably increased by the [an-
ticipation] method, and the sole excuse for its adoption should be
that the final yards are incapable of and cannot be made capable of
doing economically all of the classification work which would be
thrown upon them under a modification of the [deferment] method of
classification (Byers, 1908, p. 538-539).

Surprisingly enough, the method of anticipation, of which Byers is so critical, comes closer to describing present-day classification systems than does his method of deferment. Indeed, one modern writer, describing the classification policy of the Baltimore and Ohio, states, "The railroad's aim is to classify cars into destination blocks [i.e. groups] *as completely as possible near points of origin*, so that blocks (and sometimes whole trains) may be run without break-up through intermediate terminals to destination" (Coughlin, 1952, p. 45; italics ours).

9.3. Comparison of Assignments
when the Scheduling Policies Are Fixed

As a compromise between his two extremes, Byers recommended a method we have already described in Section 7.5 for the purpose of demonstrating our policy terminology. At this point the reader is invited to turn back to the description of this compromise plan, which, in addition to being of interest in its own right, is noteworthy for its uniqueness in the literature. Except for the two extremes described above, it is the only explicit and completely general proposal of a set of policies for a system of yards.

This plan, and especially that part of it which deals with the work a yard is to do after completing its "normal" work, serves as a good introduction to our discussion. A yard, according to Byers, should do sorting work on a through train above and beyond the normal amount specified by the deferment policy whenever it has available yard-engine time before the departure of the train. While nothing explicit is said about the scheduling policy, it is clear from this statement that "through" trains are dispatched by timetable, and that the particular timetable to be used has already been selected. The proposal therefore deals only with part of the problem of policy selection, and the assumption implicit in the discussion is that the best selection of scheduling policies has been accomplished. It is true that these policy suggestions have an interesting dynamic element which we have so far ignored. That the classification policy of a yard on a day of heavy traffic should be different from the policy on a day of light traffic is a very plausible consideration, but one we have felt justified in overlooking until the easier case of a constant policy has been more fully explored. We shall therefore assume that traffic flows are *about* the same from day to day, and proceed to examine Byers' suggestions under such conditions. It might be objected that under these conditions no yard would ever have any spare time in which to do extra work, for the schedule of trains would be tightened up throughout the system so as to eliminate the spare time. Such a tightening-up procedure would reduce the system of policies to one very much like the first extreme method; no account would be taken of the superiority, due to facilities or traffic, of one yard over another in the carrying out of classification work. We prefer to interpret the plan literally for the case of traffic flows that are fairly stable. We shall assume that for some unspecified reason the scheduling policies, i.e. the timetables, have been selected so as to leave some spare time at various places in the system. Since the spare time at any particular yard will under these conditions be constant, the amount of extra work this yard can do will be constant, and as a result its grouping and make-up policies will be fixed.

Let us suppose the schedules are arranged so as to allow yard A (Figure 7.6) enough spare time to carry out the first modified policy and the other yards no spare time at all. Then, if the plan is a good one, two implications become clear. The first is that the additional costs[2] incurred at A in carrying out the extra work are more than offset by the reduction in costs at B that result from A's sharing B's work load. The second implication of the plan is that the grouping of the through train at A, namely

$$
\left\{
\begin{array}{l}
\text{B} \quad \text{and local beyond B} \\
\text{C} \quad \text{and local beyond C} \\
\text{D} \quad \text{and beyond} \\
\text{D}' \quad \text{and beyond}
\end{array}
\right\} ,
$$

is better, in terms of system costs, than some other grouping that could also be accomplished in the time allowed by the schedule, for instance,

$$
\left\{
\begin{array}{l}
\text{B} \\
\text{local beyond B} \\
\text{E}' \text{ and local beyond E}' \\
\text{All others}
\end{array}
\right\} .
$$

As we saw in the last chapter, one of the most important influences of a policy change on yard costs operated through the variable "cuts per car." Clearly the modification of A's grouping policy increases cuts per car at that point. At the same time the number of cuts per car at B is reduced, because with the change in A's policy trains that previously arrived at B in a rather scrambled fashion are now grouped to a greater extent. Sorting costs therefore increase at A and decrease at B. Make-up costs will also increase at A since only two groups were put into the through train before the change, while now four are. Whether on balance the costs to the system go up or down depends on the sorting facilities at A and B. If A is a hump yard, and B a flat yard, then we should have good grounds for believing that the policy modification is a good one, for we know that an increase in cuts per car at a hump yard only slightly increases costs, while a reduction[3] in the same variable for a flat yard lowers costs considerably.

---

2. We are purposely ignoring Byers' stipulation that the extra work must not involve "increased cost," for additional work will always give rise to *some* cost at the yard that does the work. If we interpret his "cost" as system cost, then of course his condition begs the question of policy selection.

3. The increase in cuts per car at A will not in general be the same as the reduction in cuts per car at B. This point will become clearer in the discussion of Chapter 10.

But what if B is the hump yard and A the flat yard? In this case Byers' scheme seems to move us away from, rather than toward, an optimal assignment of classification work. At this point it could be argued that one of the functions of the scheduling policy is to timetable trains in such a way that only the most efficient yards have spare time remaining after the completion of their normal work. With respect to the considerations introduced so far this seems to be a legitimate argument. As we shall see later, however, when we begin to take accumulation delays into more explicit account, this approach to an optimal assignment which involves selecting scheduling policies first and grouping and make-up policies afterward is not satisfactory in general.

The second implication of Byers' plan is more difficult to defend. There seems to be no a priori reason why the grouping he suggests should result in less cost to the system than the arbitrary grouping we have suggested for purposes of comparison. While a more detailed examination of a problem similar to this one must be deferred to the next chapter, it is tempting to guess at Byers' reasons for selecting the particular grouping policy for A that he did. If traffic is evenly distributed throughout the network, and if long trips occur less frequently than short ones, the grouping proposed by Byers will cause all of the groups in a train to be of about the same length. Under the same circumstances our arbitrary grouping will bring about groups of very unequal lengths. The Group "E' and local beyond E'," for instance, will be small, and the group "All others" will be large. Now, group length is probably not a very important factor in yard costs, but the relative flow magnitudes of the various traffic classifications specified by the grouping policy are, and these are fairly well represented by group lengths. The relative levels of these flows influence sorting cost through their effect on the number of cuts per car, as we shall see at a later point. Thus whether or not Byers' grouping policy is to be preferred depends on the levels of the various traffic flows, and on the effect of these levels on the cuts-per-car variable.

For purposes of illustration let us suppose that Yard A in Figure 7.6 is a very large and efficient hump yard, while all the other yards in the system are small, ill-equipped flat yards. In this case, it is conceivable that there will be put into effect not only Byers' third policy modification but perhaps even a fourth or fifth such modification. Yard A will be doing some of the normal work of all the other yards in Figure 7.6. Group lengths on trains departing from A will become very much smaller than under a policy of less preclassification, and the question arises as to whether the relief afforded other yards does not begin to diminish as preclassification is carried beyond a certain point. If A puts cars bound for E' and local points beyond E' into a single group, this will not provide much saving of work at the next yard that groups this traffic, for the group from A (unless E' is an important destination) will be so small that the difference between the number of sorting operations when E' cars are grouped and when they are not is also small.

9.4. Extending Preclassification
at the Cost of Additional Accumulation Delay

By changing its make-up or scheduling policy (or both) A has still another means of saving sorting work for yards farther along the line in the direction of traffic. If a train with the E' group in it is scheduled to depart from A somewhat later than before, at the time of departure more E' cars than before will have accumulated at A, and the E' group in the outbound train will be longer than previously. Longer groups mean fewer cuts per car at an advance yard (say B) whose grouping policy does not contain finer classifications than that of A.[4]

The length of the E' group in an outbound train can also be increased — and this is probably the more important method — by changing the make-up policy at A so as to exclude E' traffic from some of the trains in which it was previously dispatched, and to exclude some of the other traffic from the trains that still contain E'. Thus perhaps before the change the make-up of several trains leaving A was[5]

$$\{ \ldots . |E|E'|\ F| . \ldots \} \ .$$

If this is changed for some trains to

$$\{ \ldots | E| \ldots \}$$

and for others to

$$\{ \ldots . |E|F| \ldots \} \ ,$$

then the group lengths of E, E', and F will all be longer than before and cuts per car at the advance yard will again be reduced. The cost at A will of course be in terms of accumulation delay to each of these components of traffic. Carried far enough this process leads to the "solid-train" type of make-up described earlier. The "maintracker" type of train, whose make-up is restricted to an extent that enables it to bypass some yards entirely, is another example.

---

4. The effect of longer groups on cuts per car is one of the "end effects" which for simplicity is assumed away in Chapter 10.

5. The dots are to be interpreted as groups which are not affected by the change. To save space, we have listed the groups horizontally rather than vertically as in Chapter 7.

Chapter 10

DIVISION OF SORTING WORK BETWEEN YARDS

10.1. Introduction

In this chapter we are concerned with the *sorting* work of yards. We shall show that because of the different characteristics of hump and flat yards it is sometimes useful to do sorting work at one yard which could possibly be done at another. Our object is to give a quantitative method for deciding when sorting should be transferred in this way. To develop such a method, we must know in more detail what determines the work required to carry out the sorting at each of the two types of yards.

We have seen that flat yards and hump yards differ in the way the cars are actually put onto the classification tracks. The assumption we shall make in the case of a hump yard is that no more work is involved in the humping operation whether there are few cuts in the train or many, that is, whether the order of the cars is scrambled up or not. There is some evidence (see Section 8.1.2) from actual yard data that if there are many cuts the operation takes longer, but since this effect of cuts in hump-yard operation is small relative to the same effect in flat-yard operation we shall ignore it in the case of a hump yard.

In the case of a flat yard we shall assume that the more scrambled up an incoming train is, that is, the more cuts there are in the train, the more work the switch engine will have to do, and the more time it will take to do it. To start with, it seems justifiable to take as a measure of the work done on a train the number of cuts in the train.

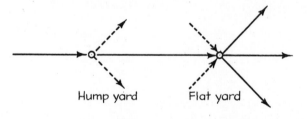

Hump yard   Flat yard

Figure 10.1

The situation we will consider is represented in Figure 10.1. Some of the traffic through the flat yard has previously passed through the hump yard. By recognizing more categories of traffic at the hump yard, that is, by finer sorting, it would be possible to save some of the work at

the flat yard. However, if cars are to depart in the same trains as before the change in grouping policy, this will involve additional make-up
work at the hump yard, for the outgoing trains will contain more groups
than before. We want to find some approach to the problem of balancing
these costs. We also want to find which of the categories at the flat
yard should be sorted out at the hump yard.

Preclassifying at the hump yard means that instead of all the traffic
for the flat yard going on a single classification track at the hump yard,
it goes onto two or more tracks. For example, if it goes on to two
tracks, on one of these tracks will be put traffic which goes on one group
of tracks in the flat yard, while traffic for the remaining group goes on
the other track. Thus the hump yard will do some preliminary sorting
for the flat yard. It may be that traffic for a single track at the flat yard
is sorted out with a classification track all to itself at the hump yard.
We will show, in fact, that under some circumstances this is the best
way for the hump yard to save work for the flat yard.

10.2. A Probability Representation of Trains

The composition of trains varies from train to train, even with
trains coming from the same point. Also, for any given classification
policy, the number of cuts (in a sense, the degree of scrambledness) of
trains varies. We will suppose that for simplicity of operation the
grouping policy will remain the same from train to train — that is, the
same classifications will be recognized despite these variations. Thus
the amount of work to be done in sorting at the flat yard will vary from
train to train. The work we shall be considering will be the average
over many trains.

We still have to find some useful way of representing the composition and order of cars in trains coming into the hump yard. There is a
strong analogy between an unsorted train and an unsorted pack of playing
cards. A shuffled pack of cards can best be represented by probability
methods, and this suggests that the order of cars in a train can be supposed to be represented by a similar type of probability model. However, the representation which we will use is rather different from that
used to represent the order of a pack of playing cards. Let us suppose
that the various suits in a pack represent the different categories of
cars. Then, in the train of 52 cars whose order the pack is supposed to
represent, there will always be exactly 13 of each of the four different
types of car. This would be a very unrealistic restriction in attempting
to describe the order and composition of a train. Consequently the first
and simplest probability description we use is the following one. Instead of supposing the trains to be represented by the shuffling of a pack,
we suppose they can be represented by drawing a sequence of cards in
order from a pack, replacing each card after it has been drawn and re-
shuffling after each drawing. Thus the proportion of cars of different
categories can change from train to train. Sequences obtained by this
method (they are called *multinomial* sequences) can easily be studied.

We have found them to give adequate representations of the composition of trains in several cases we have examined, provided the proportions of cards of different types are made to correspond with the data. However, the way in which trains are assembled suggests that such a representation will not always be adequate. Many shipments are in more than carload lots, so that, for example, three or four or perhaps more cars will stay together throughout the trip. If there is much of this prior grouping, cut lengths may well tend to be longer than the previous hypothesis (the multinomial hypothesis) admits. Even if cut lengths are changed, there is still a simple way of describing the cuts themselves as well mixed (as we expect them to be in an unsorted train). Our results extend to the case where the sequence of *cuts* is the same as the sequence of cuts in a multinomial sequence, though the number of cars in the cuts may be different from those in a multinomial sequence, so that the sequence of *cars* is not necessarily the same as that of a multinomial sequence.

10.3. The Best Sorting Policy

Suppose, for the moment, that it has been decided just how many categories to recognize at the hump yard; that is, the grouping policy is known. Suppose as an example we are to give over four of the tracks at the hump yard to preclassifying for the flat yard. Then we shall see that it would be best to sort out the three categories with the most cuts separately onto three of the tracks, and put all the rest of the cars onto the fourth track. If the number of cuts is roughly the same for all the categories, however, it does not matter what sort of preclassification policy is used, provided four tracks are actually used.

It should be emphasized that these results hold only if all the cuts come from the same type of sequence. If, as often will happen, the various incoming trains from various origins differ very much in their composition, the work function given below will have to be averaged over the different types of trains.

We should calculate this work function for each possible number of tracks of the hump yard devoted to preclassification. With each increase of this number, the extra work saved the flat yard diminishes, and the work involved in assembling trains at the hump yard increases. Thus at some point it becomes uneconomical to do further preclassification.

10.4*. Derivation of the Work Function for a Multinomial Sequence

The situation we will consider is represented in Figure 10.2. Traffic for a flat yard F passes through a hump yard H. At the flat yard n different categories are recognized, represented by $i = 1, 2 \ldots n$. The hump yard H is to do some preclassifying for F, and will recognize m different categories of traffic going beyond F. The problem is first to choose the categories to be recognized at H in order to save as much work as possible at F. We also have the problem of determining just how much work this saves at F, so that this work saved can be weighed against increased costs at H. Finally, choice of the best value of m is still another problem.

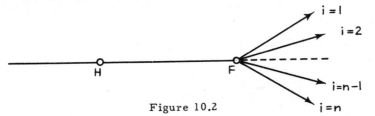

Figure 10.2

We take as a measure of work at F the average number of cuts per car for traffic coming in to F. A cut consists of an uninterrupted sequence of cars of the same category. It is the same as a run in probability theory. For example: for the sequence of cars 2 2 1 3 1 1 1 3 3 2 there are 6 cuts, so cuts per car equals 0.6.

Suppose at first that the sequence of cars coming over the hump at H, and bound for F, is a multinomial sequence with probabilities p_i. The sequence is assumed to be long, so that we can neglect the end effects both of the original sequence and the sequences into which it is divided by the preclassification. (As already indicated, we shall later suggest a more general hypothesis, which allows for the fact that shipments are often made in more than carload lots.)

For a multinomial sequence, the probability that any designated car is the first car of a cut of i's is $p_i(1 - p_i)$. Therefore the probability that a car is the first car of any cut is $\sum_{i=1}^{n} p_i(1 - p_i)$. It follows that the mean number of cuts per car equals $1 - \sum_{i=1}^{n} p_i^2$, and this is an index of work at F if H does no preclassifying.

If H preclassifies the traffic bound for F into m classes, these classes are formed by a partition of the categories $1, 2, .., n$ into m mutually exclusive subsets $\mu_1, \mu_2, \ldots, \mu_m$. This partition defines F's grouping policy for traffic bound to H and beyond. The cars now arrive at F in a series of runs, each run consisting of cars belonging to a μ_j $(j = 1, .., m)$.

If we ignore end effects of such runs, the mean number of cuts per car for cars of μ_j is

$$(10.1) \qquad 1 - \sum_{i \in \mu_j} \left(\frac{p_i}{\sum_{i \in \mu_j} p_i} \right)^2 \quad .$$

But a proportion $\sum_{i \in \mu_j} p_i$ of all the cars belong to μ_j. Therefore the mean number of cuts per car for all cars is

$$(10.2) \quad \sum_{j=1}^{m} \left[\sum_{i\epsilon\mu_j} p_i \right] \left[1 - \sum_{i\epsilon\mu_j} \left(\frac{p_i}{\sum_{i\epsilon\mu_j} p_i} \right)^2 \right] = 1 - \sum_{j=1}^{m} \frac{\sum_{i\epsilon\mu_j} p_i^2}{\sum_{i\epsilon\mu_j} p_i} \ .$$

The difference between this and $1 - \sum_{i=1}^{n} p_i^2$ is

$$(10.3) \quad \sum_{j=1}^{m} \frac{\sum_{i\epsilon\mu_j} p_i^2}{\sum_{i\epsilon\mu_j} p_i} - \sum_{i=1}^{n} p_i^2$$

and represents an index of the amount of work the given grouping policy saves for F.

We wish to find what partition $\mu_1, \ldots, \mu_m$ will leave the minimum work to F. Let us renumber the classification so that $0 < p_1 \leq p_2 \leq \ldots \leq p_n$. Then for any partition $\mu_1, \ldots, \mu_m$ of the numbers $1, 2, \ldots, n$, we can show that

$$(10.4) \quad \sum_{j=1}^{m} \frac{\sum_{i\epsilon\mu_j} p_i^2}{\sum_{i\epsilon\mu_j} p_i} \leq p_n + p_{n-1} + \ldots + p_{n-m+2} + \frac{\sum_{i=1}^{n-m+1} p_i^2}{\sum_{i=1}^{n-m+1} p_i} \ .$$

That is, the partition which maximizes the left-hand sum and thus maximizes the saving to F is $[1, 2, \ldots, n - m + 1], [n - m + 2], \ldots, [n - 1], [n]$. First we will prove the result for $m = 2$; that is, the n classifications are divided into two groups, μ_1 and μ_2. Let μ_2 be the group that contains n, the most frequent classification, and let μ_2' be the remainder of μ_2. Furthermore, let

$$(10.5) \quad \sum_{i\epsilon\mu_1} p_i \equiv \alpha \quad \text{and} \quad \sum_{i\epsilon\mu_2'} p_i \equiv \beta$$

and

$$(10.6) \quad \frac{\sum_{i\epsilon\mu_1} p_i^2}{\sum_{i\epsilon\mu_1} p_i} \equiv a \quad \text{and} \quad \frac{\sum_{i\epsilon\mu_2'} p_i^2}{\sum_{i\epsilon\mu_2'} p_i} \equiv b \ .$$

Note that

$$(10.7) \quad a \sum_{i\epsilon\mu_1} p_i = \sum_{i\epsilon\mu_1} p_i^2 \leq \left(\sum_{i\epsilon\mu_1} p_i \right)^2 = \alpha \sum_{i\epsilon\mu_1} p_i \ ,$$

so that $a \leq \alpha$. Also,

$$(10.8) \quad \sum_{i\epsilon\mu_1} p_i^2 \leq \sum_{i\epsilon\mu_1} p_n p_i = p_n \sum_{i\epsilon\mu_1} p_i \ ,$$

so that $a \leqq p_n$ and, similarly, $b \leqq p_n$. Substituting these values in (10.4), we are to show that

$$(10.9) \qquad a + \frac{p_n + b\beta}{p_n + \beta} \leqq p_n + \frac{a\alpha + b\beta}{\alpha + \beta} \quad .$$

Multiplying by $\frac{1}{\beta}(p_n + \beta)(\alpha + \beta)$, which is positive, (10.9) becomes

$$(10.10) \qquad ap_n + a\beta + \alpha b \leqq bp_n + \alpha p_n + p_n\beta \quad .$$

Adding ab to both sides, this can be written

$$(10.11) \qquad - (p_n - b)(\alpha - a) - (p_n - a)(b + \beta) \leqq 0 \quad .$$

All four of the quantities in parentheses are positive. Hence the inequality must hold, proving (10.4) for the case m = 2.

Now consider any partition $\mu_1, \mu_2, \ldots, \mu_m$, and let μ_1 be the group containing the most frequent classification n. Applying the theorem of (10.4), just proved for m = 2, to the universe consisting of $\mu_1 + \mu_2$, the expression on the left-hand side of (10.4) will not be diminished if we replace $\mu_1, \mu_2, \ldots, \mu_m$ by $\mu_1', \mu_2', \ldots, \mu_m'$, where $\mu_1' = (n)$, $\mu_2' = \mu_1 + \mu_2$ $- (n)$, $\mu_3' = \mu_3, \ldots, \mu_m' = \mu_m$. Again, let μ_i' be the group containing classification n - 1. Replace μ_i' and μ_j' ($i \neq j$, $i \neq 1$, $j \neq 1$) by $(n - 1)$ and $\mu_i' + \mu_j' - (n - 1)$ respectively. The inequality (10.4) follows after m such steps.

From this theorem we see that it is best under these conditions to select the m - 1 classes with highest probabilities and preclassify them separately. Note though that if $p_1 = p_2 = \ldots = p_n = \frac{1}{n} \equiv p$, then both sides of (10.4) reduce to mp, and it becomes quite immaterial what preclassification policy we use.

10.5*. *Extension to a More General Type of Sequence*

Although the multinomial sequence can often give quite a good representation of the incoming car sequence, it is rather restrictive. This can be seen especially if loads are shipped in more than carload lots. Then a run of cars is kept together throughout a trip, and in fact treated as a single car for sorting purposes. Thus mean cut length will tend to be longer than that expected from the multinomial distribution. However, the results of previous sections apply to a more general incoming sequence which will include this case.

This generalization is achieved by thinking of the incoming sequence as a sequence of cuts rather than individual cars. We will call a group of cars which form a cut before sorting a *segment* to distinguish it from a group of cars forming a cut after sorting. The latter we will still call a cut. Let A_i be a segment of incoming cars of type i. By the definition of a segment, no two segments of the same type can be together in the incoming sequence. Suppose the sequence of segments is generated by a Markoff chain with constant transition probabilities

$$(10.12) \qquad p_{ij} = \frac{p_j}{1 - p_i} \qquad (i \neq j)$$

$$= 0 \qquad (i = j)$$

(as in the case where the incoming cars are a multinomial sequence). We shall allow the number of cars within segments to be distributed in any manner whatever. Suppose now that the A_i are classified, as in the previous sections, by partitioning the i into m groups $\mu_1, \ldots, \mu_m$. After sorting, each cut will contain one or more segments. It is therefore possible to talk of cuts per segment. Let x be the mean number of cars per segment, and let y be the mean number of cuts per segment after sorting. Then $\frac{y}{x}$ equals the mean number of cuts per car after sorting.

We can find y as follows. If the original sequence is multinomial, as in the previous less general case, then the segments before sorting will be generated by a Markoff chain of type (10.12). In the case of the multinomial sequence, the mean number of cars per segment equals

$$(10.13) \qquad x_0 = \frac{1}{\sum_{i=1}^{n} p_i(1-p_i)} \quad ,$$

and we saw from (10.2) that the mean number of cuts per car after sorting equals

$$(10.14) \qquad \frac{y_0}{x_0} = 1 - \sum_{j=1}^{m} \frac{\sum_{i\epsilon\mu_j} p_i^2}{\sum_{i\epsilon\mu_j} p_i} \quad .$$

We have used the subscript *zero* to indicate that the values refer to a multinomial sequence.

For the multinomial sequence we now have

$$(10.15) \qquad y_0 = \frac{y_0}{x_0} = \frac{1}{\sum_{i=1}^{n} p_i(1-p_i)} \left\{ 1 - \sum_{j=1}^{m} \frac{\sum_{i\epsilon\mu_j} p_i^2}{\sum_{i\epsilon\mu_j} p_i} \right\} \quad .$$

But the insertion of additional cars in the various segments (or their removal, provided at least one car is left in each segment) in no way affects the relation of cuts to segments after classification, so that this result must hold for the general sequence in which the lengths of the segments may have any distribution. For the general sequence, therefore, the mean number of cuts per car after sorting equals

$$(10.16) \qquad \frac{y}{x} = \frac{y_0}{x} = \frac{1}{x\sum_{i=1}^{n} p_i(1-p_i)} \left\{ 1 - \sum_{j=1}^{m} \frac{\sum_{i\epsilon\mu_j} p_i^2}{\sum_{i\epsilon\mu_j} p_i} \right\} \quad .$$

This new work function, considered as a function of the partitioning of the classification, differs only by a constant factor from the function for the simpler case and is therefore minimized for the same partition as before.

Chapter 11

SCHEDULING OF TRAINS
TO MINIMIZE ACCUMULATION DELAY

11.1. Introductory Remarks

In the preceding chapters we have discussed classification policy
without much explicit reference to the scheduling of trains between
yards. In the present chapter, we shall discuss scheduling policy without much reference to the other aspects of classification policy. In addition, we disregard any restrictions on schedules that may result from
limited track capacity. The integration of the study of classification and
scheduling under conditions of limited track capacity is a task that sur-
passes the scope of the present studies.

Implicit in the analysis of this chapter are therefore the assumption
that track capacity is sufficient to accommodate without congestion any
schedule under consideration and the further assumption that none of the
schedules considered will raise classification costs by creating congestion at yards.

In fact, even if the scheduling problem is thus artificially isolated
from the other operation problems, it still has great complexity. In
this chapter we shall consider in some detail only the case of a network
consisting of a single line on which each train is reclassified at each
terminal, and on which traffic flows in one direction only. After that,
we shall make some more general comments on maintrackers (trains
that by-pass intermediate terminals), on two-way traffic, on lines with
side branches, and on networks containing circuits.

11.2. A Simple Scheduling Problem Considered

Let us first consider a network consisting of four terminals only,
labeled i = 1, 2, 3, 4 and arranged along a single line as shown in Figure 11.1. We shall consider given amounts of traffic (denoted by x_{ij}),
expressed in numbers of cars per unit period (day, week), from any
terminal i to any terminal j east of it (that is, such that $i < j$). Ignoring westbound traffic in the discussion means assuming that there is no
interference of opposite flows on tracks or in classification operations.
It also means assuming that there are no "side branches" to our network. The presence of a side branch out of a certain terminal would
place a premium on coordinating train departures from that terminal in
opposite directions among the main line with the arrival of a train to
that terminal from the side branch.

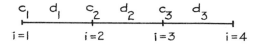

Figure 11.1.
Network Consisting of a Single Line

Of course continuing flows of eastbound traffic need to be offset by equal flows of loaded or empty cars in the opposite direction in order to keep the same pool of cars in operation. We shall not include the cost of this return flow of cars in our considerations, but assume that any saving of car-days by greater economy of scheduling eastbound flows, resulting on the average in earlier arrival of cars at destinations, will be a gain that is not offset by delays in the westbound return flow.

We shall assume further that trains run only from any one terminal to the immediately following one. The time required for the trip from i to $i + 1$ will be denoted d_i. It is assumed to be constant and independent of the length of the train. At any terminal, arriving trains are broken up, cars destined for that terminal are removed, and cars originating in that terminal for destinations east are added. The time needed for this operation is again assumed independent of the number of cars involved and is denoted by c_i, if i labels the terminal in question. If a train is scheduled to leave from terminal i at time t_i, cars can be incorporated in it if and only if delivered for classification, whether from local origins or from incoming traffic, not later than $t_i - c_i$.

We shall discuss only periodic schedules. By this we mean a list of departure times for trains eastbound from each terminal which repeats itself with a constant period. While this might be thought of equally well as a week, or as a two-day period, we shall speak of it for simplicity as a "day."

Let us assume that the given program specifies the following daily flows of cars from i to j, where $i < j$:

(11.1)

x_{ij}	$j=2$	3	4
$i=1$	45	15	20
2		110	25
3			50

It is useful also to register for each of the three stretches of line the total daily flows arising from these figures,

(11.2)
$$\begin{cases} \text{on } (1,2) & x_{12} + x_{13} + x_{14} & = 80 \\ \text{on } (2,3) & x_{13} + x_{14} + x_{23} + x_{24} = 170 \\ \text{on } (3,4) & x_{14} + x_{24} + x_{34} & = 95 \end{cases}$$

For simplicity, we shall assume further, against better knowledge, that these cars become available at each originating terminal at an even rate around the clock. This assumption will enable us to consider more effectively other aspects of the scheduling problem. Ultimately, of course, it will have to be replaced by a more realistic specification.

The first question arising in making up a schedule is how many trains per day to run on each of the three stretches. On the basis of the figures in (11.3), let us somewhat arbitrarily decide that we shall schedule one train daily on the stretches (1,2) and (3,4) and two trains daily on (2,3). Then the trains on (1,2) and (3,4) will contain 80 and 95 cars, respectively, while the two daily trains on (2,3) will average $\frac{170}{2}$ = 85 cars. A possible daily schedule, which has the appeal of simplicity and symmetry, is that represented by Figure 11.2. The slanted straight lines represent actual travel of trains at constant "speed." However, the straightness of the lines and the interpretation of the vertical axis as "distance" from terminal 1 are immaterial. All that matters is that there is a constant travel time d_i on each stretch, and a constant minimum classification time c_i for inclusion in each train.

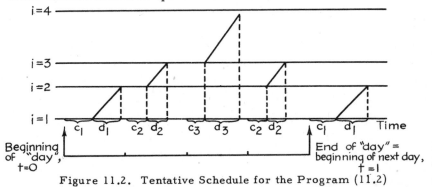

Figure 11.2. Tentative Schedule for the Program (11.2)

Before going into the question of the suitability of this schedule for the program (11.2) at hand, it will be useful to introduce a simplification in the treatment of time. For simplicity, let the point marked "beginning of day" at terminal i = 1 correspond to midnight. Then we decide to measure time at terminal 2, for the purposes of our analysis, on a clock which shows midnight when it is actually $(c_1 + d_1)$ beyond midnight, that is, at the earliest possible time of arrival at the terminal 2 in question of a train for which classification operations are started at terminal 1 at midnight. Similarly, at terminal 3, we measure time on a clock showing midnight at a still later time, later by the corresponding interval $(c_2 + d_2)$ between starting classification at terminal 2 and earliest possible arrival at 3, etc. Let us call this artificial time scale (which is different in different terminals) "referred time" and denote it by the symbol s. This is a time measurement "referred" to actual time at terminal 1, in the sense that at 11 AM actual time, say, the referred time at some terminal i is measured by the latest actual time at which a car could conceivably enter classification at terminal 1 and by an uninterrupted sequence of classification operations and travel in suitably scheduled trains reach terminal i at 11 AM. If actual time is denoted by t, actual and referred time are related as follows:

$$(11.3) \quad \begin{cases} \text{at terminal 1,} & s = t, \\ \text{at terminal 2,} & s = t-c_1-d_1, \\ \text{at terminal 3,} & s = t-c_1-d_1-c_2-d_2, \\ \text{at terminal 4,} & s = t-c_1-d_1-c_2-d_2-c_3-d_3 \quad. \end{cases}$$

In a single-line network with n terminals, referred time at the i-th yard is similarly given by

$$(11.4) \quad s = t-c_1-d_1-c_2-d_2- \ldots -c_{i-1}-d_{i-1} \quad.$$

The advantage of the use of referred time lies in the fact that the referred times of the starting of classification of a train at a terminal i and of its arrival at the next terminal i + 1 are the same. Hence, in Figure 11.3 eastbound trains can now be represented by vertical arrows. Each such train is fully defined by its referred "timing" s and by the stretch (i, i + 1) on which it travels. The times required for classification and travel (by assumption constant!) no longer clutter up our diagram. For a car to make a connection between trains at a given terminal, all that is necessary is that the arrow representing the incoming train is not to the right of the arrow representing the outgoing train. From here on, we shall often omit the word "referred" in the phrases "referred time" and "referred timing."

Let us now have a close look at the particular schedule of Figure 11.2, represented in referred time by Figure 11.3. We shall first ask the question whether this schedule could be improved without adding or taking out trains, merely by changes in the timing of trains. If we take

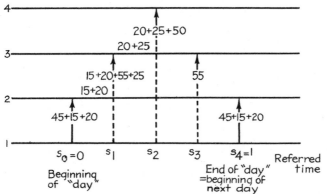

Figure 11.3. Schedule of Figure 11.2.Expressed in Referred Time

the day as the unit of time, we can write $s_0 = 0$ and $s_4 = 1$ for the timing of the (1,2)-train at "beginning" and "end" of day. The quantities to be chosen then are the timings s_1, s_2, s_3 of the first (2,3)-train, the (3,4)-train, and the second (2,3)-train, to be repeated periodically on subsequent days. The choice is to be made in the light of the effect of changes in these timings on various costs.

In the present simple example, the main effect is on accumulation delay, here represented as the waiting of cars for classification operations to start for the next train, although in actual operation this waiting may occur as well after classification. There are two categories of such cars, which we shall call locally originated cars and cars in transit. At any yard i the number of locally originated cars (i.e. originated at i) that are waiting increases with time, by assumption at a constant rate, until classification starts, at which time the number falls to zero and thereafter grows again. For schedules with equal time intervals between trains on each stretch, as exhibited in Figure 11.3, the average number of waiting cars in this category depends, for a given rate of local origination, only on the frequency of trains (one, two, or more per day), but is independent of the timing of the first train in each day. Hence, as long as we keep $s_3 = s_1 + \frac{1}{2}$, we can change s_1 and s_2 without affecting the number of cars waiting in this category.

More interesting is the second category of cars, those waiting for connections between trains. Figure 11.3 shows with each arrow the number of cars assignable to the corresponding train. It also shows the number of cars waiting in transit (in the second category), written in with the time interval during which they wait. (The figure does not record the variable numbers of waiting cars in the category of locally originated cars.)

A moment's reflection will show that in the present simple case there is no need for any waiting between connections. If we make $s_2 = s_1 = 0$ (and keep $s_3 = s_1 + \frac{1}{2} = \frac{1}{2}$) as in Figure 11.4, we cut out all the accumulation delay between connections at terminals 2 and 3 without incurring any costs elsewhere. Obviously, then, the schedule of Figure 11.4 is superior to that of Figure 11.3. Of course, s_2 should not be made less than s_1, or s_1 less than zero, because in that case connections are missed, and accumulation delay greatly increases.

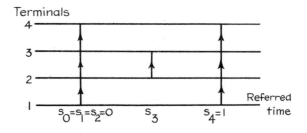

Figure 11.4. Improved Schedule for Program (11.2)

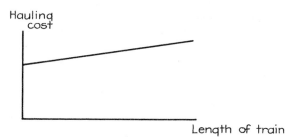

Figure 11.5.
Hauling Cost and Length of Train

Let us finally ask whether $\frac{1}{2}$ is the best value for s_3. Variation of s_3 affects the accumulation delay of locally originated cars at terminal 2. It may also affect hauling cost on the stretch (2,3). Making s_3 larger shifts cars from the 115-car train timed at $s_4 = s_1 + 1$ to the 55-car train timed at s_3. This will save hauling cost if the cost of an extra car to a long train exceeds that of an extra car to a short one. Beyond a certain length of train this will undoubtedly be the case. For the present, we shall assume that on each stretch, within the range of train lengths considered, the hauling cost of an extra car is independent of the length of the train. This is indicated by the constant slope of the hauling cost curve in Figure 11.5. In that case, changes in s_3 have no consequences for hauling cost.

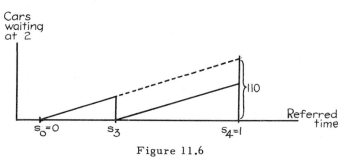

Figure 11.6
Minimization of Accumulation Delay

It remains to trace the effect of a change in s_3 on accumulation delay. In Figure 11.6 the total of this delay incurred each day is represented by the sum of the areas of two triangles bounded by the horizontal axis and the straight-line segments representing number of cars waiting at any time. This sum equals

(11.5)
$$\frac{1}{2} s_3 \cdot (110\ s_3) + \frac{1}{2} (1 - s_3) \cdot 110\ (1 - s_3)$$
$$= 55\ [\,s_3^2 + (1 - s_3)^2\,]\ ,$$

where the figure 110 represents the daily flow of (2,3)-cars according to the program (11.2). It is easily seen by means of calculus that this expression is minimized by $s_3 = \frac{1}{2}$ — that is, by making the intervals between successive trains equal.

The reader may wonder why the 25 cars originating daily at terminal 2 for terminal 4 have not been included in this calculation. A moment's reflection will show that this would not have affected the outcome. It is readily seen from Figure 11.4 that cars in this flow could not arrive at terminal 4 any earlier by taking the train timed at s_3 as far as 3. This would merely transfer the location at which (and the "category" in which) a part of their waiting time is incurred, not the total amount of waiting. For this reason, we have in Figure 11.3 arbitrarily assigned all such cars to the s_1-train to avoid ambiguity in the definition of categories.

In order that the meaning of the "best" schedule in Figure 11.4 be entirely clear, we translate it back to natural time in Figure 11.7.

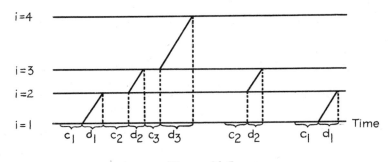

Figure 11.7.
The Schedule of Figure 11.4 in Natural Time

The simple case considered so far suggests that if on two successive stretches we schedule trains with equal frequency, there is no reason for introducing time intervals between arrival and departure of "connecting" trains beyond the minimum necessary for the classification operations that permit cars to make the connection. It also suggests that if more than one train a day is scheduled for a flow or group of flows in a program that permits us to look at this scheduling problem in isolation, constant rates of origination during the day call for equal time intervals between successive trains.

The latter inference does not extend to cases where traffic flows extend over successive stretches, whenever trains run on these stretches with different frequencies neither one of which is an integral multiple of the other. For instance, while the schedule of Figure 11.8 would be optimal for a program with three terminals such that $x_{13} = 0$, $x_{12} = 180$, $x_{23} = 270$, the introduction of a positive flow x_{13} straddling both stretches of line would call for s_3 and s_4 to approach each other (see

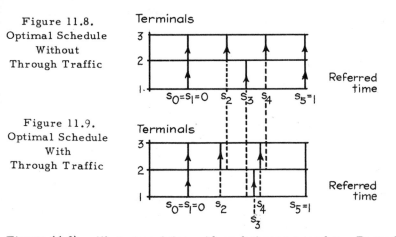

Figure 11.8.
Optimal Schedule
Without
Through Traffic

Figure 11.9.
Optimal Schedule
With
Through Traffic

Figure 11.9), with s_2 remaining midway between s_0 and s_4. Beyond a certain critical amount of (1,3)-traffic density s_3 and s_4 would actually coincide.

The broad outlines of the scheduling problem on a single line with constant rates of origination begin to show up from the preceding discussion. Daily frequency of trains on a given stretch is to be related to the total amount of traffic using that stretch. There is an advantage in running trains on successive stretches as closely timed as possible without causing cars to miss connections. This advantage is stronger, the larger the amount of traffic using several successive stretches. On the other hand, there is an advantage in equal spacing of successive trains on the same stretch. This advantage is stronger, the less the through-flows of traffic tying the scheduling on this stretch up with that on other stretches where different frequencies of trains are more economical. Thus where local traffic is relatively high, trains will tend to be spaced out evenly over the day; where through traffic is high at least some trains will be scheduled to meet connections more closely.

In the next section, we illustrate how, through the use of calculus and of computation procedures based on trial and error, the best compromise between these considerations can be found when they pull in different directions. This section can be passed over by the reader who is not interested in mathematical aspects of the problem.

11.3*. Schedules of Given Structure
that Minimize Accumulation Delay

In this section we shall maintain the assumptions of a one-way single line network, with terminals $i = 1, 2, \ldots, n$; of constant rates of origination x_{ij} on all routes such that $1 \leqq i < j \leqq n$; of constant classification times c_i and travel times d_{ij}; of a periodical schedule; and of a hauling cost on each stretch which depends linearly on length of train. The discussion in the preceding section has suggested that it will often be economical to telescope trains on successive stretches of line. Let us therefore call a *run* any (maximal) sequence of trains on successive stretches timed so as to leave only the minimum interval needed for classification between arrivals and departures at connecting terminals. In terms of referred time, a run is a (maximal) sequence of trains on successive stretches with identical referred arrival times, to be called also the (referred) *timing* of the run. A run will be denoted by $(s; i, j)$ where s is the (referred) time of arrival anywhere, i the terminal of departure of the first train of the run, j the terminal of arrival of the last one, $1 \leqq i$, $i \leqq j - 1$, $j \leqq n$. These terminals will be called beginning and end of the run. The word "maximal" is inserted in the definition because, in the schedule of Figure 11.4 for instance, we do not wish to consider the sequence $(s_0; 1, 3)$ as a run, since it can be extended to a larger sequence $(s_0; 1, 4)$ which also meets the other specification in the definition. The latter sequence is regarded as a run because no further such extension is possible. A single train can also be a run, namely, if there is no connecting train with the same (referred) timing at either its departure or arrival point.

A (periodic) schedule can now be regarded as a statement of all runs $(s_r; i_r, j_r)$, $r = 0, \ldots, R - 1$ provided for in one day. The periodicity can be expressed by the requirements

$$(11.6) \qquad s_{r+R} = s_r + 1, \qquad i_{r+R} = i_r, \qquad j_{r+R} = j_r,$$

and the time-scale can be made definite by requiring

$$(11.7) \qquad s_0 = 0 \quad .$$

It appears natural to label runs in order of increasing s_r. However, this would still leave an ambiguity when two runs have identical timing, and anyway it would be more restrictive than is desirable. For purposes that will become clear below, we will permit any labeling of runs such that within the set of all runs that "contain" any given terminal i, that is, of all runs r such that

$$(11.8) \qquad i_r \leqq i \leqq j_r \quad ,$$

the timing s_r shall increase whenever r increases. Under this rule any of the three schedules in Figure 11.10 are properly labeled, even though in each of them the labels $r = 2$ and $r = 3$ could as well have been interchanged.

Another suggestion implied in previous discussions is that it may be useful to separate the problem of determining the precise timing of the runs in a schedule from the problem of how many runs to have, which terminals to select as their end points, and in what order to place these runs on the referred time scale. To express the latter choices we shall introduce the notion of the *structure* of a schedule. We shall say that two schedules have the same structure if we can label the runs

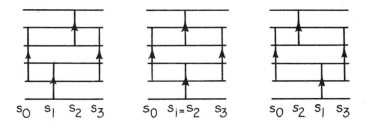

Figure 11.10. Three Schedules with Identical Structures

of each, consistently with the above rules of labeling, in such a way that corresponding runs (i.e. runs with the same label) have identical beginning and end points. Under this definition the three schedules of Figure 11.10, for instance, have identical structures. On the other hand, the two schedules in Figure 11.11 have different structures. Thus any two schedules of which one is obtainable from the other by horizontal displacements of arrows without any two arrows either touching or overlapping during the displacement, have the same structure. Any two schedules for which this is not possible have different structures.

Figure 11.11. Two Schedules with Different Structures

We now recall our assumption that hauling cost on each stretch is a linear function of train length. Total daily hauling cost therefore depends only on the number of trains per day scheduled for each stretch, and not on how the daily quota of cars on each stretch is distributed over successive trains. In particular, then, hauling cost is the same for all schedules with the same structure, and that irrespective of how cars are assigned to trains with any given schedule.

With hauling cost constant, the problem of finding the most economical schedule of given structure (the most economical timings for its runs) is a problem of minimizing the accumulation delay incurred daily in carrying out the given program. We shall show that this problem is equivalent to solving a system of R-1 linear equations in an equal number of unknowns: the timings of all runs in a day except the first. We shall also indicate how the data of the problem — that is, the given transportation program x_{ij} and the given structure of the schedule — enter into the coefficients of the equation system. Algebraic expressions will apply to a line with n terminals and an arbitrary schedule structure.

The latter is represented by a set of R runs $(s_r; i_r, j_r)$ of which the end points (i_r, j_r) are given for $r = 0, \ldots, R - 1$, and of which the timings are restricted, apart from the periodicity requirements (11.6) and (11.7), only by the stipulation that for any terminal i the timings s_r of those runs that contain i, as defined by (11.8), form a sequence increasing as r increases.

Before studying the minimization of accumulation delay by proper choice of a schedule from among those of given structure, we must consider for a moment the assignment of cars to trains in a given schedule (that is, with timings of runs given as well). Even here there is a problem, although a trivial one, of minimizing accumulation delay. Waste of car-days would result if cars by being held over to later trains would miss connections and thereby arrive at destinations later than they could have. A simple rule that is sure to avoid this mistake would be to let each car proceed with the first (eastbound) train that leaves. However, for purposes of analysis only we prefer to specify another assignment rule which likewise avoids the kind of waste we are now considering. This rule has the advantage of giving us readily a simpler formula for the minimum accumulation delay associated with a given schedule. It specifies that a car originating in i at some time s for destination j should be incorporated at i in the latest train that permits it, through subsequent connections if necessary, to arrive at j at the earliest possible moment.

A situation where this rule differs from the earliest-possible-departure rule was already encountered in Figure 11.4. A car originating at 2 just before s_3 with destination 4 has an earliest arrival time s and can achieve this by leaving 2 either at time s_3 or at s_4. In practice, of course, such a choice would be determined by other considerations, such as the lengths of the trains in question. Where under our simplifying assumptions these considerations are inactive, we choose our assignment rule merely to help the analysis forward. The rule as given does not always completely specify the assignment. At some connection point k between i and j another situation may arise where the passing up of a departing train does not delay earliest possible arrival at j. While it would be easy to extend our assignment rule to create definiteness at all intermediate points, we will not need to do so for our present purpose.

We shall now define, for each traffic flow x_{ij} between given terminals i and j, what we shall call critical departure times v_q^{ij} from i and critical arrival times w_q^{ij} at j, where $q = 1, 2, \ldots Q_{ij}$. We shall illustrate the definition with the example of $(i,j) = (1,5)$-traffic in the schedule of Figure 11.12. Let r_i be the label r of the lowest-numbered run $(s_r; i_r, j_r)$, in the schedule $r = 0, \ldots, R - 1$, containing a train that leaves i. In Figure 11.12, we find $r_1 = 0$, because the first train in the run labeled $r = 0$ leaves terminal $i = 1$. We define w_1^{ij} as the earliest possible arrival time at j for a car available at i at time s_{r_1}. In Figure 11.12 we find $w_1^{15} = s_0$ because run (0; 1, 5) reaches as far as terminal $j = 5$. We also define v_1^{ij} as the latest departure time from i that

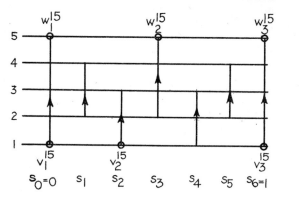

Figure 11.12.

Example of a Schedule

permits a car to arrive at j at time w_1^{ij}. In Figure 11.12 this is again $w_1^{15} = s_0$.

Next we define w_2^{ij} as the earliest arrival time at j of a car originating at i immediately following the critical time v_1^{ij} for earlier arrival, and v_2^{ij} as the latest departure time from i permitting arrival at j at time w_2^{ij}. In Figure 11.12, we have $w_2^{15} = s_3$, and $v_2^{15} = s_2$. In this manner we go on until we reach the end of the daily schedule. In Figure 11.12, $w_3^{15} = w_1^{15} + 1$, and hence we define $Q_{15} = 2$ as the number of critical (departure and arrival) times found within one day's schedule. That is, we choose Q_{ij} so that $w_{Q_{ij}+1}^{ij} = w_1^{ij} + 1$. It is clear that the number Q_{ij} and the location in time of critical points can vary with the pair of terminals (i,j) considered. For instance, for $(1,4)$-traffic in Figure 11.12 we have $Q_{14} = 3$.

The accumulation delay sustained by (i,j)-cars under our assignment rule can now be expressed as follows. During the first "critical interval" at i, that is during the time period

(11.9) $v_1^{ij} < s \leq v_2^{ij}$,

the number of n of (i,j)-cars waiting at time s is a linear function of s,

(11.10) $n = x_{ij}(s - v_1^{ij})$.

Expressed in car-days, the total delay incurred by these cars in this interval is (omitting temporarily the subscripts and superscript i,j)

(11.11) $\int_{v_1}^{v_2} x(s - v_1)\, ds = \frac{1}{2} x (v_2 - v_1)^2$.

At time v_2 a block of $x(v_2 - v_1)$ cars is ready to leave. Before it reaches j at the critical arrival time w_2, each car sustains another delay of length $(w_2 - v_2)$, where the place incurred (but not the length) of this delay may depend on further assignment decisions that we have not bothered to specify. Total delay of this kind, in car-days, therefore equals

(11.12) $x (v_2 - v_1) (w_2 - v_2)$.

The two types of delays represented by (11.11) and (11.12) have to be added up for all critical intervals in one day's schedule, to give us the accumulation delay y for any one traffic flow

$$(11.13) \qquad y = x \sum_{q=1}^{Q} \left[\frac{1}{2} (v_{q+1} - v_q)^2 + (v_{q+1} - v_q)(w_{q+1} - v_{q+1}) \right].$$

Finally, to obtain total accumulation delay Y, indices i,j designating the traffic flow have to be restored to this expression, whereupon these amounts need to be summed over all traffic flows (i,j),

$$(11.14) \qquad Y = \sum_{i=1}^{n-1} \sum_{j=i+1}^{n} x_{ij} A_{ij} ,$$

where

$$(11.15) \qquad A_{ij} = \sum_{q=1}^{Q_{ij}} \left[\frac{1}{2} (v_{q+1}^{ij} - v_q^{ij})^2 + (v_{q+1}^{ij} - v_q^{ij})(w_{q+1}^{ij} - v_{q+1}^{ij}) \right].$$

The expression for Y we need to minimize is given by (11.14) and (11.15). We note that it is a quadratic function of the unknown timings s_r, which occur in the guise of critical arrival or departure times associated with particular flows (i,j). None of the unknowns is missed, because the timing s_r of any run $(s_r; i_r, j_r)$ always coincides with a pair of critical departure and arrival times for all flows (i,j) between terminals contained in that run, and we would not include in a proposed schedule any run on which there is no traffic between any two terminals of the run (i.e. any run (s; i,j) for which $x_{m,n} = 0$ for all m,n such that $i \leq m < n \leq j$).

For any given schedule structure, the expression (11.14) can be set up by a graphical procedure which we illustrate in Figure 11.13, based on a schedule of the structure exhibited in Figure 11.12. Dotted lines immediately to the left of the vertical lines that represent runs are traced upward, those to the right downward. Dotted lines immediately

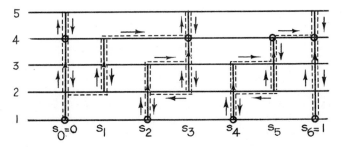

Figure 11.13. Determination of Critical Times for the
Schedule of Figure 11.12.

above the horizontal lines that represent terminals start from the end point of a run and are traced to the right up to the next run that reaches further. Dotted lines immediately below horizontal lines start from the starting point of a run and are traced to the left back to the nearest preceding run that starts at an earlier terminal. No dotted lines are traced along the horizontals for the first and last terminals $i = 1$ or 5. For any flow (i,j), the critical times v_q^{ij}, w_q^{ij} are found as pairs of points, at the levels i and j respectively, such that from each point of a pair, the other can be reached by following dotted lines in the direction indicated by the arrows. As an additional example, in Figure 11.13 these pairs of points have been encircled for $(i,j) = (1,4)$, showing that

$$(11.16) \qquad w_1^{14} = v_1^{14} = s_0 = 0, \quad v_2^{14} = s_2, \quad w_2^{14} = s_3, \quad v_3^{14} = s_4,$$
$$w_3^{14} = s_5, \quad v_4^{14} = w_4^{14} = s_6 = 1, \text{ etc.}$$

The system of dotted lines serves simultaneously for the determination of critical points for all flows (i,j). It is interesting to note that although we are considering traffic in only one (eastbound) direction, the construction of critical times is entirely symmetrical as between departure and arrival times.

Each of the expressions (11.15) is a quadratic function of the timings s_r in the schedule, and can therefore be written as

$$(11.17) \qquad A_{ij} = \sum_{r,r'=1}^{R} a_{ij,rr'} \, s_r s_{r'} \quad ,$$

in which we are free to make the matrix $a_{ij,rr'}$ symmetric by specifying

$$(11.18) \qquad a_{ij,rs} = a_{ij,sr} \quad .$$

Because $s_0 = 0$, the value $r = 0$ does not occur in the summations over runs. However, the summation has been extended to include $r = R$, where $s_R = 1$, in order to include in it terms linear in the unknowns $s_1, \ldots s_{R-1}$ and a constant term $a_{ij,RR}$. These terms arise as follows. Because of the periodicity of the schedule (omitting affixes i,j), we have

$$(11.19) \qquad v_{Q+1} = v_1 + 1 \quad .$$

While both v_1 and v_{Q+1} occur in the summation (11.13), they depend on at most one unknown s_r. The use of (11.19) to express this fact will in general introduce linear and constant terms in (11.17). Other such terms arise if a certain w_q, $q \leq Q$, coincides with a certain s_r, $r \geq R$.

In the notation of (11.17), the expression for total accumulation delay incurred daily, which is to be minimized, is

$$(11.20) \qquad Y = \sum_{i=1}^{n-1} \sum_{j=i+1}^{n} x_{ij} \sum_{r,r'=1}^{R} a_{ij,rr'} \, s_r s_{r'} \quad .$$

It is apparent from the method of their derivation that the coefficients $a_{ij,rr'}$ depend only on the structure of the schedule. The problem of minimizing accumulation delay for a schedule of a given structure therefore involves setting up the coefficient system $a_{ij,rr''}$, evaluating the sums

(11.21)
$$\sum_{i=1}^{n-1} \sum_{j=i=1}^{n} x_{ij}\, a_{ij,rr'} = b_{rr'} = b_{rr'}\ ,$$

say, and solving the linear equation system

(11.22)
$$\frac{\partial Y}{\partial s_m} = \frac{\partial}{\partial s_m} \sum_{r,r'=1}^{R} b_{rr'}\, s_r\, s_{r'} = 2\sum_{r=1}^{R} b_{mr}s_r = 0,$$

$$m = 1,\ldots,R\text{-}1\ .$$

Before a solution $\hat{s}_r$, $r = 1,\ldots, R - 1$, say, to this equation system can be looked upon as a most economical schedule of the given structure, it needs to pass two tests. In the first place, it should represent a minimum of accumulation delay, not a maximum or a saddle-point. The outcome of this test is controlled by the coefficients b_{rr}. If these make up a so-called positive definite matrix, the solution represents a minimum of the function being minimized. If the matrix $[b_{rr'}]$ were to be indefinite, it would be an indication that there exists another structure containing fewer runs and no more trains, permitting a smaller accumulation delay than the structure under examination.

Secondly, even if $[b_{rr'}]$ is positive definite, the solution $\hat{s}_r$ found represents the minimum accumulation delay achievable with the given structure only if $\hat{s}_r$ defines a schedule that actually has the structure specified. If this fails to be true, the solution has no meaning, because outside the domain of the given structure, the function minimized does not represent accumulation delay. However, if such a meaningless solution is obtained, it again indicates that there is another structure containing fewer runs and no more trains, permitting a smaller accumulation delay.

It is likely that the special way in which the coefficients $b_{rr'}$ are obtained will make it possible to find short cuts in examining the positive definiteness of $[b_r]$ and in solving the equations (11.22). In this exploratory study of the general nature of the problem, we have not attempted to look for such short cuts.

As an illustration, we will tabulate the coefficients of the equation (11.22) for the schedule structure of Figure 11.12. The first step is to record the critical departure and arrival times for all traffic flows (i,j). In Table VI, for each i and j, we tabulate the run labels of the successive pairs of critical points. By this we mean the numbers $r(q)$ and $\bar{r}(q)$, say, which when used as subscripts to s make

(11.23)
$$v_q^{ij} = s_{r(q)}, \quad w_q^{ij} = s_{\bar{r}(q)}, \quad q = 1,\ldots, Q_{ij}\ .$$

Table VI

Run Labels of Critical Departure and Arrival Times
for the Schedule Structure of Figure 11.12

Terminal of Origin	Terminal of Destination			
	j=2	3	4	5
i = 1	q = 1 2 3 $r(q)$ = 0 2 4 $\bar{r}(q)$ = 0 2 4	1 2 3 0 2 4 0 2 4	1 2 3 0 2 4 0 3 5	1 2 0 2 0 3
2		1 2 3 4 5 6 0 1 2 3 4 5 0 1 2 3 4 5	1 2 3 4 0 1 3 5 0 1 3 5	1 2 0 3 0 3
3			1 2 3 4 0 1 3 5 0 1 3 5	1 2 0 3 0 3
4				1 2 0 3 0 3

To obtain the coefficients b_{mr} of (11.22), we derive from (11.14)

$$(11.24) \qquad \frac{\partial Y}{\partial s_m} = \sum_{i=1}^{n-1} \sum_{j=i+1}^{n} x_{ij} \frac{\partial A_{ij}}{\partial s_m} ,$$

where, omitting again the indices i,j,

$$(11.25) \qquad \frac{\partial A}{\partial s_m} = \sum_{q=1}^{Q} \frac{\partial A}{\partial v_q} \frac{dv_q}{ds_m} + \frac{\partial A}{\partial w_q} \frac{dw_q}{ds_m} .$$

From (11.15) we have

$$(11.26) \qquad \frac{\partial A}{\partial v_q} = w_q - w_{q+1} , \qquad \frac{\partial A}{\partial w_q} = v_q - v_{q-1} ,$$

whereas the quantities $\frac{dv_q}{ds_m}$, $\frac{dw_q}{ds_m}$, each of which is 0 or 1, can be determined from Table VI for each (i,j). For instance, for $i = 1$, $j = 4$, we have (11.27). No rows need to be provided for $m = 0$ in these tabulations because, since $s_0 = 0$, no differentiation of Y with respect to s_0 is needed.

(11.27)

$\dfrac{dv_q^{14}}{ds_m}$	q=1	2	3	$\dfrac{dw_q^{14}}{ds_m}$	q=1	2	3
m=1	0	0	0	m=1	0	0	0
2	0	1	0	2	0	0	0
3	0	0	0	3	0	1	0
4	0	0	1	4	0	0	0
5	0	0	0	5	0	0	1

Using (11.27) in (11.25), and also using (11.26) with the v_q and w_q translated into s_r with the help of Table I, we find

(11.28)

$$\frac{\partial A_{14}}{\partial s_1} = 0, \quad \frac{\partial A_{14}}{\partial s_2} = s_3 - s_5, \quad \frac{\partial A_{14}}{\partial s_3} = s_2,$$

$$\frac{\partial A_{14}}{\partial s_4} = s_5 - 1, \quad \frac{\partial A_{14}}{\partial s_5} = s_4 - s_2 \ .$$

Similar calculations for other (i,j)-pairs lead to similar results, which we put together in Table VII in a statement of the coefficients of s_r in $\dfrac{\partial Y}{\partial s_m}$, derived from the information in Table VI on the basis of (11.24), (11.25) and (11.26). The reader is invited to examine how the placement of the various entries in Table VII is determined from Table VI.

11.4. Most Economical Schedules

If a schedule is found that minimizes accumulation delay in a given structure, this does not necessarily mean that the most economical schedule has been found. There may be another structure containing a more economical schedule. However, because different structures may involve different hauling costs as soon as they differ in the number of trains on each stretch, this question can only be considered if we introduce further assumptions as to how hauling cost depends on the structure of the schedule. For instance, we may use the very simplest assumption incorporated in Figure 11.5 that hauling cost on each stretch is a given linear function of train length, which is independent of the timing of the train in relation to that of other trains on the same or other stretches.

If this function is expressed in dollars per train, it will still be necessary also to place a dollar value on the car-day, and on the day's delay to freight, before a balancing of haulage cost and accumulation delay is possible. All these things being given, the problem of finding a most economical schedule is one of trial and error, where one examines alternative structures, determines the haulage cost for each, the minimum accumulation delay for each, and chooses that structure for which the sum of accumulation delay cost and haulage cost is as small as possible. While again the particular circumstances of the problem are likely to permit short-cuts that reduce the number of comparisons

Table VIII

Coefficients of s_r in $\dfrac{\partial Y}{\partial s_m}$

	r = 1	2	3	4	5
m=1	$2x_{23}+2x_{24}+2x_{34}$	$-x_{23}$	$-x_{24}-x_{34}$		
2	$-x_{23}$	$2x_{12}+2x_{13}+2x_{23}$	$x_{14}+x_{15}-x_{23}$	$-x_{12}-x_{13}$	$-x_{14}$
3	$-x_{24}-x_{34}$	$x_{14}+x_{15}-x_{23}$	$2x_{23}+2x_{24}+2x_{25}+2x_{34}+2x_{35}+2x_{45}$	$-x_{23}$	$-x_{24}-x_{34}$
4		$-x_{12}-x_{13}$	$-x_{23}$	$2x_{12}+2x_{13}+2x_{23}$	$x_{14}-x_{23}$
5		$-x_{14}$	$-x_{24}-x_{34}$	$x_{14}-x_{23}$	$2x_{23}+2x_{24}+2x_{34}$

between alternative structures that needs to be made, we will not press the search for such short-cuts here.

11.5. Scheduling on a Network with Circuits

In the cases considered so far there is only one way in which a car can go from a terminal i to a terminal j, where $j > i$. This is done by joining successively a train from i to i + 1, a train from i + 1 to i + 2, and so on, and finally a train from j - 1 to j. This feature of our model made it possible to introduce the concept of referred time and thereby to achieve a simplification of the analysis.

In the present section we shall consider a number of extensions of the analysis which are best discussed and understood as scheduling problems on networks that contain circuits, even if at first glance this does not always seem to be the case in a literal sense. We shall only give an exploratory discussion of a few such extensions, without attempting a formal analysis. The concept of referred time is likely to be less useful in most of these cases. In principle, one would need to distinguish at a terminal j as many different concepts of "time referred to i" as there are ways in which a car could travel from i to j. We shall therefore use only "natural" time in our discussion. We shall continue to assume that classification and travel times are independent of the flows of cars being classified or traveling and that limitations of track capacity do not rule out any of the schedules that are otherwise considered.

It is also unrealistic, on more complicated networks, to ignore the problem of assignment of empty cars to next loading points. This problem is analyzed in more detail in Chapter 12. Here we shall assume that besides the flows of loaded cars prescribed by the program, which we shall here denote by $\bar{x}_{ij}$, most economical flows $\bar{\bar{x}}_{ij}$ of empty cars have already been determined. The scheduling problem thus is that of most economical scheduling of trains to accommodate the flows

$$x_{ij} = \bar{x}_{ij} + \bar{\bar{x}}_{ij}$$

of all cars, loaded and empty. This assumption ignores possible "interaction" between the empty car assignment problem and the scheduling problem. It also ignores possible differences between loaded and empty cars in classification or travel times.

The analysis of Section 11.4 is still approximately valid for a network consisting of one double-track line, of which each track is traveled in one direction only. Perhaps the weakest spot in the assumptions made there is the assumed even flow of car originations from loading or discharging. The schedule itself indicates that cars are delivered for these operations in bunches. In order that releases of cars from these operations can be treated as an even flow, one would have to assume that there is either enough natural variability in loading or discharging times, or enough congestion in these operations, to convert a bunched input to these activities into an evenly flowing output. In the second case, one would have to recognize congestion delays at loading or discharging tracks as an additional cost of the bunching of cars in trains.

Further complications arise if the line considered has side branches. In the network of Figure 11.14, with two-way traffic on each stretch, there will be an advantage, at terminals A and B, in scheduling train arrivals and departures in *both* directions of the "main line" in such a way that

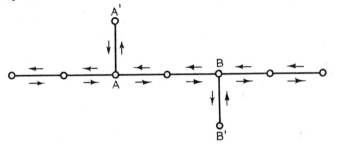

Figure 11.14. Main Line with Branches

with suitably coordinated arrivals and departures of trains on the side branches, cars from A' or B' for either direction, and cars for A' and B' from either direction, can make connections with little accumulation delay at A or B. That this is essentially due to the presence of circuits in the network comes out more clearly if, in Figure 11.15, we draw the same network with a separate line for each direction of flow.

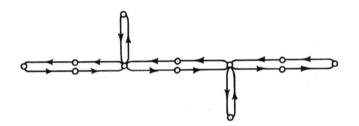

Figure 11.15. Network of Figure 11.14 Drawn with One-Way Lines

Circuits also arise, even on a single line with one-way traffic only, if the structure of the schedule includes maintrackers, that is, trains which by-pass certain intermediate yards. The network of Figure 11.16 illustrates such a case. Diagrams in natural time of the type of

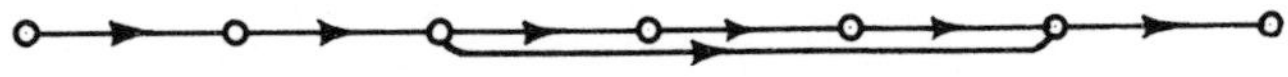

Figure 11.16. Single-Line, One-Way Network with Maintrackers

Figure 11.7 can be used to analyze scheduling problems on networks such as that in Figure 11.16, even with two-way traffic, and with main-trackers between several pairs of terminals. The limitations of two-dimensional diagrams begin to show up in networks with branches such as that of Figure 11.14, and are fully apparent with regard to networks such as that in Figure 11.17, in which circuits occur even if one disregards direction of flow.

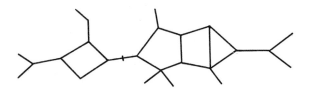

Figure 11.17. Network Containing Circuits

The method for determining a most economical schedule of given structure under constant rates of origination, which was described in preceding sections of this Chapter, can probably be extended without essential difficulties to arbitrary networks containing any number of circuits. However, the more complicated the network is, the more the essential part of the scheduling problem shifts to that of determining the *structure*, rather than the timing, of the schedule. The reason is that in rather complicated networks often a slight change in the timing of some given train will cause some traffic flow x_{ij} to miss a connection previously made, or permit it to make a connection previously missed, in either case changing the structure of the schedule. Thus on networks as complicated as the United States railroad system, or even a major railroad company network, the first and foremost problem is that of choosing between a finite but very large number of alternative schedule structures. Problems of this type are classified in mathematics as "combinatorial" problems. While basic mathematical tools to deal with combinatorial problems have been developed by many mathematicians, their application in computational procedures for solving complicated practical problems is still in its first beginnings.[1]

In conclusion we wish to offer a few intuitive remarks on ways of approaching the problem of choice of schedule structure on networks with many circuits. It would seem natural to split this problem into two parts. First, one would find a good schedule on what may be called the "core" of the network. In the core we include all routes that are part of one circuit or another. If this were to form a disconnected set of routes (as in the network of Figure 11.17, where the routes belonging to circuits form two separate networks) we add the minimum number of connecting routes necessary to make the core into one connected network.

---

1. For a survey of computational aspects of combinatorial problems see Tompkins (1952).

Figure 11.18 shows the core so derived from the network of Figure
11.17. The route A B C has been added to reconnect the core.

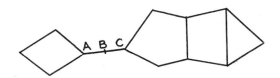

Figure 11.18. Core of the Network in Figure 11.17

If we remove the core from a network, we are left with a number of
isolated branchings which we shall call trees (in accordance with established mathematical terminology). The six trees of the network in
Figure 11.17 are shown in Figure 11.19. The point where a tree feeds
into the core will be called its feeding point, shown by a circle in Figure 11.19.

Figure 11.19. Trees of the Network in Figure 11.17

Now a first approximation to the scheduling problem on a network
with circuits could be obtained by treating programmed traffic flows to
and from all terminals of a tree (other than the feeding point) as if they
were programmed to and from a single terminal. The network of Figure 11.17 is thereby simplified to that of Figure 11.20, in which the
ramifications of the trees are ignored. The underlying idea is that the

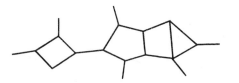

Figure 11.20. Simplification of the Network of Figure 11.17

scheduling on a tree is not encumbered by circuit problems and can
therefore perhaps be adjusted to whatever schedule is found to be best
on the simplified network. Implicit in this is the assumption that speedy

turnaround of engines at the dead ends of the trees is a problem of secondary importance, that can be neglected in a first approximation.

Even after this simplification, the scheduling problem is bound to be complicated if several circuits are present. A further simplification may be achieved by first concentrating on routes with heavy traffic and thereafter filling in the schedule on the more sparsely traveled routes. This procedure will be even more natural if track capacity on the heavily traveled routes is a limiting factor. Of course any of the simplifications suggested entails a cost by preventing one from finding the theoretically very best schedule -- which however may be too costly to compute anyway.

One other thought may be advanced very tentatively as a suggestion for further research. It is conceivable that a solution of the scheduling problem could be made easier by the introduction of fictitious prices on the cars, which vary with the location of the cars in such a way that they increase as the car comes nearer to its destination. As cars accumulate at a certain terminal on the way, a point in time will be reached where the gain in "locational" value from running a train to the next terminal will be enough to make up for the cost of that train.

Another aspect of the scheduling problem has not been mentioned at all yet. This is random fluctuations, in travel times, in classification times, and in traffic flows. Safety margins to allow for such fluctuations will be needed in any realistic schedule. We have not attempted to introduce this consideration in the present exploratory discussion of the scheduling problem.

Chapter 12

SHORT-HAUL ROUTING OF EMPTY BOXCARS

12.1. Purposes of the Study

12.1.1. Demands of a Transportation Program
on the Freight-Car Fleet

Throughout our study of railway operations a great deal of emphasis has been laid on the time required to carry out a shipment. As was pointed out in Chapter 6 the importance of time arises not only through its effect on the inventories customers need to carry and on railroad operating costs, but also through its effect on the amount of rolling stock the industry needs in order to carry out a given amount of business. Thus if we had estimates for some future year of the number of car miles and car loadings, and if we knew, from studies such as that of the Federal Coordinator of Transportation, discussed in Chapter 6, how long it took to load a car, to haul it so many miles, etc., we would have a very good start on estimating the amount of rolling stock that would be needed. An important part of this problem, however, remains to be discussed. This is the relation between the set of traffic flows from each place to each other place and the number of empty car miles required to sustain this set of flows.

Hultgren (1948, pp. 111-120) has shown that loaded car-miles and empty car-miles rise and fall together, but not in the same ratio. The swings of empty car-miles seem to be proportionately less than those of loaded car-miles. One could estimate the level of empty car-miles corresponding to a given set of traffic flows by using ratios like those in Hultgren's study. There are, however, serious shortcomings to such an approach and in addition several reasons for investigating a more direct one.

To give an idea of the magnitudes involved: in 1951 loaded car-miles for Class I railways were 20.6 billion and empty car-miles were 10.6 billion (ICC, *Statistics of Railways in the United States,* 1951). The ratio of loaded to total car-miles fluctuates between 60 and 70 per cent (Hultgren, 1948, p. 118, Chart 52). The predominant movement of traffic in the United States is eastward. This arises from the fact that most manufacturing takes place in the East and most farming in the Midwest and West; so we have bulky raw materials moving east and compact manufactured goods moving west. The result is that empty freight cars for Western loading must be supplied from Eastern terminals, and a considerable amount of empty-car mileage is brought about in the process. Now if one year's transportation program is very much like another year's we should expect the empty-car mileage to be about the same for the two years; and if the two years were proportionately the same, that is, if the A to B traffic changed in the same ratio as the C to D traffic, etc., then we should expect that empty-car mileage would also vary in the same proportion. It is quite clear though that changes in the program which are *not* proportional can give rise to very radical changes in empty mileage, even though the total loaded car-miles remain nearly the same as before. If we desire, therefore, to make any statements as to the adequacy of freight car supply for these more unusual changes, we must develop a more direct method of calculating the empty mileage associated with the given program.

12.1.2. A Means of Evaluating the Existing Car Service Procedures

Except for "system cars" (cars on their owners' tracks) within the confines of a single railroad, the movement of empty freight cars is governed by three things. First is the set of so-called *Car Service Rules* agreed upon by the various railroad companies and administered by the Car Service Division of the Association of American Railroads. Second are the *Per Diem Agreements*. "Car Service Rules and Per Diem Agreements are established for the purpose of providing an improved movement of cars interchanged between railroads, to minimize the movement of empty cars, to coordinate equipment so that an improved car supply can be had by shippers, to facilitate general movement of loaded cars, and to establish uniform charges for cars on lines of other than the owners, commonly known as Per Diem Charges" (*Freight Traffic Red Book*, 1950, p. 951). The third controlling factor consists of special directives issued by the Car Service Division. These represent a cooperative attempt on the part of the different railroads to predict the time, place, and extent of extraordinary needs for loading, and to take measures to supply these needs by directing that empty cars be moved in certain ways, often contrary to those specified by the Car Service Rules. These directives can be interpreted as a recognition of the fact that the Car Service Rules and Per Diem Agreements do not by themselves lead to the most efficient use of the freight car fleet. While the application of these rules can become quite involved, the main idea they express with regard to the movement of empties (that is, cars for which no load is available) is that these cars should be moved in the direction of the home road. In a brief space it is difficult to avoid doing the rules an injustice, for they are not quite this rigid,[1] but it is nevertheless true that car ownership is given a more important role than considerations of the needs for and availabilities of empty cars at various locations.

In the present chapter we shall examine these needs and availabilities at different times and we shall attempt to discover how empty cars

---

1. "If empty, ... cars ... may be moved locally in an opposite direction from the home road ... if to be loaded for delivery on or movement via the home road." Rule 2(c), Code of Car Service Rules, *Freight Traffic Red Book*, 1950, p. 952.

should be routed if the only consideration were that empty car-miles be minimized. It should be emphasized at this point that while for simplicity car-miles are the only cost we consider in this routing, many others, such as the costs of congestion, might very legitimately be brought in.

Once these hypothetical short-haul routings were known, it would in principle be possible to compare them with the actual routings brought about by the three agencies mentioned earlier and in this way facilitate an evaluation of existing car service procedures. Because, however, our study is a rather crude one and because information on actual empty-car flows is sparse, we must be satisfied for the present with a somewhat more modest goal, as follows.

12.1.3. Stability of the Short-Haul Routing Patterns

We shall compare the short-haul routing patterns that are derived for empty cars for several different years and for the four quarters of one year. If the pattern should be found to be a very unstable one we would consider this as evidence of difficulties that the car service procedures must overcome. In this case we would not expect a set of rules as simple as the Car Service Rules to provide efficient direction; judgment, organized flows of information, and special directives would carry most of the burden. If on the other hand a high degree of stability should be found, a simple set of rules might be found to suffice.

12.2. The Data

The data published by the Interstate Commerce Commission on commodity movements by rail are, generally speaking, of two sorts. For brevity we shall refer to these two as *program data* and *flow data*. Each relates to a given period of time. The program data tell us, for instance, how much corn traffic originated in Illinois in 1949, and how much terminated in the same period. The flow data tell us how much corn moved from Illinois origins to Pennsylvania terminals.

While it is clear that program data can be obtained from flow data, the reverse is not the case unless some assumption is made which gives us a rule to use in assigning the supplies of, say, corn in one state to the demands for corn in other states. If we wished to carry out this process, market prices would provide one such rule. Namely, Illinois will ship to Pennsylvania if the price of corn in Illinois plus the cost of transporting corn to Pennsylvania is less than the price of corn in Pennsylvania. That is to say, those shipments will be made which are profitable. [2]

Notice, however, that the flow pattern which would result from such a calculation is a purely hypothetical one; it might or might not agree with the actual flow data, depending on the validity of the assumptions made.

---

2. In Fox (1953) this approach is applied, with the additional complication that the program itself depends on prices. Demand and supply curves are given for each location, and flows, program, and prices are solved for simultaneously.

As far as carload commodities are concerned, both program and flow data are available, in various degrees of detail. The program data are the result of complete tabulations of traffic by individual railroads and are published by the ICC for several degrees of classification. The flow data consist of estimates derived from a one per cent carload waybill sampling procedure of the Commission. The classifications are years, states, and commodities in detail.

The one commodity, however, with which we are particularly concerned here appears in none of the published programs or flow data. This "commodity" is the empty freight car, and any information on its movements must be inferred from data on the movements of commodities proper.

We have seen above that the program data for any particular commodity could be used to set up a hypothetical flow pattern for that commodity. This is the procedure we shall follow in determining the flows for empty cars, with the added complication that the program data must also be estimated before we can start. These latter data will be derived from the program data for all other commodities.

12.3. Surpluses and Deficits of Empty Boxcars

If the number of empty freight cars that originates in a region during a given period is greater than the number that terminates there, the region will be called a freight-car *surplus* region. Conversely a *deficit* region will be one where the number of empties terminating is the greater. Finding the program for a given year, then, is simply a matter of determining the levels of the year's surpluses and deficits for all the regions. If all freight cars were equally useful for all purposes, this determination would be much easier than it actually is. We must, however, take account of the fact that an empty gondola car is of no use to a shipper who wants to load oranges. Surplus and deficit figures relating simply to freight cars would not be very meaningful, for later, in the process of deriving flows, we might unwittingly assign one region's surplus, consisting mostly of boxcars, to the filling of another region's deficit, consisting mostly of flat cars. To reduce these errors due to the summing up of different kinds of things, we shall confine our whole discussion to the movement of boxcars alone. Precisely the same procedure could be applied to each of the other types of freight car. By thus confining our study to a relatively more homogeneous group we reduce the seriousness of these objections, and by concentrating on boxcars we still have in our study a sizable fraction of the whole freight car population. The total cars in active service in 1950 and the breakdown by types of car are shown in Table VIII, where it can be seen that boxcars constitute more than a third of the total stock of rolling equipment. While we can be a little more comfortable with the assumption that every boxcar is like every other than with the assumption that all cars are alike, it should be realized that even this restricted simplification is far from true. If by some standard it is thought that too much

Table VIII

Freight Cars on or about Dec. 31, 1950
(Class I Line-Haul Railways Plus Private Lines)*

	Number	Per cent
Boxcars	717,424	36.16
Flatcars	65,196	3.28
Stock cars	47,971	2.42
Gondolas and hoppers	866,489	43.67
Tank cars	149,330	7.53
Refrigerator cars	127,210	6.41
Other freight-carrying cars	10,594	.53
Total	1,984,214	100.00

*Source: ICC, *Statistics of Railways in the United States*, 1950, Table 24, p. 29.

distortion is introduced into the final estimates of empty car flows by this assumption of homogeneity, the class of cars examined could be still further reduced. As we shall see below, however, such a procedure would very quickly lead to diminishing returns, quite apart from the fact that computations would increase if the same number of cars were to be included in the study. The reason is that the estimates of the program for the type of car being studied quickly deteriorate if this car is not one of the main classifications for which related information is published by the ICC.

We shall now describe the method used to derive from the program data for all commodities the estimated boxcar program of surpluses and deficits for the different states in the U.S. for a period of a year.

Unfortunately, for our purposes, the unit of the published origination and destination figures is not the carload but the ton (Table 51-A, ICC, Statistics of Railways in the United States, 1940-52). Thus it is necessary to convert these figures to carloads through the use of statistics of average tons per car for the various commodities. While the latter are available for each of the 500 commodities in the ICC classification, we shall for computational ease use only the ones corresponding to the coarse six-commodity classification: Products of Agriculture; Animals and Products; Products of Mines; Products of Forests; Manufactures and Miscellaneous; and Forwarder Traffic.[3] Table IX lists these tons-per-car figures by year and by commodity group.

---

3. "The term 'forwarder traffic' means freight traffic consigned by or to a forwarder, i.e., a company, firm, or individual recognized as engaged in the business of collecting and accumulating less-than-carload shipments into consolidated carloads without an ownership interest in the property so handled." ICC, *Statistics of Railways in the United States*, 1950, p. 40.

Table IX

Tons per Car of Carload Revenue Freight Originated
by Commodity Group, 1940–1950*

Year	Products of Agriculture	Animals and Products	Products of Mines	Products of Forests	Manufactures and Miscellaneous	Forwarder Traffic
1940	27.6	12.9	53.8	31.6	27.8	12.1
1941	28.4	13.4	54.2	31.7	28.3	12.7
1942	30.7	14.6	54.4	33.0	30.7	17.4
1943	34.1	15.4	54.8	34.5	32.1	19.1
1944	32.9	15.5	55.2	34.5	31.4	18.7
1945	33.4	15.0	55.5	34.3	30.9	18.2
1946	32.6	14.2	55.6	34.5	29.7	17.8
1947	34.7	14.3	55.9	34.1	30.5	17.5
1948	34.5	14.5	56.3	34.3	30.8	17.2
1949	34.4	14.2	56.9	34.0	30.1	15.9
1950	33.8	14.3	57.3	33.8	30.1	14.3

* Source: ICC, *Statistics of Railways in the United States*, 1950, Table 49, p. 41.

The first important thing to notice in the table is the absence of any mention of the state concerned. These are U.S. averages; where the true figures differ between states we have a source of error in our conversion from tons to cars. The second feature to notice is the wide difference in the averages between the several commodities. This difference is somewhat reassuring with respect to the source of error just mentioned. By treating heavy commodities such as Products of Mines separately from light commodities such as Animals and Products we are ensuring to some extent against the chance that a tons-per-car figure for a mining state exceeds the U.S. average for the same complex of commodities while at the same time a similar figure for a cattle-raising state falls below the U.S. average. Using these average load figures then, the following conversion from tons to cars can be made for each state and each commodity:

$$\frac{\text{Tons of Commodity Group X Terminated} - \text{Tons of Commodity Group X Originated}}{\text{Tons of Commodity Group X Per Car}} = \frac{\text{Car Surplus Due}}{\text{To Commodity X}}$$

A negative surplus is taken to be a deficit.

Thus we have for each state six car-surplus estimates, one for each commodity group, from which we must now derive estimates of boxcar surpluses (or flatcar surpluses, etc., if we so desired).

Through the early years of our study no data on the relative uses of boxcars and other cars were published. In 1949, however, the ICC began presenting in their *Carload Waybill Analyses* some very valuable information on the distribution of car types in the haulage of each commodity in the Commission's detailed classification.

From this source we learn for example that of the 36,965 freight cars in the sample which were used in the carload transportation of Products of Agriculture in 1952, 27,532 were boxcars, 7,127 refrigerator cars, 63 stock cars, 791 gondolas, 797 hoppers, 1 flat, 617 special cars, and 37 tank cars (ICC, *Carload Waybill Statistics*, 1952, Statement 5354, File 40-C-8, p. 1). These statistics, like all others in the *Waybill Analyses*, are based on a one per cent sample of the audited waybills of Class I railroads and are consequently subject to sampling errors. Furthermore, the errors in an estimate, as the *caveat* in the introduction to each of these reports states, will tend to be larger when the number of cars (i.e. number of waybills) to which it corresponds is smaller. This need not worry us too much here, however, for our commodity groups are very broad and the sample, while from a percentage point of view small, is in absolute size large indeed. It is well known that the absolute size of a random sample controls the accuracy of estimates derived from it much more decisively than does the ratio of the sample size to the whole population. Table X lists for the years 1949, 1950, and 1951, the ratios of boxcars used to freight cars used in the transportation of each of our six commodity groups. It can be noticed

Table X

Ratios of Boxcars Used to Freight Cars Used,
by Commodity Group, 1949-51*

Year	Products of Agriculture	Animals and Products	Products of Mines	Products of Forests	Manufacture and Misc.	Forwarder Traffic
1949	0.750	0.081	0.064	0.526	0.578	0.962
1950	0.725	0.094	0.062	0.523	0.585	0.964
1951	0.739	0.083	0.055	0.558	0.558	0.964

*Source: ICC, *Carload Waybill Statistics*, 1949, 1950, 1951, Statements 5058, 5159, 5255 File 40-C-8.

first that the variation in the ratio for any one commodity group from year to year is very small. This is fortunate, for we have no information about the ratios for earlier years, 1940-48. We shall use the 1949 ratios for each commodity as estimates for these earlier years. On the other hand, the variation of these "boxcar per car" figures between commodity groups is seen to be very substantial, as we should expect. The lowest figures are those for Animals and Products and for Products of Mines, both of the major parts of which call for special purpose cars -- stock and refrigerator cars in the first case and gondolas and hoppers in the second.

These figures, like the tons per car figures, are derived from data for the U.S. as a whole and therefore introduce errors into our calculations whenever they differ from the corresponding (unknown) figures for the individual states.

We can now translate the freight car surpluses into boxcar surpluses by multiplying by the appropriate boxcars per car figure. The final formula is:

$$\frac{\text{Tons of Commodity Group X Terminated} - \text{Tons of Commodity Group X Originated}}{\text{Tons of Commodity Group X per Car}} \times \begin{array}{c}\text{Boxcars per Car} \\ \text{for Commodity} \\ \text{Group X}\end{array} = \begin{array}{c}\text{Estimated Boxcar} \\ \text{Surplus Due to} \\ \text{Commodity Group X}\end{array}.$$

These six surpluses (some of which may of course be negative) can now be summed to give the final boxcar surplus for the year and state being considered. The results of these calculations for the eleven years in our study are printed on the maps in Figures 12.3 through 12.13. For simplicity the states have been aggregated into the twelve regions described in Table XI and Figure 12.1.

The derivation of the program of boxcar surpluses and deficits from the programs for all other commodities is now complete. The next step is to build up from these program data a hypothetical system of empty boxcar flows which brings about the least amount of empty boxcar mileage possible. Before we can go on to this routing problem,

Table XI

Regions and Representative Points

Region	States Included	Representative Point
I	Maine New Hampshire Vermont Massachusetts Rhode Island Connecticut	Boston, Massachusetts
II	New York New Jersey Canada	New York, New York
III	Ohio Pennsylvania Michigan West Virginia	Cleveland, Ohio
IV	Maryland Delaware Virginia District of Columbia Florida Georgia North Carolina South Carolina	Columbia, South Carolina
V	Indiana Illinois Wisconsin	Chicago, Illinois
VI	Alabama Arkansas Kentucky Mississippi Tennessee Louisiana	Jackson, Mississippi
VII	Minnesota North Dakota South Dakota	Minneapolis, Minnesota
VIII	Colorado Iowa Kansas Nebraska Missouri	Kansas City, Missouri

Table XI continued

Region	States Included	Representative Point
IX	New Mexico Texas Oklahoma	Fort Worth, Texas
X	Wyoming Utah Idaho Montana	Ogden, Utah
XI	Arizona Nevada California	Monterey, California
XII	Oregon Washington	Portland, Oregon

however, a short discussion must be devoted to the assumed distances between regions.

12.4. A Simplified Rail Network

Table XI describes the twelve-region division of the U.S. and lists for each region a representative point. This grouping of states has been done by weighing the following factors: geographical proximity, similarity of economic status and product, pattern of railway facilities, and the possibility of selecting a single center for the area which would dominate other possible centers as a focal point for shipping. The purpose of picking representative points is to establish an origin from which to measure rail distances. The cities selected do not necessarily represent important gateways or rail centers; these would often be less satisfactory for present purposes than the points chosen. The criteria of selection are admittedly rather vague, but they include some of the following considerations. Since we are interested in the distances to and from *ultimate* origins and destinations of traffic, large centers of population are not necessarily the points to choose. One would expect this to be the case especially in the farm states. Wheat is not grown in large cities. Secondly, unless there is very good reason to think that originations and destinations are concentrated along the edge of a region, a point in such a place should be avoided, in order not to favor flows to the region bordering this edge. This consideration excludes St. Louis in Region VIII. One should attempt in setting up the regional classification to avoid bipolar regions such as Region XI which includes Los Angeles and San Francisco. Since the state-by-state character of our data precludes this, we picked an intermediate representative point. If we had for a region complete information about where empties arose or where they were needed, and in each case the precise number, it

Table XII

Rail Distances Between Regions*

Region	I (Boston)	II (New York)	III (Cleveland)	IV (Columbia)	V (Chicago)	VI (Jackson)	VII (Minneapolis)	VIII (Kansas City)	IX (Fort Worth)	X (Ogden)	XI (Monterey)	XII (Portland)
I (Boston)	0											
II (New York)	229	0										
III (Cleveland)	678	571	0									
IV (Columbia)	930	701	846	0								
V (Chicago)	1018	911	340	867	0							
VI (Jackson)	1463	1234	965	668	738	0						
VII (Minneapolis)	1424	1317	746	1273	406	1144	0					
VIII (Kansas City)	1469	1362	791	1111	451	695	490	0				
IX (Fort Worth)	1905	1676	1244	1110	961	442	1000	510	0			
X (Ogden)	2496	2389	1818	2281	1478	1801	1330	1170	1359	0		
XI (Monterey)	3298	3191	2620	2785	2280	2117	2132	1873	1675	802	0	
XII (Portland)	3217	3110	2539	3066	2199	2649	1793	2018	2207	848	953	0

* Source: Italicized figures from Rand-McNally, *Commercial Atlas and Marketing Guide*, 84th Edition, 1953; others derived from italicized figures by finding shortest route.

Figure 12.1. Regions and Representative Points

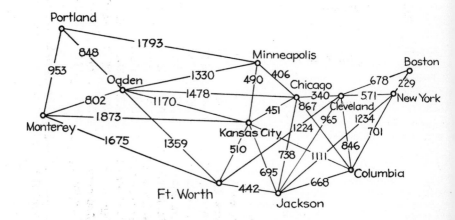

Figure 12.2. A Simplified Rail Network
with Distances in Miles

might be possible to specify our representative point more closely in mathematical terms. Since in any case such information is not available, it is perhaps best to think of the point roughly as a traffic center of gravity for the region.

Table XII gives the assumed representative distances between regions. The italicized entries in the table are short-line rail distances between representative points; the other entries are rail distances between representative points which differ only slightly from short-line ones; they are derived from the italicized entries by finding the shortest route over these links. The reason for not using short-line distances between all the points is that we have a somewhat simpler rail network as a result. As far as our final routing calculations are concerned this small change has no effect. The conceptual rail network corresponding to the distances of Table XII is shown in Figure 12.2.

12.5. Finding the Short-Haul Routing Patterns

Once the surpluses and deficits are known, the short-haul routings can be computed by the so-called "simplex" method of Dantzig.[4] We shall not describe the method beyond stating the condition which is necessary and sufficient for the solution. This condition was first formulated by Koopmans[5] in relation to the problem of finding the most economical routing of empty ships. It is quite similar to those conditions developed in Chapter 4 for the efficient use of a highway network. Here it is somewhat simpler because we have disregarded congestion. If in the present problem we were concerned with the routing of *all* traffic, this simplification would have less justification.

Our condition is that there must exist a set of fictitious prices or "potentials,"[6] one for each of our representative points, which has the following two characteristics. (1) The difference in potentials between any two points must not exceed the distance between these points, and (2) if the boxcar flow between any two points is positive, the potential at the receiving point must exceed the potential at the sending point by an amount just equal to the distance between the two points. Of course, *distance* is used here as a substitute for *cost of empty movement,* on the simplifying assumption that the latter is proportional to the former. Dantzig's method consists essentially in showing how to proceed in a systematic manner from an arbitrary initial routing pattern for which such a set of potentials does not exist to a routing pattern for which one does.

4. Dantzig (1951e, pp. 359-374). For a description of the development of this problem, see our introduction.

5. Koopmans (1947). See also Koopmans and Reiter (1951).

6. A term suggested by an analogous problem in the flow of electricity through a network of conductors.

12.6. Results

Figures 12.3 through 12.13 show the short-haul routing patterns of empty boxcars for the programs of each of the years 1940-50, and Figures 12.14 through 12.17 the same for the four quarters of 1949. Surpluses for each region are shown as the boxed figures alongside each representative point, and the magnitudes of the various flows (in hundreds of cars) are shown alongside each segment of the pattern.

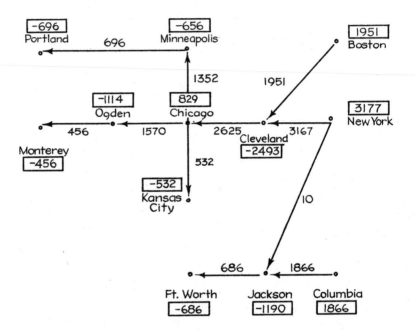

Figure 12.3. 1940

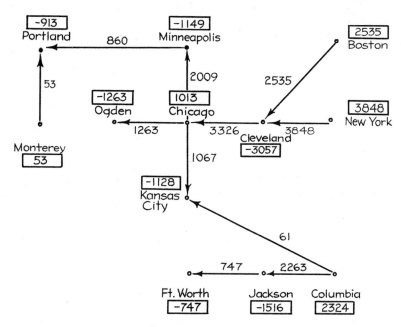

Figure 12.4. 1941

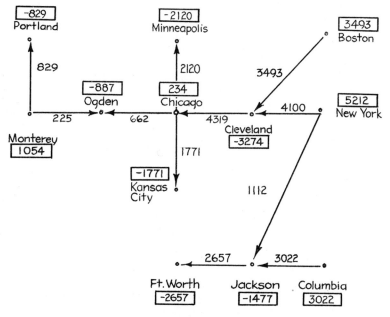

Figure 12.5. 1942

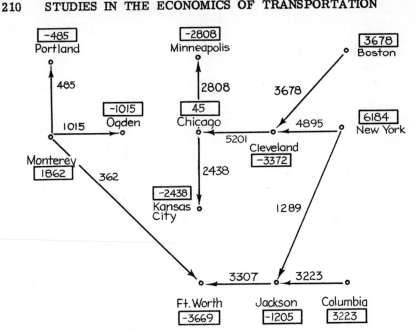

Figure 12.6. 1943

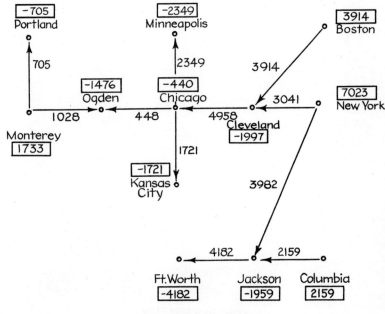

Figure 12.7. 1944

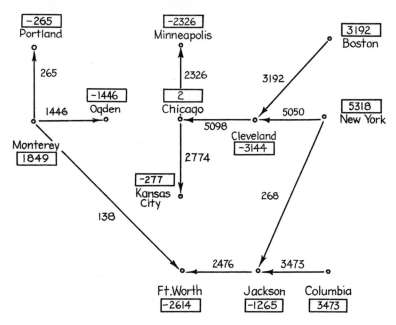

Figure 12.8. 1945

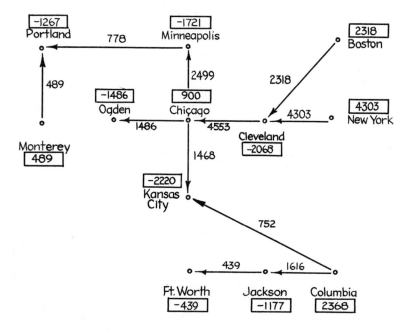

Figure 12.9. 1946

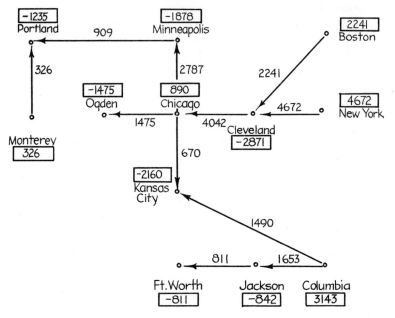

Figure 12.10. 1947

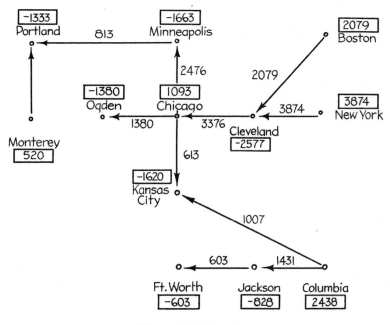

Figure 12.11. 1948

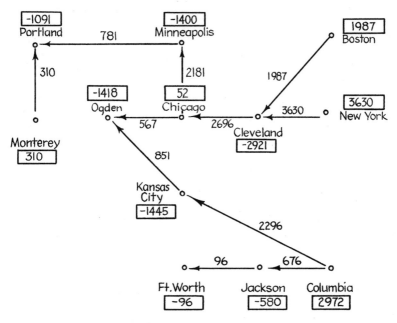

Figure 12.12. 1949

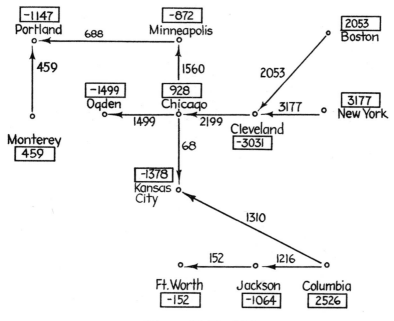

Figure 12.13. 1950

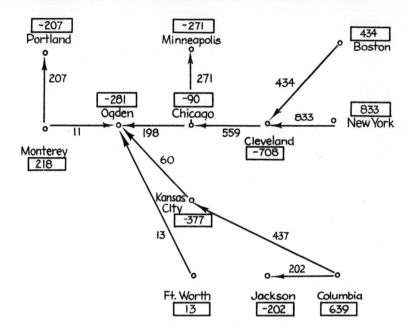

Figure 12.14. 1949 - First Quarter

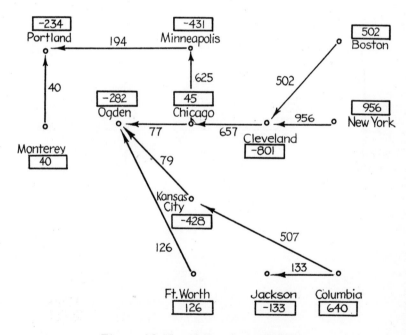

Figure 12.15. 1949 - Second Quarter

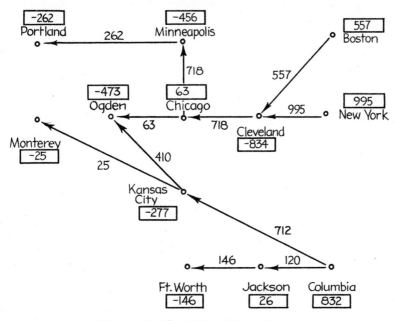

Figure 12.16. 1949 - Third Quarter

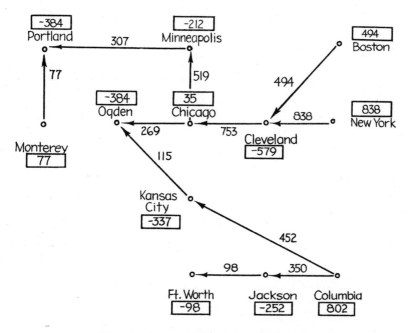

Figure 12.17. 1949 - Fourth Quarter

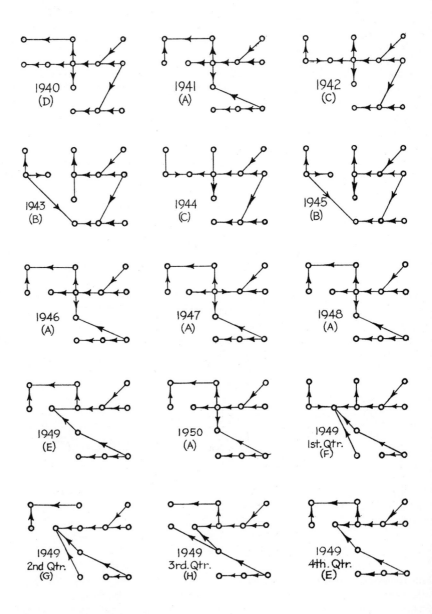

Figure 12.18. Short-Haul Routing Patterns

12.7. Conclusions with Respect to Stability

In Figure 12.18 we have reproduced all of the resulting short-haul routing patterns on a single page, where they can be seen at a glance for easy comparison. Since a judgment as to whether one pattern is very different from another is to some extent a subjective matter, we shall leave part of the final decision concerning stability to the reader. Notice, however, that in the eleven years only five different yearly patterns arise: 1941, 1946, 1947, 1948, and 1950 are of one type, let us say type A, 1943 and 1945 of type B, 1942 and 1944 of type C, 1940 alone of type D, and 1949 alone of type E. While the fourth quarter of 1949 is of the common type E, the other quarters of 1949 are unlike each other and unlike any of the yearly patterns. While the peacetime years taken by themselves and the wartime years taken by themselves do seem to show a fair amount of stability, the quarterly patterns for 1949 seem to indicate that seasonal instability warrants a closer inspection of other years than we have given them. One encouraging aspect of our results is this. The stability found to exist seems sufficient to justify the hope that incremental-cost freight rates that take into account a shipment's contribution to empty-car movement can some day be put into effect. Short-haul empty-car routing patterns like the ones we have examined in this chapter are a prerequisite to the administration of such a rate structure. The computations for such purposes would have to be a good deal more detailed than the simple one we have carried out here, but it is clear that the complexities of the problem are not so great as to carry it beyond the reach of existing techniques.

12.8*. Appendix. Formal Description of the Surplus-Deficit Computation Procedure

In this section the exact procedure used in deriving the surplus-deficit estimates is described. It differs from the verbal account in 12.3 only insofar as some adjustments of the initial data are concerned.

Since only Class I line-haul railroads reported, there was a discrepancy between tons originated and tons terminated for the whole U.S., within each commodity group. If one had summed originations and terminations for any commodity group over each state and Canada, he should have found that total originations equaled total terminations within each commodity group. The actual discrepancy between the two was undoubtedly caused by error and by "leakage" of freight tonnage on to the Class II and Class III railroads (i.e. railroads which do not gross over \$1,000,000 a year). Since no data were available for the true originations and terminations, it was decided to adjust the figures initially so that tons originated would equal tons terminated. The initial adjustment was carried out as follows: Let $\bar{O}_i^M$ and $\bar{T}_i^M$ equal the number of tons in commodity group M reported originated and terminated in state i, respectively. Then for each M

(12.1) $$\sum_i \bar{O}_i^M - \sum_i \bar{T}_i^M = C^M$$

where C^M equals the discrepancy between the two. To adjust $\bar{O}_i^M$ and $\bar{T}_i^M$ to find O_i^M and T_i^M, respectively, we divide C^M evenly and apportion each half among the $\bar{O}_i^M$ and $\bar{T}_i^M$ according to their percentage of $\sum_i \bar{O}_i^M$. That is,

$$(12.2) \qquad O_i^M = \bar{O}_i^M - \frac{C^M}{2} \cdot \frac{\bar{O}_i^M}{\sum_k \bar{O}_k^M} = \bar{O}_i^M \cdot \frac{\sum_i \bar{O}_i^M + \sum_k \bar{T}_k^M}{2 \sum_k \bar{O}_k^M} \; ;$$

$$(12.3) \qquad T_i^M = \bar{T}_i^M + \frac{C^M}{2} \cdot \frac{\bar{T}_i^M}{\sum_k \bar{T}_k^M} = \bar{T}_i^M \cdot \frac{\sum_k \bar{O}_k^M + \sum_k \bar{T}_k^M}{2 \sum_k \bar{T}_k^M} \; .$$

Clearly, $\qquad \sum_i O_i^M = \sum_i T_i^M \; .$

The transformation of the adjusted tons originated and tons terminated was carried out as follows: Let α^M equal the proportion of boxcars to all cars used in shipping commodities in group M for a given year. Let β^M equal the reciprocal of the average number of tons per car for commodities in group M and for a given year. Then

$$(12.4) \qquad \sum_M \alpha^M \beta^M (T_i^M - O_i^M)$$

gives us an estimate for surplus or deficit box cars attributable to each state i.

BIBLIOGRAPHY

Adams, W. F., "Road Traffic Considered as Random Series," *Journal of the Institution of Civil Engineers, 4* (November, 1936), 121-130.

American Railway Engineering Association, *Proceedings, 53* (1952).

Arrow, K. J., T. E. Harris, and J. Marschak, "Optimal Inventory Policy," *Econometrica, 19* (1951), 250-272.

Association of American Railroads, Car Service Division, *Revenue Freight Loaded and Received From Connections*, Statement CS-54A.

Beakey, John, "The Effect of Highway Design on Vehicle Speed and Fuel Consumption," *Oregon State Highway Commission Technical Bulletin*, No. 5 (1937).

Beakey, John, and F. B. Crandall, "The Effect of Surface Type, Alignment, and Traffic Congestion on Vehicular Fuel Consumption," *Oregon State Highway Commission Technical Bulletin*, No. 17 (1944).

Beckmann, Martin, "A Continuous Model of Transportation," *Econometrica, 20* (1952), 643-660.

Beckmann, M., T. C. Koopmans, C. B. McGuire, and C. B. Winsten, "The Allocation of Switching Work in a System of Classification Yards," *Proceedings of the Railway Systems and Procedures Association* (December, 1953), 94a-94j.

Bonnesen, T., and W. Fenchel, *Theorie der konvexen Körper, Ergebnisse der Mathematik und ihrer Grenzgebiete*. Berlin, Julius Springer, 1934; New York, Chelsea Publishing Co., 1948. Vol. 3, No. 1.

Brockmeyer, E., G. L. Halstrom, and A. Jensen, *The Life and Works of A. K. Erland*. Copenhagen, Copenhagen Telephone Company, 1948.

Byers, M. L., *Economics of Railway Operation*. New York, Engineering News Publishing Co., 1908.

Charnes, A., W. W. Cooper, and B. Mellon, "Blending Aviation Gasolines — a Study in Programming Interdependent Activities in an Integrated Oil Company," *Econometrica, 20* (1952), 135-159.

Cooper, W. W. *See* Charnes, A., *et al.*

Coughlin, E. W., "How Can Carriers Secure Better Car Handling in Yards and Terminals?" *Railway Age, 132* (May 26, 1952), 44-47.

Crandall, F. B. *See* Beakey, John, and F. B. Crandall.

Crane, Roger, "Some Examples of Operations Research Work," *Proceedings of the Railway Systems and Procedures Association* (December, 1953), 97–113.

Dantzig, George B. (1951a). *See* Wood, Marshall K., and George B. Dantzig.

Dantzig, George B. (1951b), "The Programming of Interdependent Activities: Mathematical Model," Chapter II in Koopmans (1951).

Dantzig, George B. (1951c), "A Proof of the Equivalence of the Programming Problem and the Game Problem," Chapter XX in Koopmans (1951).

Dantzig, George B. (1951d), "Maximization of Linear Function of Variables Subject to Linear Inequalities," Chapter XXI in Koopmans (1951).

Dantzig, George B. (1951e), "Application of the Simplex Method to a Transportation Problem," Chapter XXIII in Koopmans (1951).

De Sylva, H. A., and T. W. Forbes, *Driver Testing Results.* Boston, Works Progress Administration, 1937.

Dorfman, Robert, "Mathematical, or 'Linear' Programming: a Nonmathematical Exposition," *American Economic Review, 43* (1953), 797–825.

Droege, John A., *Freight Terminals and Trains.* 2d ed. New York, McGraw-Hill, 1925.

Dupuit, Jules, "De la mesure de l 'utilité des travaux publics," *Annales des Ponts et Chaussées, 2d. ser., 8.* (1844). Reprinted and translated as "On the Measurement of the Utility of Public Works," in International Economic Association, *International Economic Papers,* No. 2. New York, Macmillan, 1952.

Dvoretzsky, A., J. Kiefer, and J. Wolfowitz, "The Inventory Problem," *Econometrica, 20* (1952), 187–222, 450–466.

Enke, Stephen, "Equilibrium among Spatially Separated Markets: Solution by Electric Analogue," *Econometrica, 19* (1951), 40–47.

Erlang, A. K. All of Erlang's papers (translated into English) will be found in the work listed under Brockmeyer, E., *et al.*

Erickson, Elroy L. *See* Greenshields, Bruce D., *et al.*

Farkas, J., "Über die Theorie der einfachen Ungleichungen," *Journal für reine and angewandte Mathematik, 124* (1901), 1–27.

Fenchel, W. *See* Bonnesen, T., and W. Fenchel.

Flood, Merrill M., "On the Hitchcock Distribution Problem," *Pacific Journal of Mathematics, 3* (1953), 369–396.

Flood, Merrill M., "Applications of Transportation Theory to Scheduling a Military Tanker Fleet," *Journal of the Operations Research Society, 2* (1954), 150-162.

Forbes, T. W., "Speed, Headway, and Volume Relationships on a Freeway," *Proceedings of the Institute of Traffic Engineers* (1952). Reprint No. 13, Institute of Transportation and Traffic Engineering, University of California, 1952.

Forbes, T. W. *See* De Sylva, H. A., and T. W. Forbes.

Fox, Karl A., "A Spatial Equilibrium Model of the Livestock-Feed Economy in the United States," *Econometrica, 21* (1953), 547-566.

Freight Commodity Statistics. Interstate Commerce Commission, Bureau of Economics and Statistics. Washington, Government Printing Office, various years.

Freight Traffic Red Book, 1950. Comp. and ed. C. J. Fagg, Walter W. Weller, and Arthur B. Strunk. New York, Traffic Publishing Co., 1950.

Freight Traffic Report. Washington, Federal Coordinator of Transportation, 1935. Appendix I.

Gale, David H., H. W. Kuhn, and A. W. Tucker, "Linear Programming and the Theory of Games," Chapter XIX in Koopmans (1951).

Garwood, F., "An Application of the Theory of Probability to the Operation of Vehicular-Controlled Traffic Signals," *Supplement to the Journal of The Royal Statistical Society, 7* (1940-41), 65-77.

Glanville, W. H., "Operational Research and Road Research," *Proceedings of the Manchester Joint Research Council, 25* (1949), 105-127.

Greenshields, Bruce D., Donald Schapiro and Elroy L. Erickson, *Traffic Performance at Urban Street Intersections.* Yale Bureau of Highway Traffic, Technical Report No. 1, 1947.

Greenshields, Bruce D., and F.M. Weida *Statistics, with Applications, to Highway Traffic Analysis.* Saugatuck, Connecticut, Eno Foundation, 1952.

Harris, T. E. *See* Arrow, K. J., *et al.*

Herrey, Erna M. J., and Hermann Herrey "Principles of Physics Applied to Traffic Movements and Road Conditions," *American Journal of Physics, 13* (1945), 1-14.

Herrey, Hermann. *See* Herrey, Erna M. J., and Hermann Herrey.

Hess, V. F., "The Capacity of a Highway," *Traffic Engineering, 20* (1950), 420-421.

Hess, V. F., and M.S. Raff, "Letters," *Traffic Engineering, 21* (1950), 49.

Hitchcock, F. L., "The Distribution of a Product from Several Sources to Numerous Localities," *Journal of Mathematics and Physics* (Massachusetts Institute of Technology), *20* (1941), 224-230.

Hotelling, H., "The General Welfare in Relation to Problems of Taxation and of Railway and Utility Rates," *Econometrica*, *6* (1938), 242-269.

Houthakker, H. S., "Electricity Tariffs in Theory and Practice," *Economic Journal*, *61* (1951), 1-25.

Hultgren, Thor, *American Transportation in Prosperity and Depression*. New York, National Bureau of Economic Research, 1948.

Interstate Commerce Commission, *Carload Waybill Sample Statistics*, Statements Nos. 5058, 5159, 5256, File 40-C-8. Washington, ICC, 1949, 1950, 1951, 1952.

John, F., "Extremum Problems with Inequalities as Subsidiary Conditions," in *Studies and Essays Presented to R. Courant on His 60th Birthday*. New York, Interscience Publishers, 1948. Pp. 187-204.

Kantorovitch, L., "On the Translocation of Masses," *Doklady Akad. Nauk SSSR*, *37* (1942), 199-201.

Kendall, D. G., "Some Problems in the Theory of Queues," *Journal of the Royal Statistical Society (Series B)*, *13* (1951), 151-185.

Kiefer, J. *See* Dvoretzsky, A., *et al.*

Knight, Frank H., "Some Fallacies in the Interpretation of Social Cost," *Quarterly Journal of Economics*, *38* (1924), 582-606. Reprinted in F. H. Knight, *The Ethics of Competition* (New York, Harper, 1935), pp. 217-236; and in American Economic Association, *Readings in Price Theory* (Chicago, Richard D. Irwin, 1952). Pp. 160-179.

Koopmans, T. C. (1947), "Optimum Utilization of the Transportation System," *Proceedings of the International Statistical Conferences*, *5* (1947), 136-146. Reprinted as supplement to *Econometrica*, *17* (1949), 136-146.

Koopmans, T.C. (1951), ed., *Activity Analysis of Production and Allocation*. New York, John Wiley, 1951.

Koopmans, T. C., and S. Reiter, "A Model of Transportation," Chapter XIV in Koopmans (1951).

Koopmans, T. C. (1953). *See* Beckmann, M., *et al.*

Kuhn, H. W., and A. W. Tucker, "Non-Linear Programming," in *Proceedings of the Second Berkeley Symposium on Mathematical Statistics and Probability*. Berkeley, University of California, 1951.

Kuhn, H. W. *See* Gale, David, *et al.*

Marschak, J. *See* Arrow, K. J., *et al.*

McGuire, C. B. *See* Beckmann, M., *et al.*

Mellon, B. *See* Charnes, A., *et al.*

Mitchell, Robert B., and Chester Rapkin, *Urban Traffic*. New York, Columbia University Press, 1954.

Moyer, R. A., "Braking and Traction Tests on Ice, Snow, and Bare Pavements," *Proceedings of the Highway Research Board, 27* (1947), 340-360.

Normann, O. K., "Preliminary Results of Highway Capacity Studies," *Public Roads, 19* (1939), 225-232, and 240-241.

Normann, O. K., "Highway Capacity," *Proceedings of the Highway Research Board, 21* (1941), 379-392.

Normann, O. K., "Highway Capacity," *Proceedings of the 28th Annual Highway Conference, 43* (February, 1942), 107-122. Ann Arbor, University of Michigan.

Normann, O. K., and the Division of Highway Transport of the Public Roads Administration, "Results of Highway Capacity Studies," *Public Roads, 23* (June, 1942), 57-81.

Normann, O. K., W. P. Walker, and the Committee on Highway Capacity of the Highway Research Board, "Highway Capacity: Practical Applications of Research," *Public Roads, 25* (1949), 201-277. Reprinted as *Highway Capacity Manual*. Washington, U.S. Department of Commerce, Bureau of Public Roads, 1950.

Palander, Tord, *Beitraege zur Standorttheorie*. Uppsala, 1935.

Palm, C., "Intensitatsschwankungen in Fernsprechverkehr," *Ericsson Technics, 44* (1943), 1-189.

Parmelee, Julius H., *The Modern Railway*. New York, Longmans, Green, 1940.

Pigou, A. C., *The Economics of Welfare*. 4th ed. London, Macmillan, 1932.

Pipes, Louis A., *A Proposed Dynamic Analog of Traffic*. Los Angeles, University of California. Institute of Transportation and Traffic Engineering Special Study, July 11, 1950.

Raff, Morton S., "The Distribution of Blocks in an Uncongested Stream of Automobile Traffic," *Journal of the American Statistical Association, 46* (1951), 114-123.

Raff, Morton S., *A Volume Warrant for Urban Stop Signs*. Saugatuck, Connecticut, The Eno Foundation for Highway Traffic Control, 1950.

Raff, Morton S. *See* Hess, V. F., and M. S. Raff.

Raff, Morton S., and the Eno Foundation Staff, *Turn Controls in Urban Traffic*. Saugatuck, Connecticut, The Eno Foundation for Highway Traffic Control, 1951.

Rand-McNally Commercial Atlas and Marketing Guide. 84th ed., 1953.

Rapkin, Chester. *See* Mitchell, Robert B., and Chester Rapkin.

Reiter, S. *See* Koopmans, T. C., and S. Reiter.

Reuschel, A., "Fahrzeugbewegungen in der Kolonne," *Oesterreiches Ingenieur-Archiv, 4* (1950), 193-215.

Samuelson, P. A., "Comparative Statics and the Logic of Economic Maximizing," *Review of Economic Studies, 14* (1946-47), 41-43.

Samuelson, P. A., *Foundations of Economic Analysis.* Cambridge, Mass., Harvard University Press, 1948.

Samuelson, P. A., "Spatial Price Equilibrium and Linear Programming," *American Economic Review, 42* (1952), 283-303.

Schapiro, Donald. *See* Greenshields, Bruce D., *et al.*

Statistics of Railways in the U.S. Interstate Commerce Commission, various years.

Stewart, J. Q., "The Development of Social Physics," *American Journal of Physics, 18* (1950), 239-253.

Tanner, J. C., "The Delay to Pedestrians Crossing a Road," *Biometrika, 38* (1951), 383-392.

Tinbergen, Jan, *Econometrics.* Philadelphia, Blakiston, 1951.

Toll Roads and Free Roads. 76th Congress, 1st Session. Message of the President, House Document 272. Washington, Government Printing Office, 1939.

Tompkins, C. B., "Discrete Problems and Computers," National Bureau of Standards, INA-53-5, November 17, 1952.

Train Classification. Terminal Department of the Baltimore and Ohio Railroad Co., August 15, 1950.

Trueblood, D. L., "The Effect of Travel Time and Distance on Freeway Usage," *Public Roads, 26* (1952), 241-50.

Tucker, A. W. *See* Gale, David, *et al.*

Tucker, A. W. *See* Kuhn, H. W., and A. W. Tucker.

Vickrey, William S., *The Revision of the Rapid Transit Fare Structure of the City of New York.* Finance Project, Mayor's Committee on Management Survey of the City of New York, Technical Monograph No. 3, New York, February, 1952.

Walker, W. P. *See* Normann, O. K., W. P. Walker, *et al.*

Wardrop, J. G. (1952a), "Traffic Capacity of Town Streets," *Roads and Road Construction* (February and March, 1952).

Wardrop, J. G. (1952b), "Some Theoretical Aspects of Road Traffic Research," *Proceedings of the Institution of Civil Engineers*, Pt. II, Vol. *I* (1952), 325-378.

Weida, F. M. *See* Greenshields, Bruce D., and F. M. Weida.

Winsten, C. B. *See* Beckmann, M., *et al*.

Wolfowitz, J. *See* Dvoretzsky, A., *et al*.

Wood, Marshall K., and George B. Dantzig (1951a), "The Programming of Interdependent Activities: General Discussion," Chapter I in Koopmans (1951).

Working Book No. 19. Transportation Department of the Baltimore and Ohio Railroad Co., December 1, 1951.